RELENTLESS

'Dean's journey from the Special Boat Service to
intrepid adventurer is truly inspirational.'
Sir Ranulph Fiennes

'An extraordinary tale of courage and adventure.
Dean's story is inspirational.'
Levison Wood

'Dean's relentless determination to help those who
face many mental health battles is incredible
and admirable – he's a hero to many.'
Bear Grylls

Dean Stott is a former British Special Forces Soldier who left the military after suffering a severe knee injury in a parachuting accident in 2011. He then established a distinguished career in the private security sector. He was renowned for his willingness to take on any job, no matter how dangerous.

However, in 2016 Dean was ready for a new project and wanted to use this to help others. He began training to cycle the longest motorable road in the world – The Pan-American Highway.

Always on the lookout for his next challenge, Dean continues to live by the Special Forces' ethos of 'the unrelenting pursuit of excellence'.

RELENTLESS

DEAN STOTT

With Geraint Jones

HEADLINE

First published in 2019 by
HEADLINE PUBLISHING GROUP

First published in paperback in 2020 by
HEADLINE PUBLISHING GROUP

1

Cataloguing in Publication Data is available from the British Library

ISBN 9781472266910

All photographs © Dean Stott

Designed and typeset by EM&EN
Printed and bound in Great Britain by Clays Ltd, Elcograf S.p.A.

The views and opinions expressed are those of the author alone and should not be taken to represent
those of Her Majesty's Government, MOD, HM Armed Forces or any government agency.

HEADLINE PUBLISHING GROUP
An Hachette UK Company
Carmelite House
50 Victoria Embankment
London EC4Y 0DZ

www.headline.co.uk
www.hachette.co.uk

For my Brothers, who are continually stepping out the door into the darkness, making sacrifices and putting their families through it.

'A true SF operator won't care what the public's opinion of them is; they only care that the public remain free to have that opinion.'

And to my darling wife, Alana, and beautiful children, Mollie and Tommy, who sacrificed so much of our time together to ensure I fulfilled my mission.

'There is no hero without her.'

'The Unrelenting Pursuit of Excellence'
– *Special Forces ethos*

'The only thing necessary for the triumph of evil
is for good men to do nothing.'
– *Edmund Burke*

PROLOGUE

I'd made a mistake that was going to cost me my life.

I turned to the man beside me. He was a Yemeni, we called him H and he was the only passenger in the beat-up local car I was driving. The air around us was stiff with heat and tension, the vehicle almost rocking as the press of humanity outside began to shove towards me, pointing. I kept my eyes down, not out of fear but so that they didn't get a good look at them through the dirty glass.

I knew exactly what had happened. How they'd spotted me. I was dressed head to toe as a local, from flip-flops to a turban. I had a dyed beard, my skin coloured so that I looked like that bloke from *Bargain Hunt*, but what I hadn't added to my disguise was my brown contact lenses, and now my bright blue eyes were drawing the locals in to point and stare. I knew it was only a matter of minutes before the neighbourhood bad guys started slipping out of their hiding places, and tonight I could look forward to an orange boiler suit. The last thing the world would see of me was the image of a former Special Forces soldier about to meet his end courtesy of an enemy unfamiliar with the Geneva Convention.

Bollocks.

I wanted to talk to H. I wanted the local man's opinion, but if the people outside saw my lips moving in a funny way, then we were truly fucked. And so instead I raised an eyebrow, and hoped that people would just think I was commenting on the traffic that had packed us into the bustling marketplace. H gave a shrug in reply, as if to say, 'What can you do?'

What could I do? Get my head chopped off or go out fighting. Those seemed to be the choices. I knew which one I'd choose if it came down to it, but I couldn't help but hear that voice in the back of my head. The voice that had told me: 'You'll never last two minutes in the army.' Well, if this *was* the end, I'd show them how wrong they were there.

I'd been showing them for years.

This wasn't my first covert mission as a civilian, and I hadn't come into this job because I was anything less than the best. I had cut my teeth as a Special Forces soldier, and as such I'd had my mettle tested again and again. I tried to remember that as yet another local pointed at me and began waving towards my door. I pretended to be busy looking ahead at the traffic, and checked my mirror behind me.

No sign of our second car.

I wanted to rub at my eyes. Despite the danger I was knackered. Maybe that's why I'd made the mistake. Maybe that was why I had to get on my radio, hidden away out of sight of the Yemenis who continued to walk by, peering in and pointing at me.

I kept my message short, trying to move my lips as little as possible. 'I've been compromised.'

My mate Sam came on the net from the second vehicle. He was out of sight but I was sure that he couldn't be more than a hundred metres away.

'Are you compromised, over?'

I confirmed that I was.

'Are you happy with the immediate action drill, over?'

I knew that drill off by heart – the key to Special Forces soldiering is that we train and drill relentlessly, putting in the repetitions just like a bodybuilder does in the gym, and I'd brought that ethos with me into the civilian world. The first part would involve me pulling a snub-nosed machine gun from beneath my seat and emptying a full magazine into the windscreen. This would send a very loud signal that it was a good idea for people to get away from me. It would buy me seconds to grab my wrapped-up assault rifle, wedged between the seat and the door, and exit the vehicle. Then me and my flip-flops would be racing for my nearest safe house.

Sam came back on the net. 'Your call. Out.'

My call. When it comes down to it, the biggest moments in your life always are.

I thought about letting out a deep breath, but looking ice-cool in front of H was important to me. Fear is contagious, and so I put mine on a shelf until I'd got clear of the situation. Instead, I imagined everything that was about to happen in this shitstorm.

Bloody hell, I almost laughed to myself. All this over a pair of contact lenses.

I looked at H. Gave him the slightest of nods. He was probably sending up a prayer at that point. Maybe more than one. My own thoughts went to my wife and children. If someone wanted to stop me seeing them again, then I promised it would be a fight like no other.

And then, with the thought of my family pumping like fire through my veins, I reached below my seat and took hold of my weapon.

1. PAD BRAT

As you might imagine, it's a long ride from my entry into the world as a baby to ending up in Yemen, seconds away from going full Jason Bourne in a busy market street, but maybe I had a shorter road than most people do into the military. In fact, I took my first breaths and screamed my lungs out for the first time at the hospital of RAF Wroughton, an air force base not far from Swindon.

The reason for that was my father. He was a career squaddie based in Tidworth, and like so many 'pad brats' – kids belonging to those in the service – my early childhood was a blur of packing and unpacking boxes, and various homes in the army's drab versions of council estates as we relocated every few years. After Tidworth, it was Germany, but I was too young to remember much of that. Then came Bradford, and I do remember when the football stadium burnt down. Like a lot of kids, it was sport that got etched into my early memories, and little wonder – my dad was a player, manager and coach of the army's football team. After Bradford, we were moved down to Aldershot, then a huge garrison town, and close by was 3 Royal School Mechanical Engineering, with whom my father was a squadron sergeant major at Gibraltar Barracks. Looking back on those days, I can remember him standing at the head of his formation of young soldiers, while I looked on with my hair close-cropped to my head like the rest of them. Queen Elizabeth Avenue ran through the heart of the garrison, and it was here that I watched my dad play football at the army's ramshackle stadium, my eyes often drawn to the skies where the Paras tested the mettle of their recruits by making them jump from a hot-air balloon floating above the drop zone.

I loved being in that environment of soldiers, tanks and trucks – I suppose that most kids would – but not all my memories are pleasant. My mum and dad fought a lot. I never saw them physically hit each other, but their words cut. With my two sisters, I'd wait out the storms. I was the oldest and they looked to me for answers – what could I tell them at that age? I was as confused as they were. Confused and scared. Not for myself but for my family. There were a lot of kids with only one parent around the garrison. I didn't want to be one of them, but life doesn't always care about what we want.

It happened when I was seven years old. It was New Year's Eve, which was also my dad's birthday. They were going at it again, but this time the intensity was cranked up to a whole other level. Eventually the door slammed, my dad left, and finally our hearts slowed down and we slept. In the morning, Mum woke us, and I was instantly nervous. I'd never seen her so animated. So fidgety.

'We're moving to Manchester,' she said simply. 'I'm leaving your dad.'

She was our mum, and so we went.

Manchester was her home town, but she didn't have a home there now. We were put into a bed-sit, sharing a building with a bunch of other families who seemed on edge and miserable. I didn't realise it then, but it was a shelter for the homeless.

I try not to think too much about that time. Not because it was so terrible for me but because I try not to dwell on the down points in life. I'm a positive person. Looking back, I remember the dirt of the place. A damp smell that was eventually over-powered by the stink of burnt fat when one flat had a pan fire. The building wasn't much to look at, or to smell, but there were good people there – people who had fallen on hard times, victims of harsh circumstances. Thinking about it now, I'm glad to have had that experience, as it taught me not to judge those less fortunate than myself. People often see somebody who's homeless and they judge and criticise, but who knows what that person has been through? Who knows what horrible things might have happened in their life? What battles they have fought, or are still fighting?

Of course, I didn't think that at the time.

I was too busy trying not to get the shit kicked out of me.

Our shelter was in Moss Side, which at the time was probably the roughest part of the UK. I was the only white kid, and I wasn't even from Manchester, so you can imagine how I stuck out when I got to school. Like any big brother, I wanted to protect my sisters, and so there weren't many days where I wasn't coming home with bruised knees and skinned knuckles. You're probably thinking that the guy who went on to be a Special Forces soldier was some kind of karate kid at a young age. If only. I threw my legs and fists around like the Tasmanian Devil but there was a lot of them and only one of me, and usually I needed the quick reaction of a teacher coming to pull me out of the melee before I got any permanent damage. I reckon I must have drunk a lot of milk as a kid, because despite all the batterings I didn't ever have a broken bone.

It was a strange place, that school, and the neighbourhood. Later, working on operations, I'd feel that same vibe in the air as I had in Moss Side – a sense that something dangerous could occur at any time, for any reason. I remember one day I was in the playground, waiting for my next shoeing, when a kid threw something over the fence that hit a woman. I don't even know what the object was, but in no time her son had arrived, a beard on his face and a knife in his hand. The headmaster, who looked like Gerry Adams, came out to try and quiet things down, but this was one peace process that wasn't going to happen – the young lad grabbed the headmaster in a headlock and held the knife on to him until the police arrived.

That was Moss Side, but my weekends at that age couldn't have been more different to my school days. On Fridays, my dad would make the four and a half hour drive to Manchester to collect me and my sisters, and then we'd head back down south to spend the weekend with him in Aldershot. It must have run up the clock on his car and then some, but I appreciated it. As the boy in the family, I felt closest to my dad, and I loved playing in the woods or playing football with my old friends – I'd got used to being the one taking the boot, so it was nice to be the one doing the kicking for a change!

I was a lot happier in Aldershot than I was in Manchester. It wasn't so much that I preferred one parent over the other, but when the judge hearing our custody case asked me which one I'd like to live with, the choice was clear for me. I said my dad, and my days of being a punchbag were over.

Or so I thought.

My dad was a 'tracksuit soldier', meaning that he spent much of his time in the army doing sports, which of course is one of the perks of the military and a big draw for recruits. If you're good at a particular sport or discipline, you can spend most of your time out of green kit, living a kind of semi-professional sporting lifestyle. Though my dad was a squadron sergeant major, he spent most of his time in Aldershot running and training the football team. He may have worn a tracksuit, but its creases were razor sharp – and he was as old school as you like when it came to my education.

'You're going to Wavell,' he told me. It was a school outside Aldershot; none of my friends would be going there. I told him so.

'There's more to the world than Aldershot,' he said, and it was only as I got older that I realised he wanted me to see beyond the pad, and the Paras and the parades. Though I was living in a sea of green, the army was not something that was about to be pushed on to me.

That first day of school was tough. Dad may not have been pushing the army on me, but he was certainly putting forth their standards. You could cut bread with the edges of my blazer's sleeves, and my briefcase was spotless. I looked like that gimp from *The Inbetweeners*, and I got welcomed like him too. The other kids didn't know anything about pad brats, and if my 'uniform' didn't stand me out, then my close-cropped hair did.

Yet again, the school yard was a battleground for me. After Moss Side, though, this was nothing, and before long it was me who was getting the upper hand. I thought that was a good thing, until I got suspended.

When Dad's service ended, I was given a clean slate: we moved to a small village in the Surrey countryside. For once, nobody seemed interested in kicking the shit out of me. I had thought school was about watching my back and counting down the minutes until the end of the day, but now I got into the sports on offer, and I did OK in the classroom. I wasn't about to be welcomed into the Premier League or Mensa, but I was a solid all-rounder.

'What are you gonna do when you finish school?' my dad asked me one day.

I'd had the answer for a while. 'Fireman,' I told him confidently. It looked like a job where you could stay fit, and the money was decent. Truth be told, I was thinking with the thing between my legs – what girl doesn't like a firefighter?

My dad didn't have much to say about my career choice. I think he was just relieved that I had my eyes on something and wasn't about to start drifting when my formal education finished.

I enjoyed those final few years of school. I felt like my fighting days had been left behind me in Aldershot. I was well liked in this new environment, and the location suited me too. Being out in nature was where I felt at home. I had one friend who lived on a trout farm, and another who lived on a cattle farm, and I spent a lot of time with both of them, helping out, just for the fun of it. It was also in these years that I began to surf. It was my dad who took me; we'd catch waves either in Cornwall or the

South of France. Even though the sea is a dangerous place and the power of the waves is not to be underestimated, there is a real tranquillity out on your board. It helps you realise your place. Clear your thoughts. Perhaps this is why I had chilled out a lot since the 'playground' of Moss Side.

I left school in 1993, and soon found that my dream of becoming a firefighter was just that – there were thousands of applicants for every one space. Not much chance of a seventeen-year-old sprog getting to the front of the line. I'd never really thought of an alternative, and so I did what a lot of young men do when they're without a job and it's summer – I went to the coast to chase women.

I chased waves too. Newquay was a hell of a spot, and as my mates spent their days on the piss, I spent mine in the swell. I didn't want the dream to end, but even staying at hostels and eating cheap I was running out of money.

Then, one day as I was waiting to catch a wave, I began talking to a young Norwegian guy.

'I've been here all summer,' he told me.

'How the hell do you afford that?'

'Easy. Silver service. I wait at breakfast, then I get to eat for free. I surf all day, then go back and do the same at dinner. They pay me thirty pounds in cash a day, and it costs me ten to stay at a hostel.'

I wasn't Archimedes, but even I could do that maths. 'You eat for free, surf all day and you still get twenty quid in your hand?' I couldn't believe it. When he told me that he'd lend me a suit so that I could get started, I almost tap-danced on my board.

And so that was how I passed the summer. They were some of the best days of my life, and when my dad came to collect me and my friends, he found that I wasn't there to go back with them. That was a bit of a selfish move on my part, but in my defence, the waters were warm and the women were warmer. I was living a dream, and I suppose that Dad felt it was his duty to be my alarm clock. Eventually, he came back out to get me. If you've ever been a young adult disagreeing with a parent, or vice versa, then you'll know that it wasn't a happy reunion.

'You've thrown away your education!' he told me in the car. 'It's too late for you to try and get into somewhere now. What will you do?' We both knew that I had about as much chance of becoming a fireman as I did of winning Miss World.

And then, without even thinking, I said, 'I'll join the army.'

My dad scoffed. 'The army? You wouldn't last two minutes.'

And something in those words – something in his tone – hit my pride like a hammer, and I knew in that moment that I would prove him wrong.

I'd join the army.

I'd become a soldier.

And I'd be a great one.

2. BASIC TRAINING

My journey into the army began the next day.

It was a short walk to the Armed Forces Careers Office. The night before – still a little in shock that I planned to go ahead with what I had said – my dad had told me that I should get the most that I could out of the army, instead of them just getting the most out of me. No doubt expecting that I would bail on this new career path as soon as possible, he suggested that I join a corps where I could learn a trade that would help me on civvy street.

Instead I joined the Paras.

'You've done *what*?' My dad shook his head when I gave him the good news.

The Paras were a fixture in Aldershot, and I'd always fancied a crack at jumping out of their balloon. I was cocky, and I knew I had the bollocks. Surfing on the ocean gave me an amazing adrenaline rush. I figured jumping out of a plane would be more of the same. And I'd be getting paid for it.

My dad shook his head until I was worried it would fall off. 'You're not joining the Paras,' he told me in that tone that a son knows not to argue with. 'Listen,' he went on, 'there's other places in the army where you can jump out of planes.'

Outside the sporting side, my dad had never really talked to me much about the military directly. As I said, I never had the army pushed on me, but now he outlined a few options where I could secure a trade *and* step out of a perfectly good aircraft.

'Nine Para Squadron are here in Aldershot,' he explained. 'They're part of the Royal Engineers. So are Five-nine Commando.'

'Commando?' I asked, suddenly interested. What young lad hasn't pictured himself on daring raids behind enemy lines?

'They're Royal Engineers,' he told me, 'but they operate with Three Commando Brigade. You'd be working with the Marines. If you went to Five-nine, you could get your dagger as well as your wings.'

I liked the sound of that, and so I told my dad that I'd go back to the careers office to change my paperwork.

He stood up, taking no chances. 'Not without me you won't.'

A few weeks later, I went to the camp at Pirbright for my assessment. There was a lot of running around, lots of shouting instructors who were trying not to smile, and lots of rain. We talked to some of the recruits who were already undergoing their training, but they looked to the instructors before giving every answer. It was like those videos where the hostage says that the terrorists are treating him well, and I suppose the recruit would have been on the end of a beasting if he'd said, 'It's shit! Don't come!'

At the end of that assessment we were called in by the staff who had been overseeing us and given a grade. I received an A, and I couldn't wait to show it to my dad. I could see the pride in him, but more than that, I think he realised for the first time that I was actually serious about going ahead with this career. Looking back, maybe it was the first time that I realised it myself.

Having received my A-grade and passed some tests, I was good to go and free to choose any trade within the Engineers that I wanted. As a seventeen year old again thinking with his downstairs brain, I decided that bomb disposal would be the best way to woo the ladies.

It certainly didn't woo Dad – 'You silly sod!' – and for the second time I was marched back to the careers office.

The choice of roles was broken down into A and B trades. A trades paid more, but B trades offered the better civvy qualifications, like plumbing. Hindsight is 20/20, and it would have been a good decision to take on one of those B roles, but I was young, keen and desperate to join the field army.

'What's the shortest course?' I asked the careers officer. They all seemed bloody long to me, and I'd joined up to be a soldier, not a student.

'This one's six months,' he told me. 'Plant operator.'

I was shocked. 'They have gardeners in the army?'

Once he'd stopped laughing, the recruiter told me that I'd be operating machinery like JCBs. It was good enough for me, and in no time I was at Bassingbourn for my basic training.

People might be surprised to hear that, like any government organisation, the army loves paperwork. I went through a bunch of the stuff during my recruiting process, and they sent me a load back in return.

'These are your joining instructions,' my dad explained. I'd see a lot of them in my military career. Every course, every exercise, every tour came with its own stack of papers. 'It says you need to report to Bassingbourn between zero-eight-hundred and seventeen-hundred hours.'

'Anytime between them?' I asked.

'That's right.'

Brilliant, I thought. *I can turn up about half-four and have the rest of the day to relax.*

The night before I left, my dad made sure that I had a squared-away haircut and that my suit would be pristine. 'First impressions count,' he told me, helping me to pack my bag so that everything was properly folded. 'The staff will judge you as soon as you arrive. Make a good first impression and the rest of training will be easier.'

He was talking from experience, and he was right. It was a lesson that stuck with me, and one that I live by to this day. No matter the client, no matter the meeting, no matter the place, first impressions count.

And my first impressions at basic training began at 0755.

'Always be somewhere five minutes early,' Dad said, teaching me an unofficial rule of the army.

Then, once my name had been ticked off the attendance sheet by an instructor, I learnt another one: hurry up and wait. I was the first recruit to arrive, and for the next nine hours I stood on parade in the rain, watching as the other recruits trickled in from across the country. I wasn't impressed at being soaked to my skin, but then I noticed that the recruits who had made it in last were already being harried by the instructors and asked for their names – better to be wet than beasted, I realised quickly. Better to be cold than conspicuous.

There's not much else to say about basic that hasn't been said a thousand times already. It's a universal experience, which is what makes it unifying between soldiers, regardless of country and regardless of race and religion. I enjoyed the physical training, and surprised myself by how competitive I was, both as an individual and in a team. If we lost and I didn't think someone had been pulling their weight, then they'd know about it. Very quickly I was realising that not everyone who joined the army was self-motivated, and though there was a sense of satisfaction in pulling people through, I felt myself gravitating towards the company of those who were as motivated as I was and aspiring to win whatever was in front of us, be it marksmanship or cross country.

When it came to Phase Two training, I found myself in familiar territory, back in Gibraltar Barracks, where my dad had been a squadron sergeant major. It meant that I was close to home and could go there on weekends. I felt sorry for the poor buggers who lived too far away, in towns like Inverness and Aberdeen. 'Why would anyone want to live up there?' I'd laugh at them – karma would come back at me for that one!

Like Phase One, Phase Two training wasn't anything that pushed me to my limits. It was enjoyable, and so was seeing my dad's face every weekend when I told him that I was loving it. In my mind, I'd already lasted two minutes. 'You're not even out of training yet,' the career soldier would chuckle to himself.

I didn't have a driving licence, and so I was sent to Leconfield to complete my training in everything from a Ford Fiesta to an artic wagon. This probably wasn't a good thing for a young man on a driving course to know, but I found out that the local town of Beverley had a large number of pubs, and so the course ended up being a lot of fun. At the end of it, I was now qualified for my position, and I called home to tell them about my first posting.

'I'm going to Two-eight,' I told my dad's partner, meaning

28 Engineer Regiment, and couldn't understand why she burst out crying.

My dad came on the line. 'You're going to Kuwait?' he said incredulously.

'Two-eight!' I laughed. 'Two-eight!'

The regiment was in Germany, and so I was now back in the same town that held hazy memories of my early life.

And just like in childhood, I found my days occupied with playing football. Two-eight were the army champions, and I had been sent here because I was Stotty's son and it was assumed that I must be a half-decent player myself. I was good enough to make the team, and was soon finding myself in the 'tracksuit soldier' role that my father had had.

'I'm hardly ever going to see you.' My first sergeant major shook his head. 'So I might as well send you on a PTI course.'

I almost laughed. The Physical Training Instructor course was conducted at Fox Lines in Aldershot. I felt like I had a bloody magnet in my forehead.

The course was a blast, though. Beastings. Assault courses. Sports. It was right up my street, and it was the first time in my army career where I was doing something that most other soldiers can't or won't do. I felt that I was proving that not only was I lasting more than two minutes in the army but I was excelling too.

The course completed and a set of crossed swords added to my uniform – the mark of a PTI – I returned to Germany and took up a position in the garrison gym. I took all five of the regiment's squadrons for PT, and found myself beginning to long for more challenge; when the unit needed to qualify for its combat fitness test (CFT) – an 8-mile march in 2 hours carrying 55lbs –

I'd lead the march for each squadron, sometimes doing five CFTs in two days. I loved it, and only wanted more.

I had seen my dad's career as a tracksuit soldier, and I knew that I was a decent enough athlete and PTI that I could follow in his footsteps if I wanted to, but I kept thinking to myself that I had joined the army to wear assault boots, not football ones.

I called my dad. 'Tell me again about Nine Para and Five-nine?' I asked him, repeating the same question to the older, more experienced men in my regiment.

The more I heard, the more I became certain that I wanted to join one of the units that required an arduous selection process. I wanted challenge – no, I *needed* it – and I just wasn't getting it where I was.

'I can't decide which one to go for,' I confided in a friend, and so in the end I filled out the paperwork for both specialist units. 'Hide them behind your back,' I told him, and then I picked one of his hands and looked at the top line of the sheet of paper.

59 Commando

My unit were good to me and didn't try and hold me back from moving on to a new squadron. Unfortunately, though, I nearly did that myself.

It was just before my assessment course for the Commando Engineers that it happened. One of the squadrons from our regiment had just got back from a tour of Northern Ireland, and the sappers were gathering with their families in the NAAFI for a welcome home party. We weren't the only units on the base, however; and some infantry soldiers of the Fusiliers were visiting.

I suppose that lads join the infantry to fight, and without an enemy to hand they'd taken this out on the local town, and so they were confined to camp. Now, full of lager, they wanted to make the NAAFI the next battlefield, and they started hurling insults at the wives of the returning sappers.

We may all have been part of the same army, but it was squadron first, then regiment, then corps. Our fellow Engineers were under attack and so we started throwing punches. I got some good licks in on the infantry before we were pulled apart and sent our separate ways. Fights were hardly uncommon in the garrison, and as I went to bed I didn't think much more of it.

I certainly thought more about it when I woke up to find the military police standing by my bed.

I was taken down to the base's cop shop. Apparently, a few of the Fusiliers were in hospital, and I'd been pinged as one of the people that had put them there. I tried to protest my innocence, but they weren't having it: 'They all recognised you from the gym.'

Bollocks.

'There's going to be a follow-up to this,' the RMP promised me.

'But can I go now?' I asked. 'My beat-up training starts next week.' I tried not to smile at that – apparently I was already pretty skilled when it came to beat-ups, but this wasn't a drunken fight in the NAAFI. It was four weeks of getting beasted up and down mountains in Devon and Wales in preparation for the All Arms Commando Course.

I could have kissed them in relief when they let me go. I flew through the beat-up training and loved the All Arms course at Lympstone. It was just the challenge that I'd wanted from the army, and I wore my green beret with pride. There were times during the course when I really had to dig in, and during those moments I would think of my dad's words to me on that car journey: 'You won't last two minutes.' And I pushed through. Was it healthy to draw inspiration from that? I don't know, but it fucking worked and I walked away from Lympstone and its honking beastings on Bottom Field as a Commando.

I reported to Barnstaple, Devon, proudly wearing the dagger on my sleeve and my green beret. I felt ten foot tall and couldn't wait to join my new unit.

But first there was shit to deal with at the old one.

'The squadron's going across the water,' the OC told me, meaning Northern Ireland, and I couldn't have been happier; an operational tour!

Maybe he saw my smile. 'Not you,' he said. 'You're going across the other water, to Germany. From there, because of your fight with the Fusiliers, you're probably going to do a spell in Colchester.'

The words hit me like a blow to the stomach. I was gutted. I wanted to soldier, and instead I might be going to the army's prison.

I was still feeling that way when I arrived in Germany and went in front of the CO. The Colonel looked me over and saw my regret. 'Look, Sapper Stott, I was going to give you sixty days, but because you did so well on the Commando course I'm going to knock it down to fifty-six.'

My head raised a little then. I felt my spirit coming back. This officer had once been a member of 9 Squadron, and I just couldn't help myself. 'How many days off would I have got if I'd gone airborne, sir?' I asked with a straight face.

Thankfully, the CO laughed and I didn't feel a pace stick getting rammed up my arse by the regimental sergeant major behind me. Instead, the Regimental Police entered, and I was marched at double-quick time to the guard room, to await my transportation to military prison.

Having been a PTI with a good work ethic, I was well known and well liked in the regiment despite being only a junior soldier, and so I wasn't surprised when one of the regimental PTIs asked me if I wanted to go for a run.

Captivity didn't seem so bad as we ran through the town's streets. It seemed even better when my squadron mates caught sight of me through a pub window and called me over.

'I can't drink,' I told them. 'I think I'm under arrest.'

Someone pushed a pint into my hand. 'All the more reason then, yeah?'

I could hardly argue with that logic. Neither could I argue with the charges when I was found passed out in an Irish bar the next morning, still in my PT kit. At some point during the night I'd tried to lean out of a window to take a piss and lost my balance. Now my wrist was the size of an orange.

'It's broken,' they told me at the hospital, and now the regimental staff had a dilemma – could I still be sent to Colchester with a broken wrist?

In the end they decided that I could, and so began my imprisonment at the pleasure of Her Majesty's Armed Forces.

The impression that everyone has of Colchester's military prison is that it's all shouty-shouty and in your face. That's certainly what it's like when you first get there, but I think that's just to make an impression on your escorts, who will carry the story back to your unit and put off other would-be naughty boys. I found the staff there to be respectful and pleasant. I even got a doughnut on my first evening.

Drink was a big problem in the Forces at that time – I'd be surprised if it isn't still – and so when I was interviewed by the officer of the prison, I was grilled on my alcohol consumption.

'You were drunk when you hit the other soldiers, correct?'

'Yes, sir.'

'So you have a drinking problem?'

'No, sir, I'd have hit them anyway.'

'Hmm. What happened to your wrist?'

'I fell out of a window, sir. Trying to urinate, sir.'

'Were you drunk?'

'Well . . . yes, sir.'

'Hmm. So you have a drinking problem?'

I didn't really know what to reply to that one. As far as I saw it, it was just part of army life. Part of being a squaddie. If I had a drinking problem, then maybe the whole army did. Personally, I felt it was just boys being boys. The officer dismissed me.

Strangely enough, I actually found that I enjoyed Colchester. Perhaps the dirty homeless shelter was the reason, but I was meticulous when it came to tidiness and cleanliness, and so I wasn't bothered at all by the stringent inspections. If anything, I liked the fact that everyone had to have their locker squared away in exactly the same fashion. The prisoners with the cleanest and most tidy rooms were allowed a radio for two hours in the evening, and my competitive spirit came out – I wanted to win that radio each and every night, and I would be pissed off at myself if I didn't.

There were different kinds of prisoners at Colchester. Many were like me, there because they'd done something stupid, and we were treated differently to the shitbags who showed no signs of remorse or redemption. They just wanted out of the army, and there was a separate wing for them. In my wing, it was split between those serving more than four weeks and those serving less time, and of course we looked down on the short-timers – I can get competitive about *anything* and I had flashbacks to the Christmas board games in my childhood. Those games nights were loaded with as much pressure as the Cuban Missile Crisis, no one wanting to back down or lose.

In the end, I got a third off my sentence because I was a good prisoner and tried my hardest. We had plenty of PT, plenty of military lectures, and I soaked it all up. If it hadn't been for the fact that my pay was stopped while I was inside, I'd have been happy to stay longer.

But that wasn't to be. I was on my way to 59 – and we were going to deploy.

3. COMMANDO

I couldn't have asked for a better beginning to my time at 59. The admin officer took one look at my report from Colchester, seemed happy with what he saw and ripped it up.

'Fresh start,' he said.

But it was a lonely start. The rest of the squadron was in Northern Ireland, finishing the tour that I had missed out on due to my time in Collie. I was gutted not to be a part of that, but it ended up working in my favour.

'We're sending you on the diving aptitude course,' the rear party sergeant major told me. 'Usually guys have to wait years to get on this, so consider yourself lucky.'

I did. Surfing had made me a strong swimmer and I felt at home in the water, so taking that to a new level was an amazing experience for me. It was a highly sought-after course for a reason, and I loved the challenge of working in a new environment beneath the waves.

I was back in camp just in time for the squadron to get back from Ireland. Being new to a unit always gives you a bit of an uneasy feeling, like the first day in a new school, but when guys are coming back from a deployment you know that the testosterone's going to be cranked up another level. To be honest, after putting lads into hospital and Colchester I was a bit full of myself too, but thankfully nothing got out of hand. There was the usual sniffing around each other, trying to establish the pecking orders that exist outside the army's official chain of command, but no violence. At least, not until I volunteered to be part of the squadron's boxing team.

There were a couple of reasons I did this. I thought it would be a good way to get accepted quickly by my new squadron mates – and it was – but there was also that itch inside me. That need to be constantly pushing myself. What better way to do that than to go up against someone who was trying to take my head off my shoulders? At least this time I wouldn't be fighting in a blazer, with one hand on my *Inbetweeners* briefcase.

There was one fight in particular that cemented my reputation as a 'good bloke', one who was welcomed into his new unit. During the army's boxing finals I put one lad on the canvas three times inside ninety seconds. That got the approval of the 'old heads', the sweats and veterans of the unit, and once you had them on your side you were sorted.

Five-nine turned out to be everything I'd been looking for. The physical challenge was there, and without meaning to disparage anyone I had worked with previously, the people around me seemed to mirror my desire to push myself and to be pushed by others. We were competitive, confident and cut around giving it the big licks. I'm sure we were cocky too, but that comes with the territory when you have young lads in uniform, training for war.

This training took us all over the world, from golden beaches in the Caribbean to frozen forests in Norway. Three Commando Brigade would be the ones to stop the Russians if they were to mess around up in the Arctic, and so I got my first experience of jumping into a hole cut in the ice of a frozen lake. You had to recite your name and army number and answer a few questions before getting out of the hole unassisted – I can't even describe how cold that water was, but I think it was about a week before I saw my manhood again. Still, you just got on with it. Showing weakness in front of the boys was not acceptable, and so you'd put on your best smile and crack a joke.

It wasn't long into my time at Five-nine that I was selected for Recce Troop, a kind of elite within the squadron. It was a huge privilege, as Recce was known as being a great stepping stone towards the Special Forces – an idea that I'd begun to toy with, thinking about my future in the army.

Recce's job was to go ahead of the squadron and to look for vulnerable positions in the enemy's lines that could be exploited by the sappers, creating a breach for the Royal Marines to push through. To get ahead of the main body, Recce were required to be the fittest men in the squadron, and they were also required to jump out of planes.

At last! Just like the Paras I had seen floating down to Earth around Aldershot, I finally got my chance to throw myself into thin air from a perfectly good aircraft.

It was just the rush that I'd expected, and I was only disappointed that the jumps course wasn't longer. I would have quite happily gone up day after day, night after night, but instead I was back to my unit and back on the constant cycle of overseas and domestic exercises. There was a huge one in Egypt, where we acted as part of the Brigade Recce Force. This meant that we worked alongside the hardcore of the Royal Marines – their snipers and mountain leaders – which was both a great chance to learn and a hell of an incentive not to fuck up and look shit. It was also my first exposure to the heat of the Middle East, which was something I'd come to know rather intimately.

One day, I called home to the UK with news for my dad. He'd probably forgotten long ago about our 'two minutes' conversation in the car. I hadn't, and I had a big smile on my face as I gave him the news.

'I'm going to Kosovo,' I told the old soldier. 'I'm going on tour!'

4. OP AGRICOLA

In 2000, 59 Commando was deployed in full to the Balkans, a part of the world that was still torn apart by vicious war and ethnic cleansing that had claimed the lives of thousands of combatants and civilians. As a soldier, this was the kind of mission you hoped for. We knew that we were on the side of good, bringing peace to people who just wanted to live and grow up in a country without fear. While the rest of 59 was sent into Bosnia, Recce Troop joined the NATO effort in a region known as Kosovo. It was a small place, half the size of Wales, and just like the mountains where I would later attempt the first part of Special Forces selection, it was hills, hills and more hills.

We got there in the autumn, as the leaves were beginning to fall from the trees of the thick forests that clung to the sides of the steep mountains. The locals were as dogged as the plant life, and there were some among them who were not interested in peace and stability. They wanted blood and revenge, and we were there to stop that happening. We were armed, but because we were not engaged in fighting, I felt a little like a cop stuck in the middle of a gang war – except that here both sides had tanks.

This was the first independent op for Recce Troop since the Falklands War, almost twenty years before. That came with a lot of responsibility, and we wanted to do as good a job as the men that had gone before us. It also made me realise how lucky I was – not every soldier gets to go on operations, and here I was, with my mates, ready to put our training into action. We didn't have an enemy as such, but we had plenty of threats – both the ethnic Albanians and the Serbians were armed and numerous, and we knew that with the coming winter, Mother Nature would be giving us a hard time too.

Our first task on the tour was to get eyes on a group of war criminals who had set up shop in the 5km buffer zone that NATO had drawn up between Serbia and the new territory of Kosovo. In theory, there should be no troop movement within the zone by any side, but this made it a good place for some of the people behind the recent genocide to hide.

Or so they thought.

Acting on local intelligence (int.), six of us patrolled into the mountains to get eyes on the farmhouse that we believed was their home. Thinking about the terrible atrocities they had committed, the murder of innocent women and children, made you want to charge ahead and take them down, but we were professional soldiers and so we patrolled quietly and patiently, and a good thing too.

We were being followed.

We could hear it every time we paused to take a map bearing: a rustle in the leaves, like someone was tiptoeing. I looked to my mates and raised my eyebrows. They did the same back. We waited, but nobody showed themselves and eventually we had to move on.

We stopped for another map check. 'There it is again,' I mouthed silently to my nearest mate. Again we waited for the person following us to reveal himself, but nothing. My heart was beating a little faster now. I didn't know these mountains. The

Serbs and the Albanians did. Were they slipping in and out of caves? Tunnels? It was unnerving.

We got to the high ground and dug in our Observation Post (OP), where we could get eyes on the war criminals. We used high-tech optics, and wrote down anything that we saw. At night, we had early night vision – not as great as we get now, but good enough to note the comings and goings of people and cars. They had no idea we were there.

But someone did.

We could hear them tiptoeing around our position every night, but even with our night vision goggles we couldn't see anyone.

'This is giving me the creeps,' one of the lads whispered to me.

I'd given a lot of thought to who it might be hunting us. 'I think it's Predator,' I said, expecting to see Arnold Schwarzenegger come running through the trees.

We spent fourteen days in that position, getting weirded-out by Predator, pissing into plastic containers and shitting into clingfilm. You leave no trace when you're Recce, and so two weeks' worth of bodily fluids and solids would be coming with us back down the mountain; I'm not sure why they leave that tasty fact out of the recruiting brochures!

The work may not always have been pleasant, but it was rewarding, and our observations were part of building the case against these men and would go towards their eventual apprehension and takedown. I've found a lot of things in life that give me satisfaction, and knowing that I helped put monsters into cages is one of them.

It was hard work getting down off the mountain. We'd been minimising our movement for two weeks, and then we had to tab down with all our weapons, kit and the stuff that I already mentioned – not easy when you've been static in the cold for so long. When we got back, I saw people wrinkle their noses at our stink, but it didn't bother us. All part of the job.

'We think there was someone up there,' our team leader told the intelligence officer during our debrief.

The man shook his head. 'There's no fighters up there.'

'I'm telling you we heard something. Every night. Tiptoeing in the leaves.'

There was a long silence, then, 'Ah.'

My team leader leant forwards. 'What?'

'We probably should have told you this in the briefing, but . . .'

'What?'

'At this time of year the tortoises come out at night and gather to mate. That's what you'll have been hearing.'

We looked at each other, then burst into laughter. Here we were, the big bad Recce boys, and we'd lost hours of sleep because of a tortoise getting his end away. Only later did I realise that there was a very real lesson to be learnt from the experience: little details can have big consequences. We could have literally scrapped that mission, thinking that we were compromised. It showed me that when it comes to planning, there is no such thing as too 'silly' or obscure to include. You're going backpacking in North America? You'd better be prepared for bears. Trekking in the jungle? Bring along your anti-venom.

And in Kosovo?

Be aware of horny tortoises.

*

I got taught another valuable lesson soon after the first one.

There were a lot of people in Kosovo looking to settle scores. Sometimes these were ethnic divisions that went back hundreds of years, and other times it was more personal. If you'd helped out the Serbs during the fighting, you were at risk of a nasty ending. Likewise, the Serbs would send hit squads across the buffer zone to take out people who had pissed them off in the short but brutal war.

It was a mess, but it was our job to try and keep as much blood off the streets as we could. When the int. came in that a certain individual – let's call him Mr X – had been picked for assassination, we were put into plain clothes to stop it happening. We weren't his bodyguards, more like guardian angels. We'd follow him on foot. We'd wait in the back of vans. He wasn't a hard man to track, keeping to a very familiar pattern of life, day in, day out.

That's not a good idea when someone's decided to kill you.

One cold morning, it all went down. We saw the assassins coming long before they saw us. We knew their faces from the int. briefings we'd received, and they looked the part, real seasoned veterans. They were known to have blood on their hands, and it seemed as though they were about to spill more. We couldn't let that happen, and so, as they approached their man, our vehicles roared in and our guys on foot ran to the target and his would-be killers, shouting, 'Down, down, down, NATO forces!'

The two assassins did exactly as they were told and slowly dropped to the deck. They were calm. Too calm.

'No weapons on them,' a soldier said.

It took a few seconds for someone to realise why.

'This was their fucking rehearsal!' he cursed.

These guys were pros, just like us. We rehearse and rehearse before conducting a mission, and we put in our recces to gather intelligence. They had done exactly the same, and by doing a rehearsal they had discovered that this man had NATO angels on his shoulders. They backed off him for a few years after they discovered that, bided their time and eventually got him. Mr X hadn't learnt the lesson of varying his routine and putting in counter-surveillance drills, but I'd learnt mine. The Army's motto at the time was 'Be the best', and that had gone to our heads. If you are capable of doing something, then so is the person who is trying to kill or beat you. Never underestimate your enemy, be that a person, terrain or weather. Look at things from every angle. Put yourself in their shoes. If we had asked ourselves, 'How would we take out this guy as a start-to-finish operation?' then we would have realised that they were likely to rehearse. Be humble enough to know you're not the only one with a plan. Revise it, adapt it, and above all challenge it – better to be proved wrong by yourself than by 'the enemy'.

Winter in Kosovo is hard. Biting cold, icy winds and deep snows. I suppose, then, that I must have been a little wrong in the head for being excited about the idea of going into the mountains for another four weeks in an OP.

The Serbs had come to NATO and told them that there was a splinter group of the Kosovo Liberation Army inside the buffer zone. Apparently, this group had no desire for peace, only more bloodshed, and so they had set up a training camp where they thought they'd be out of sight and out of mind. Yet again, we were happy to prove them wrong.

The tab to the site of the OP was an absolute lick-out. The snow was fresh and knee deep, with a lovely thin layer of ice on top. Hard enough to trudge through when you're just carrying a snowboard, but we had bergens that required two mates to help you put on. The reason they were so heavy was that they were full of ammunition, rations and water – we'd be expected to stay in situ for up to a month. It made for hard going, but at least this time there were no tortoises to haunt us.

To remain unseen, we dug into the snow and set up our specialist tents inside the drifts. We'd had plenty of practice at this during our exercises in the Arctic, and to be honest, I loved living the simple life out of my kit. It was a camping trip on steroids. Again, we knew that the information we provided would be important, and so we put our best attention and effort into the task. The training camp was like a miniature version of Bassingbourn, and we saw their recruits getting weapon training on everything from AKs to mortars. They posted sentries, but they had no idea we were there, watching and capturing every move.

After four weeks of living in the snow, we were due to be relieved by an American SF unit. I was sent down the mountainside, with my mate B, to escort them in.

Their leader was a SEAL, about the same build as me, a little more athletic than average but no beast. The others in the team looked like NFL players.

'Ready to go?' I asked them, seeing them shoot dubious looks at the mountainside and its thick snow.

It was just ten minutes before the first of them needed to stop. Their leader looked on embarrassed as B took the man's kit. Ten minutes later we had to stop again, and this time I ended up with a set of American kit on my back. I began to worry that, with the way things were going, B and I would end up carrying all the kit, and we only had a two-hour window to get to the OP.

Thankfully, the others had more mental resilience, and when we got within a few minutes of the OP, I stopped the patrol for them to catch their breath and get their bearings. I saw B shaking his head at their lack of light discipline as torch beams lit up the mountainside.

'Is that the training camp?' one of them asked, pointing back in the direction we'd come.

To be fair to their leader, he seemed appalled, and I wondered if he'd just been saddled with these guys at the last minute. Us 'scrawny' Brits collapsed back from the OP with our military rucksacks, weighing almost the same as the people carrying them, and I heard a couple of the Americans mutter things like 'Jeez'. I'm not knocking the Yank SF – they're good at what they do – but they're just not programmed like we are. We've never had the luxury of having enough wagons and helicopters to ferry us and our kit. We have to carry it ourselves, and we better take enough because the resupply is probably coming in by foot too. Blokes carrying half a house on their backs may not make for as good a Hollywood movie, but it makes for a tough and resilient soldier. I think that any civvy putting a bet on who was stronger would have picked the bigger guys, and maybe they could smash us on the bench press, but you don't bench your way up a mountainside or through a contact with the enemy.

Train how you intend to fight, and never judge a book by its cover.

We were just about to head home from Kosovo when we were fast-balled on to a task.

'We're going to apprehend a bomb maker,' we were told, and the adrenaline began to buzz in my veins.

Sitting through the int. brief, we learnt that someone had been cooking up bombs that were being used to take out politicians. The bomb maker wasn't the one using them; he was more like a chef for hire. Understandably, NATO were keen to get him off the streets.

I wasn't the one to grab him, but a couple of the other guys bundled him into the back of our vehicle. His hands were tied behind his back, and despite our orders to keep his eyes on the floor, he kept looking up and around him.

I put a hand on the back of his head to help his concentration.

'That's bang out of order!' The man shouted, in as sharp a Mancunian accent as I'd ever heard.

My jaw dropped, and I looked around at the other guys in the team. Not for one moment had we suspected that the bomb maker could be a fellow countryman.

When we dropped him off for questioning, I bet he wished he'd stayed at home. There was a solitary chair in the centre of a courtyard with two bright spotlights shining on to it. Very James Bond.

We left the bomb maker to answer for his crimes.

It was time for us to go home.

5. LYMPSTONE

Every unit in the field army needs to provide soldiers for guards, duties and postings. Five-nine was no different, and as we shared a camp with the Commando Logistics, we split our camp stag – guard duty – with them. Fortunately for those of us in Recce Troop, our duties took us in a more interesting direction than checking IDs at the camp gate – an important but eyeball-bleeding way of spending your day – and instead of providing an NCO here and there, one member of Recce was permanently based at Lympstone as part of the All Arms Commando Course Training Team. Though I was a lance corporal when I got back from Kosovo, I was given the acting rank of a full screw (corporal), and happily went to take up my new position of screening and instructing those who wanted to earn the coveted green lid (beret) and dagger. I felt very proud to be given such an honour and responsibility, and I promised myself that I would live up to the trust put in me by my unit.

The All Arms course had changed a lot since I had gone through it, only a few years previously. We had been beasted mercilessly, and there had been little instruction. As a result, soldiers could pass the course if they were fit and could stand being cold and wet, but what the Commandos wanted was people who were a cut above the average soldier in all skill sets – and who could stand being cold and wet. Unlike my experience of the course, there was a lot of emphasis on teaching and bringing out the best qualities in those on the course. I loved this, as I'm a big believer that the best soldiers are those who can take care of themselves, think for themselves and contribute to the chain of command, rather than having everything shouted in their face.

The All Arms Commando Course lasts for ten weeks, and for my first I shadowed the outgoing instructor I was about to replace. I think this is a valuable lesson to learn from the military. Giving someone time to study under the person they're replacing is invaluable in getting to know their new position or location – we did the same kind of thing on operations too. It doesn't mean that you have to be a robot and do everything the same as the person you're replacing, but if you leave your ego at the door, you can pick up methods of executing your mission that you may never have thought of if you'd dived in headfirst. Shadowing this instructor, I got to know the training area like the back of my hand, and I was able to deliver great instruction for the next course attendees when they arrived. If I'd still been learning the ropes while I was teaching them, I would have been doing them all a disservice. Worse, because this was the military, any sloppy instruction on my part could literally have life-or-death consequences.

In a first for me, one of the soldiers on the course was a woman. Surgeon Lieutenant Y was the medical officer of a Commando unit, and she quite rightly wanted to put herself through the same course as the men that she took care of. She came in with a great reputation of just 'cracking on', and we'd heard from the PTIs who had helped prepare her for the course that she had a great chance of passing.

I had no problem with that. I had no experience of soldiering alongside females, but my attitude towards them in the forces – and in life – was this: if they can do the job, then they should be allowed to do it.

What I didn't want, however, was a drop in standards to accommodate that. I didn't care what race, gender or religion a person was. What I *did* care about was the Commando ethos, and what it took to earn the dagger and coveted green beret: the only beret that cannot be worn unless the wearer has passed the course, unlike other brigades, where it can be worn by attached personnel who haven't passed that elite unit's rite of passage. I didn't want to see the standards be allowed to slip for *anyone*. I decided off the bat that I would treat Lieutenant Y the same as I would treat any lads on the course.

One thing that the Commando course emphasises is doing the basics of soldiering, but doing them well. Simple doesn't mean easy, and a good example of this is 'wet and dry routine'.

It goes without saying that soldiers get wet – a lot. We crawl through ditches, cross rivers and spend a lot of time in the rain. In such conditions you can easily become a cold-weather casualty, and to negate the chances of that happening you need to carry out 'wet/dry routine'. Whenever you get a chance to sleep and strip off your wet clothes in a secure location – usually a harbour area in woods – you do it, and put on the spare, dry clothing from your kit before getting into your sleeping bag to warm up. Rest is in short supply, so it probably won't be long before you have to come out of that nice warm cocoon for your next sentry duty, patrol or lesson. I bet you'd like to stay in those nice dry clothes, wouldn't you?

I'm afraid not.

Take your warm and dry kit off. Then get yourself back into your honking, stinking, freezing kit that's still soaking wet. Just getting into wet clothing is an effort in itself, and the feel of it against your skin is oh so lovely. It sucks – there's no doubt about it – but it's moments of discomfort like that which will save you days of discomfort if you get lazy and allow that second set of clothing to get wet too. Then what are you going to wear when you get chance to dry off?

Like everything we did on the course, wet/dry routine was explained, demonstrated, imitated and practised. I am a huge believer that you shouldn't ask someone to do something that you wouldn't do yourself, and so I went and lay down in an icy stream for a while, getting each one in the course to step over me so that they could see I was willing to go through what they would be required to do. Once that was done, I walked in my sopping clothing to the front of the class. 'I have to get naked now,' I said, looking to Lieutenant Y. In the field, you live, breathe and shit alongside your comrades, so any issues with bashfulness would affect operational effectiveness. 'Is that going to be a problem, ma'am?'

Surgeon Lieutenant Y shook her head. 'No, Corporal. I've seen it all before.'

But she hadn't seen this.

Some of the class burst into laughter as I pulled down my soaked trousers and boxers. Others gasped, not because I'm hung like an Afghan yak but because none of them guessed that I had a piercing at the end of my cock, and on to that ring I'd attached a half dozen Karabiners that were now pulling it down towards the ground.

'Looks like a piece of spaghetti,' one of the instructors

laughed. It was a sick piece of humour, but that's what the military runs on. When you're cold, wet and tired, you need a pick me up, and a knock-knock joke doesn't cut it.

We used that prank on later courses too. Another of our favourites was to mess with them in a flooded tunnel that they had to pass through on the endurance course. The tunnel was short but completely flooded, and people were naturally scared of that claustrophobic space. Again, we demonstrated what we would ask them to do.

The course watched as the first instructor dunked me and put me into the short tunnel. What they didn't know is that I'd been down there earlier and placed a STASS bottle at the half-way point, and now I sucked on the oxygen from this hand-held cylinder as I looked at the hands on my watch. I gave it a good two minutes before I dumped it and pushed off. I was out the other end in seconds.

'Fuck me!' I gasped, as I surfaced to a sea of terrified faces. 'Whatever you do, do not go left!'

'There's different tunnels, staff?' someone blurted out, nervous as hell. They all were, and that was the reason that we set up the prank. The drill was actually extremely safe, but now the class were all fearful of it. They'd have to overcome that fear, and the more you can overcome fear, the less control it will have over you in all parts of your life. Parachute school was the same. It's not so much about learning to parachute as it is having the courage to step into thin air. Always after the demonstration I'd ask, 'Who's up first?' and that would show you who the real leaders were in the pack. Quite often, these came in the most surprising packages.

The same was true of soldiering skills. Back on that first

course I instructed, I watched as one of the aspiring Commandos went through the close quarter battle range like an absolute pro. Their use of cover was perfect, as was their movement, weapon handling and marksmanship.

'Bloody hell,' I said to my fellow instructor, 'their drills were gleamin'. Who was that?'

He shrugged, and we turned to look in the direction of the slick drilled soldier, our jaws dropping as we saw long hair coming out from beneath the helmet, swept out with a shake of the head like a shampoo commercial.

Surgeon Lieutenant Y.

'I can't believe it,' my mate said.

Neither could I, but: 'If she was the best, then she should know it.' And so he walked over to congratulate her.

Surgeon Lieutenant Y was a keen student in the lessons and well squared away on her drills. In that regard she was one of the most competent candidates I'd met, but her weakness came in the physical activity. During yomps, she would be placed at the front of the formation, where the going is easiest due to being able to keep a constant pace, unlike the people behind, who suffer from the yo-yo effect like you get in built-up traffic. Despite this, she still moaned and groaned her way through. I didn't like her chances of passing the Commando tests – a fail in any one of them and she'd not earn her lid.

One of those tests was Bottom Field, and one of the hardest parts of it is a 30m rope climb with kit. Lieutenant Y burnt out two feet from the top. I felt terrible for her, but the standard is the standard, and it exists for a reason. There were plenty of men who had failed on that part of the test too. That's just the way it was. Very few people can achieve what it takes to be a

Commando, but if Surgeon Lieutenant Y had made that climb, then neither I nor any of the other instructors would have had any issue with passing her and awarding her the green lid and dagger.

When it came to the end of the course, Lieutenant Y had failed her nemesis, the Bottom Field test on the rope – a shame as this was the only test preventing her earning the green beret.

As I said, I don't care if you're a man or woman; if you can make the standard, you make the standard.

Captain F was a great example of this. He was fifty-five years old, and as far as I'm aware, he was the first world-record-holder that I ever met. He was the oldest man to ever attempt the course – but what did age matter to the man who currently held four world bests in long-distance running? The rumour was that Captain F had some kind of condition that meant if he stopped being in top physical condition he'd be browners, but maybe that was just a mental thing. A philosophy. Either way, I think it's a good lesson for us all: when we stop moving forward, be that in learning, with challenges, or just growing as a human being, that is the point where we cease to live, and when you stop living . . . well, Dr Stott is here to tell you that you die.

I have a lot of admiration for Captain F. He was the embodiment of what I considered a soldier to be – he was just a beast, mentally and physically, and didn't have a single ounce of quit in him. I mean, he'd done P Company training seven years before I was even born, and there he was, yomping alongside me like a twenty-year-old trooper!

He was perspiring a hell of a lot though, even though he wasn't out of breath.

'You all right, sir? You're sweating like a Marine on a spelling test.' I thought he was coming down with something, but he just smiled.

'Oh, don't worry about that, Corporal. I caught pneumonia twenty years ago and it messed me up a bit, but nothing to worry about.'

Nothing to worry about?

'By the way, Corporal, when we do the thirty-miler, do you mind me telling my girlfriend where the finish line is? I'd love for her to be there.'

The finish of the thirty-miler marked the end of the Commando tests, and it was where the course attendees would receive their green berets. It was supposed to be secret, but . . . this guy was a legend.

'All right, sir, but just keep it to yourself, yeah?'

A few days later, we came around the final bend of the thirty-miler and my jaw dropped to the floor.

It looked like Portsmouth when the troops came home from the Falklands, kids jumping up and down, and banners blowing in Dartmoor's winds.

I was gobsmacked. I turned to look at Captain F but I said nothing. The man was fifty-five and had completed one of the hardest courses the British military had to offer. He deserved his banners, and his fan club.

As my time at Lympstone drew to a close, I looked back at what I'd learnt there. There were a lot of lessons, from how many Karabiners I could dangle from my willy to an eye-opener on how the armed forces' attitude towards women was changing, but the most valuable lesson I learnt was about what kind of instructor I was.

I think a lot of NCOs came into their positions on courses –
and at units – thinking that being shouty-shouty and swearing
was the way to behave because that's how it had been for them,
and perhaps they thought it made them feared.

Personally, I didn't want to scare people into learning. If
they didn't want to be there, then they'd end up failing themselves without me shouting and screaming. I found it far more
effective to use humour, and to be quiet at times when others
would shout. Using that old parents' line of 'I'm not angry, I'm
just disappointed'. Just a look would be enough. They wanted
the approval of those already wearing a green lid, and so if they
saw that they had 'failed' you, they'd double their efforts on the
next task. No need for shouting or swearing. When you fill a
void with swearing, it looks – rightly or wrongly – like it's down
to a lack of intelligence or to anger issues. Instructors are being
assessed by their students just as much as the other way around.

I also decided early on that I would share in any punishment
that I handed out. If I gave them press-ups, then I'd get down in
the mud and do them too. Not only did that earn their respect
but it gave them no excuse in their minds to feel hard done by.
At the end of the course, those that earned their coveted berets
would be serving alongside me, and so I wanted to treat them
as my equals, even if I was in a position of authority – *especially*
if I was in a position of authority. We needed each other, and
that's the same whether you're on a training exercise, in combat
or attempting a world record.

No person is an island.

6. SELECTION

By the time that I returned from Lympstone I'd been a part of 59 Commando's order of battle for about eight years and I was pulled in by the careers management officer.

'Have you thought about what you want to do next?' He asked me. Eight years was a long time to have been in 59 without posting out; technically, my time at Lympstone was a squadron duty rather than the usual two-year posting at a training centre like Bassingbourn.

'I'm thinking about PF, sir.'

PF were the Pathfinders, an airborne unit that provided the same kind of Brigade Reconnaissance Force for 16 Air Assault as our Recce Troop had been doing alongside the mountain leaders and snipers of the Marines for 3 Commando Brigade.

The older man nodded. He knew I was the right fit. 'Are you thinking of going for selection?' he asked, meaning the Special Forces.

I was – for the second time – and I felt that the experience gained in the Pathfinders would be a huge help when it came to taking on one of the hardest challenges in the military world.

'Good lad,' he said. 'I'll get them cracking on your paper-work.'

But the Army Personnel Centre in Glasgow had other ideas: there'd been a number of diving deaths in the navy, and so across the forces, all diving equipment was being replaced with new rig. This meant retraining every qualified diver in the Royal Engineers, all 300 of them. Because I was an army diving supervisor, Glasgow overruled my wish to transfer to PF and instead sent me down to Portsmouth to bring the blokes up to speed on the new gear. The courses were two weeks long, and because everyone was already a qualified diver it was seen as buckshee, with everyone on the lash most nights. I don't think there'd been any other period in my life where I had so many hangovers – and something had to change. I didn't want this to be how I spent my army career, and so I decided that I would make my second attempt at selection. Because the Special Forces were involved, Glasgow wouldn't be able to stop me.

I stopped drinking the moment I made the decision, and cleaned up my diet. The first choice I had to make was which branch of the Special Forces I'd apply for – the SAS in Hereford or the SBS in Poole. Traditionally, soldiers (even Commando-trained ones) go to the SAS and Royal Marines to Poole, but I was worried that with my dive quals I would be shoved straight into Boat Troop at Hereford, and I wanted a change.

'They'll all be divers at Poole,' I told my mate when he asked me why I finally settled on the SBS. One day I'd find out how wrong I was about that – Mystic Meg I was not!

In 2002, I'd tried SF Selection for the first time, but I'd injured my knee early on, and I decided this was down to the way that I'd prepared for selection: running up and down the side of a mountain with a house on my back. My knees were battered before I even got on the course, and so, like a lot of people, I ended up coming off with an injury.

The definition of insanity is repeating the same actions and expecting different results, so I knew that this time I needed to do things differently. To that end, I got myself on a spin bike and beasted myself until I was a mess of jelly held up by the bike frame. I pushed myself until I was on the edge of puking, but this kind of training had no impact on my knees; my cardio improved, but my joints were spared the wear and tear of the hills. I didn't worry about what would happen when I put kit on my back. For one thing, lugging the heavy dive rig around Portsmouth had kept my upper body in good shape, but I am also a big believer that tabbing – carrying heavy kit over distance, named for Tactical Advance to Battle – is as much a mental thing as it is physical. You're never going to be comfortable tabbing, no matter how much you train. Your shoulders will ache, and the straps will cut into you. It's a strong mind that will get you through that. I've seen plenty of gifted athletes ditch their kit and give in because their minds broke, not their bodies. For them, their mental discipline could not withstand the discomfort.

Before attending Special Forces selection, you are required to attend what's known as a briefing course. It's a week long and the first point at which they cut the numbers: you have to be invited back for selection itself. The SAS and SBS hold back-to-back courses and I attended both, receiving two invitations. I decided to stick to my guns and go for the SBS. I was one of the first members of the British Army to do so, which pretty much eliminated any chance of being 'the grey man' you hear many people talking about as being the best strategy for selection – the idea being that you don't want to draw the attention of the directing staff (DS).

That became evident almost as soon as I arrived for the Hills

Phase, a number of weeks of tabbing and navigation on the harsh mountains of Wales.

'Why the fuck do you wanna go Poole?' one of the DS asked me. (The Special Forces selection encompassed all those who wanted to go to the SAS or SBS.)

I knew I shouldn't give him the real answer. I didn't want to go to Boat Troop in Hereford, and I liked the way the SBS guys cut about in t-shirts, shorts and Oakleys. As a surfer, that appealed to me, and Poole would certainly put me closer to the surf spots of Devon and Cornwall.

'I love diving, staff.'

'Shit answer. Who likes divin'?' the DS snorted, picking up a rock. 'Put that in your kit, and you better fucking have it with you at the end of today.'

I had it with me *every* day. Each morning the DS would ask me the same question, and each day I'd be told to put a rock into my already heavy bergen.

Then, one day, I had an idea. My chances of being the grey man were long gone, and so I decided to deploy a bit of humour. Back in the camp that evening I got busy, and in the morning I was prepared.

Two of the DS walked over to me. They were both from Hereford, and both had been at 59. They had a keen eye for horrible rocks.

'Oi, you. Why the fuck you wanna go Poole?'

I placed my weapon down across my boots so that it was out of the dirt, and opened one of the map pockets in my trousers, pulling out a laminated photo.

'What the fuck's this?' one of them sneered.

It was a photo of Bournemouth beach during a heatwave. I'd

pulled it off Google and laminated it in the offices. 'You don't get topless girls on the beach in Hereford, staff,' I told them with a straight face, and both men burst out laughing.

I kept that photo in my pocket for the rest of the course, and I didn't carry another rock.

With hindsight, I think that the DS were giving me a bit of a hard time about my choice of Poole because they were worried that it could start a trend. After the Paras, the Royal Engineers supply the second highest number of blokes for the SAS, and I don't think they wanted to see their traditional recruiting pool heading in a different direction. I wasn't the last guy to go from the army to the SBS, but the break in tradition that maybe they feared didn't come to pass.

Despite the rocks, I did really well on the hills. The training on the spin bike worked out, and my joints felt fit and fresh; on my last basic fitness test at the dive school I even ran my fastest time ever, at twenty-eight years old. Avoiding injury on the hills is key, as there's no time for recovery. If you get hurt, you're done, that's that, and so I was pleased that I'd learnt the lessons of my first attempt at selection and adapted my plan accordingly. Having been in Recce Troop, I didn't have any dramas with the navigation side of things, and I knew that if I just kept my body together then I'd be passing this phase of selection. But without meaning to, somebody else on the course almost ruined that chance. Like many of the guys, I'd purchased my own boots, because they gave a lot more ankle support than the ones we were issued and going over on your ankle with a bergen on your back usually meant endex (the end of the exercise). I'd busted my ankle up twice as a kid, so I was particularly nervous about mine.

During Hills, you see a lot of the original two hundred or so hopefuls drop out either due to injury or because they couldn't hack it. You feel bad for them, but at the same time it just motivated me to keep going. One morning I went to the drying room to get my boots ahead of a big test, but one look at them was enough to know they weren't mine; someone binned from the course had left the night before, and with his head full of disappointment he hadn't paid attention when he'd picked up what he thought were his own boots to pack away. The ones he'd left behind were two sizes small for me, and so I would have to wear a pair of my own issue boots, which had a lot less support. I strapped the hell out of my knees and ankles, but I was still nervous.

Thankfully, I got through with those boots. Strapping goes a long way, but so does attitude. I saw a lot of lads literally break themselves, falling for the mind games of the DS. The Paras especially, because they were almost overprepared. They'd been given pre-courses and taught routes, so when something unexpected came up, it threw them, whereas someone like me, who didn't know what to expect, just cracked on.

After one long day we got to the final rendezvous. The trucks were there, and in their minds, lads began to switch off.

'Get your kit back on,' the DS said. 'This is your next grid.' He read off a map reference. It was flippin' miles away. 'Right, off you go.'

I went. So did most of the others, but for some of the lads, thinking that they'd been finished for the day, it was the straw that broke the camel's back.

'You not going?' the DS asked them.

'No, staff,' they repeated, one after the other, until each one had answered.

That was when the DS turned and called after those of us who had cracked on, 'Oi! Back here. Get on the trucks.'

It had all been a trick. A mind game. A test of mental resilience.

The lads who had fallen for it looked broken. I couldn't make eye contact with them. I couldn't even begin to imagine how awful that would feel, and I promised myself that I would never find out. Whatever happened on this course, I would not be taking myself off it.

The final part of Hills Phase was an endurance march that required us to cover 40 miles in 20 hours, carrying 70lbs of kit. Hard work on a road, but this involved traversing some of the harshest terrain that the UK has to offer.

I knew that we were lucky, though. It was January, but it hadn't rained once. This annoyed the DS so much that I imagine they held nightly rain dances. They wanted the wind to be howling and our clothes to be wet through. It had been that way for them, and now they wanted it that way for us.

Instead we got a bright white moon and not a cloud in the sky. It was a gift, and allowed those of us with good nav skills to sail through. Despite the good weather, a lot of lads were battered from the constant hill work, and one bloke was so full of painkillers he couldn't even talk – but he made it.

Not everyone did. One team of four messed up, and one lad paid a high price, falling from a cliff and badly injuring himself. It could have been even worse, but in any case he was done, and so were the three that were with him, failed for their navigation. Again, I felt sympathy for these guys, but I also felt pride and motivation from knowing that I was amongst a dwindling number. I didn't have any fear that it would be me dropping out. I wasn't stupid enough to think that I was injury proof, but I was comfortable knowing that I was controlling what I could control. I'd done my best to take it easy on my body in the beat-up while still training hard. Now I just had to execute.

At the end of the endurance phase we were loaded up into trucks and driven back to camp. You didn't need the moon to see the smiles in the back, and I'm sure I was smiling as broadly as anyone. It felt like a great achievement to have completed Hills, but as those of us who had passed the first phase of selection were gathered in the theatre to be briefed on the next stage, it didn't seem as though the DS shared our enthusiasm.

'All right,' one salty operator said. 'Selection starts today.'

That attitude was common from the DS throughout selection; they were trying to test guys. Trying to make us feel like we had accomplished nothing. There was no feedback on your performance, and a lot of the guys were not used to having to find internal validation. I think that's maybe why quite often it was guys from pretty rough childhoods who passed selection: they weren't used to anybody telling them that they were valued. They'd always had to do that themselves.

You had to be totally self-motivated. You either had the mental strength or you didn't. Unlike P Company or the Commando course, there were no shouts of encouragement from the staff. Anything the DS did say would be an attempt to undermine your confidence and to make you second-guess yourself.

My preparation for the course helped a lot, and I never doubted my decisions. I knew I'd done the work over the years to be spot on with my map and compass. I knew I'd left enough sweat in the gym to have my fitness up to the standard. I'm only human, and I'd listen to the DS's cutting criticism, but then I could calmly say to myself: 'It's just part of their mind games, mate. You're doing fine.' At times like those, I'd think back to when my dad had told me I wouldn't last two minutes in the army. He'd been wrong, and so the DS would be. I knew what I could do, and I just had to keep putting one foot in front of the other, literally, to show them. You have to put trust in your abilities, regardless of what others tell you.

During the selection process we went back to our military fundamentals, because Special Forces soldiering is about doing the basics and doing them well.

Section attacks are the eight-man building blocks that the entire forward momentum of the army is built on. There are three sections in a platoon, and one of these will attack an enemy position while another provides fire support and another is held in reserve (ready to punch through and begin the next attack). All soldiers in the army are taught this, but of course some spend less time on it than others. Section attacks are the infantry's bread and butter, and so to ensure that our newly formed sections' attacks did not go to total shit, an infantryman would be appointed to lead it. Then, a second in command (2i/c) was appointed from a non-combat trade. Attendees on selection can come from any part of the military, and so there were chefs, and tank drivers and . . .

'Sergeant Stott.' The DS was looking at paperwork in his

hand, and no doubt seeing 'dive school' written beside my name. 'You'll be 2i/c.'

With the section commander – a Pathfinder we'll call NB – I got our section together and began to distribute the ammunition between the guys. NB clearly knew his shit, and his orders were slick and to the point. Confidence oozed off him. Then, he looked at me.

'You done many of these before?'

I tried not to smile. 'I'll be all right, mate.'

We moved up to the range. Everything was live firing on selection. No blanks. If you cocked up on your weapon handling – didn't apply a safety catch or properly aim a shot – then you could be sending someone home in a body bag (which probably wouldn't do your own chances of passing much good either!).

We went into the attack, and NB sent me and my team to flank the enemy position. I picked my cover well, kept a good rate of fire going and cleared through the position in textbook fashion. Then, as was the job of the 2i/c, I cut around the blokes, getting an ammo and cas status (how much ammunition each man had remaining, and if we had any casualties). When the DS came in – acting as the platoon sergeant – to ask for my report, I had it written and on the tip of my tongue.

He narrowed his eyes. 'I thought you were a fucking navy diver?'

'Recce Troop at Five-nine, staff.'

The man snorted and shook his head. 'Fuck's sake.' There were a lot of Recce Troop guys in the Regiment. In fact, they had a 100 per cent pass rate when it came to selection. The DS had looked at the paperwork and thought he'd picked someone who would find the section attack hard going, putting pressure on not only himself but the commander and the others in the section. Instead, we'd gone through like the well-drilled professional soldiers that we were. Yet more evidence that you should never judge a book by its cover.

NB patted me on the arm. 'Good job, Grey Man.'

Over what felt like an eternity we were continually tested in the most challenging situations and environments to see if we had the mental composition and physical robustness to be an SF soldier. It was gruelling, it was draining, but . . . it was also a lot of fun. I was where I wanted to be and, as hard as it was, I loved it. Nothing in life that's worth having comes easy, and that's especially true in the military world. The numbers on the course slowly dwindled, but I was confident that I would become one of the few who would make it to the end and earn the title of Special Forces soldier.

One Friday evening, we were called into the camp's theatre to shake hands with the DS. This was the moment we were told that we were now part of the Special Forces, though a more formal ceremony would take place that night in the sergeants' mess, where the CO and RSM of the SAS officially badged their blokes.

It was a bittersweet moment for me. As proud as I was that I had passed the course, I couldn't help but feel that I wanted to be part of the moment with the SAS lads, who were all wearing big smiles and puffing out their chests. Those of us going to Poole would have to wait a few days more for our own moment like this, and it would be without the majority of blokes on the course, a lot of them now like brothers to us after all that we had gone through together. I wouldn't go as far as to say it was an anticlimax, because I was still chuffed to bits, but it did give me something to think about other than the fact that I'd just joined the world's most elite club.

An elite club it may have been, and the journey to get there incredibly difficult, but all of the other men at the squadron I now joined had done exactly the same, and so nobody remarked on it. For me, selection had been the most monumental thing in my life, but for these guys, it was a tick in the box to get me to work.

'You the new guy, are you? All right.'

Simple as that. I'd be exactly the same way, once I'd spent some time at Poole and the next cadre of new guys came in, but for now I was the new bloke, and I was about to begin one of the most intense periods of my life. It was certainly the most clandestine part, due to the fact that I had to sign the Official Secrets Act.

I totally understand that some people will be disappointed that I can't divulge details of Special Forces operations, but our country has enemies and we can't hand them information that could endanger the lives of my former colleagues, who continue to operate around the world, selflessly providing the blanket of freedom beneath which we sleep. I know you'll appreciate that, and in light of what *they* sacrifice, *we* can sacrifice some stories. Let me just say that those years gave me some of my best friends, and that I loved the job. It was everything that I wanted as a soldier, but one day, my stint taking the fight to the enemy was cut short.

We were in the desert as part of our pre-deployment training. I couldn't wait to get back out on operations, nor could any of the other guys. Being on ops was the reason we'd joined the Special Forces, and nowhere were our skills put to the test more than in the daily life-or-death battles with our enemies.

We had a couple of new guys in the squadron, and though they'd completed their jump course on squares, they still needed a tick in the box for HAHO (high-altitude, high opening). This form of parachuting meant jumping at a higher than usual altitude, and having your canopy deploy immediately on a static line (the kind that is initiated by leaving the aircraft, rather than in freefall, where a parachutist pulls the release himself). The advantage of this is that you can then steer your chutes for a very long distance. A nice way to achieve an insertion.

I loved jumping. Some guys didn't and just sucked it up, but I always wanted to be the first in the stick so that I could stand on the open tail ramp and look down at the Earth beneath me. I wanted to soak it all in before I jumped, but on the second jump that day I was put at the back of the line.

I waddled with my kit towards the door as the others left the aircraft. One guy tumbled out after the next. Eventually, it was my turn. I jumped . . .

And immediately I knew that I was in trouble.

I felt something on my leg. I looked up and saw that it was wrapped in rigging. I knew that as soon as the static line pulled up canopy that rigging would shoot up above my head and the force of it could take my leg with it.

I had about a second to get my leg clear.

WHACK!

I failed.

The static line pulled the chute.

The chute pulled the rigging.

The rigging pulled my leg.

It came up and over my shoulder like I was a yoga guru. Instantly, I felt every muscle, ligament and tendon rip and snap. I screamed in absolute agony and almost blacked out from the pain. The rigging worked its way clear, and now the leg fell back alongside the other, but I knew that I had no control over its movement. I was lucky to still have the leg. The force could easily have ripped it off, and if that had happened, I'd have bled to death within minutes and some poor local would have had a one-legged corpse landing in his garden.

Pain was racing through my body but I knew that if I didn't get my act together I could still die. I was so far up that oxygen was thin, and I could not afford to pass out. If I drifted away from my guys, I could end up in the middle of the desert or the sea. I would be browners. I had to stay awake. You'd think that the pain would have made that easy, but it was so intense that my brain was trying to send me into unconsciousness. I wouldn't let it. I just wouldn't. Instead, I fixed my focus on the descending parachutes of the stick and followed them in.

It was the longest thirty minutes of my life. Despite the physical agony, I had enough time hanging in the sky to feel emotional pain too. I knew that there would be no deployment for me now. I think I knew, deep down, that there would be no more time on operations at all. Thirty minutes is a long time to think about that when you're alone, floating through the air.

Finally, the ground was getting closer. I saw my mates landing in formation. I wanted to make a good landing out of pride, but more than that, I knew that if I landed badly I could quite well ruin my good leg too.

The ground came up to meet me. I pushed down on my toggles and flared the chute just at the right moment, dragging in enough air under the canvas to take the speed out of my descent. If you do it too early, you just stop in the sky, then drop like a sack of shit, but I came in like a feather and landed on one leg.

Then there was only one thing left to do.

'*Medic!*'

7. TRANSITION

I spent the next six weeks on my back. My leg had turned black with swelling and bruising, but I wasn't in a hospital, I was in a hotel in Oman, stuck here because some bloody volcano in Iceland had chosen this moment to erupt. I was stuck in bed with nothing to distract me except the Arabic version of *Coronation Street*.

That gave me a lot of time to think, and I didn't like what was on my mind. I didn't want to throw in the towel and admit that my military career was over, but realistically, with my whole leg in rag order, I knew that my best-case scenario would involve months of gruelling rehab work. I hadn't got to the position I was in by lacking confidence, and I knew that I could put that graft in. I wasn't a surgeon, though; I couldn't perform my own operations. Maybe if I'd known how the next year would go, I would have picked up a knife and fork and had a go.

When the ash cloud of the volcano dispersed, I could finally be aero-medded to the UK, where I went straight to Selly Oak Hospital. My girlfriend, Alana, was there to meet me, and one of the first things she said was, 'I can't believe how much weight you've lost.' I'm not built like an NFL linebacker, but you have to carry muscle to do the Special Forces job. Lying in bed for six weeks and eating whatever the hotel served up had stripped me back. My clothes were hanging off me and I felt like I'd been put into my teenage body.

When I arrived in Selly Oak, I was assuming that I'd be operated on pretty quickly. When I took my first shot at selection in 2002 and busted up my knee, I'd had my torn lateral meniscus operated on within five days. Within six weeks I was up and running again.

Unfortunately, this time things took much longer. For various reasons it ended up being a whole year before I was able to have the operation, which meant a lot of time sitting on my arse at home.

Home was Aberdeen, with Alana, the woman who would later become my wife, who I'd met in a pub while we were up there on an exercise. Her dad had been in a Scottish infantry regiment, and at first he'd thought I was 'full of shit' about being in the SBS. We get along well now, though, and Aberdeen was home. It wasn't quite the surf beaches of Devon and Cornwall, but at least it was close to the coast.

This second six weeks of injury passed a lot faster than the first, thanks to Alana's company, and I could even watch *Coronation Street* in English if I wanted to!

Instead, I started researching the private security market, a lucrative source of work for an ex-soldier, ensuring the safety of anything from individuals to oil tankers. As you'd expect, a lot of ex-SAS and -SBS guys end up in these jobs, many of them as directors of companies. I made calls, studied the news, and looked into the world's current flashpoints and where could be the next. There seemed no shortage of business, but there was also no shortage of security businesses, and so I began searching for a niche that I could exploit with my own company.

After spending my entire adult life in uniform, it felt strange to be planning to set up shop on my own, but I'd come to the realisation that I was done with the military. In the twelve months that followed my accident, the squadron had finished pre-deployment training, been to Afghanistan and come back, and had leave again before I finally went under the knife – as if seeing them deploy without me once wasn't bad enough!

Yeah, I was done with the military, and so I decided to throw myself into my new life.

I made every call I could, learnt everything I could, and Alana helped me set up my first company.

I was really lucky to have her with me at this time. I was an expert at jumping from planes and putting rounds on target, but if you'd asked me what council tax band I was, you'd have got an absent look in reply. The army had clothed, fed and paid me. I'd been taxed at source and never had to deal with any of the things that most people are sorting out regularly from the time that they leave home. I mean, *water bills*? Who knew that you had to pay for water, ha!

I think that's why a lot of blokes struggle when they leave the military. It's not so much the things you've seen that are difficult but the things you didn't learn while you were training in the role that your country required. I was lucky that I had Alana. A lot of people are all alone when they come out, and I can totally see how it could all build up on top of them in no time. It's not like the military really teach you any of it before you leave.

In a way, I was lucky that I was injured before I left service because it meant that I was basically just left alone to do my own thing. As well as the paperwork-based stuff, I took courses to make sure I was covered across the whole spectrum of private security work. I had obtained a high-level qualification in close protection (CP) since leaving the army, and I picked up things like my Ship Security Officer certificate in case I ended up doing work involving piracy. Alana did a few of these courses with me, as she was thinking of getting into the industry alongside me.

They say no plan survives contact with the enemy, and I think the same can be said of kids. We found out during this time that Alana was pregnant, and although we were both thrilled to be having our first child together, that did slap a nice bit of extra pressure on me to have my military exit plan sorted before I got the med-discharge boot and they stopped my pay.

To be honest, I found the whole thing daunting. I'd been the guy who'd stood on the back of a tailgate at 15,000 feet and jumped into thin air. I'd been a door-kicker in Afghanistan, and a stealthy ninja in Kosovo. Now here I was shitting myself in case I filed the wrong set of papers to Companies House or read my bloody water meter wrong.

There was more to it than that, of course. I wasn't leaving the Special Forces by choice. I'd been part of a clearly defined team with a clearly defined purpose. Being a Special Forces operator was everything I had wanted in my career; My best mates were there. Adrenaline rushes were there. My *identity* was there.

I still felt like a soldier. I talked like one and I thought like one, but I knew that I couldn't act like one any longer. It wasn't enough for me to follow orders now. I couldn't just wait for missions. I had to go out and find them. The success I had had in the military was because I gave my all on every challenge that I came up against. Civvy street was my new test and, like all the others I'd faced in my life, I'd give it my all.

Forty-eight hours after leaving the camp gates and becoming a civilian, I received a call.

'Can you be in Libya tomorrow?'

8. ARAB SPRING

Alana was eight months pregnant when I got that call. In a perfect world I would have turned it down so that I could be around to help during her first pregnancy, but I'm sure anyone reading this knows that the world isn't perfect. We needed money, and this was a job. I wasn't about to get offered a gig at the nearest architecture firm, was I? I didn't have qualifications or experience for most of the civilian world, but what I did have was, as Liam Neeson put it, 'a very particular set of skills'.

The job was to work with a Department for International Development project, which was the darling of David Cameron. In a nutshell, the idea of DFID was that it would go into other nations to help them structure themselves in a way that would bring them more prosperity. The kickback for the UK being that if a country is prosperous, it's less likely to harbour terrorism and it's a better place to do business with.

Gaddafi was still in one piece at the time, holed up in Tripoli. Benghazi, in the east of the country, was fully in the grip of the Arab Spring, and I wasn't expecting too much trouble there when I flew in on an RAF Hercules. On the ground, the feeling was one of jubilation and excitement rather than threat.

Because of my experience, I'd been sent ahead of the incoming DFID team to get the lie of the land, reporting back on anything from the state of the roads to where the incoming thirty CP operators could be housed.

I got a room at the Tibesti Hotel, which was crammed full of contractors. Some of these were operators, and many others were the laptop-carrying swarm that arrives in a country as soon as a war has broken out. Some of those laptops belonged to journalists, for typing up their reports, but many others belonged to oil and infrastructure companies. I didn't hold anything against them, of course. I'd also come to Libya for a cheque, not a suntan.

Having done operational tours in several different countries I felt like I had a good read on the mood of a place. On the flight in, I'd wondered about how I'd feel on the ground knowing that there was no QRF (Quick Reaction Force) in helis ready to ride in to the rescue, but seeing so many smiling faces I was soon put at ease. That didn't mean that I ceased being vigilant, but your gut instinct is usually right when it comes to assessing anything from a job offer to the possibility of getting your head snipped off.

The British Embassy staff were staying at a different hotel, and I had a little pressure from my new employers to set up the incoming DFID team with them. I made the counter-argument that if DFID were posted at the Tibesti then there would be mutual support between the two locations; one team of operators could act as the other's QRF, and vice versa. Some at the embassy felt like I was only making that recommendation because the Tibesti had a pool, but the truth was that an embassy in an unstable country – no matter how many smiles you see – is a target. And that was demonstrated in brutal fashion in Benghazi just over a year later.

I got my selection of the Tibesti approved, but then I ran into a problem: the place was chocka and I needed thirty rooms. Luckily for me, I had a well-drilled plan for such situations.

I sought out the hotel manager. 'All right, mate? I'm Dean. Good to meet you.'

We sat down and had a chat. He was a nice bloke with plenty of local gen. He was also a fan of Jack Daniels, and so when the incoming guys asked me if I needed anything else to accompany them on their flight – on a chartered C-17 carrying four armoured cars, no less – I added something extra to the list.

A couple of days later, thirty operators were put up in thirty rooms at the Tibesti.

'How the fuck did you manage that?' a friend in another company asked me by the pool. 'We're all sharing beds.'

I tapped my nose. It certainly didn't have anything to do with the crate of Jack D in the manager's office.

Being places like Libya and Afghanistan has a strange effect on you. Because you feel you're at the centre of one of the world's hotspots, you almost forget that things carry on at home without you. It almost seems as if everyone else hits pause when you get on the plane, but of course that's not the case.

There were only a couple of weeks until Alana would drop our first baby together. There was a strict no-fly zone imposed over the country, so I didn't expect to see Ryanair popping up in Benghazi to get me home.

'Don't worry about it,' my employers told me. 'We'll get you home in time.'

Yeah, right, I thought to myself. I'd heard that one often enough in the military.

Despite missing my family, there was a lot to like about Libya. After a year of being a sick-case, it felt great to be on the ground again. Even though Benghazi seemed calm, there was certainly a lot more chance of danger here than in Aberdeen. I don't think at the time I had admitted this to myself, but that sense of potential chaos was seductive, and I wanted to be somewhere where I could get my adrenaline fix. Somewhere I could put sixteen years of training and experience into use.

To be honest, places like Benghazi were where I felt like I *belonged.*

It's hard to explain that to your wife or girlfriend without causing huge offence, and so I kept my mouth shut, like most soldiers do – even the ones who are now wearing civvies. Instead I threw myself into the experience as much as I could. As I said, I had never been one to half-arse, and if this life of civvy contracting was going to be my new gig, then I'd be the best at that.

I got a huge opportunity to learn on that job. Some lads turn up for security gigs and just stick their head down, counting down the days until they get paid and get their rotation home. I soon realised that I would be rubbing shoulders with high-level government officials and successful business people. There was a lot I could learn from them, and they looked to me as their guardian angel. The Special Forces community interests people. I'd field their questions, they'd field mine. It was win-win – we both came away with more knowledge in our pockets, which is something you can never get enough of.

I got to meet some of the heads of the Arab Spring movements in the DFID meetings. They were mostly academics who had fled their home nations to escape persecution. Now they were back, hoping to lead their countrymen in governments that more closely resembled the democracies we know in the West. Unfortunately, they failed in this goal, but at the time it was exciting to be around these people. They really believed they could make life better for the ordinary citizen. I believed it too. I'd come to Libya for a pay cheque, but I soon realised that I was in a privileged position where I could not only learn but also watch history unfold.

It goes without saying that not everything in Libya worked out as people had hoped. I'm not an expert on why, but I did see mistakes being made with my own eyes.

During the meetings with the Arab Spring leaders there was quite a lot of discussion about four full shipping containers that had been supplied by a foreign government. At the time, Gaddafi was holed up in the west of the country. There were men willing to root him out, but for this they needed weapons, and that was what this foreign government had provided.

The four containers did eventually arrive in the mountains, and the newly armed men fell on their former dictator. Maybe it seemed like a good plan at the time, but there was no accounting for this weaponry, and much of it soon found its way on to the black market and into the hands of Islamist terrorists. Some of it was found in the dead hands of al-Shabaab fighters in Somalia. Even some naval mines, identified by their serial numbers, were found in the port city of Mogadishu.

Our own weaponry for protecting the DFID team was a lot more limited. The locals in Benghazi were very keen that their city should not become another Baghdad, and they didn't want heavily armed foreign security contractors on their streets – who can blame them? If anything, I felt that carrying such weapons would just stir up trouble, and that our greatest protection came from looking friendly and unthreatening. You can tell a person all you like that you are there to help his country, but when it's you with the guns in his streets and not him, what is he going to think? More to the point, what is he then going to *do*?

By far our most effective protection was through forming good relationships with the Libyans themselves. Like many African people, their culture is deeply bound in respect. If you are their guest, then they will protect you. It's as simple as that.

Instead of always eating at the hotel, I made an effort to get out and have food with my Libyan counterparts as often as I could. I was soon invited to their homes, where I met their children and joined them for dinner. It was a real pleasure to spend time with them, but I eventually had to say my goodbyes to my hosts and their families – it was time to fly back to the UK and begin my own.

9. GUINEA

My clients had told me that they'd get me back in time for the birth of my child. Similar promises in the military weren't usually held up, so I was chuffed to bits when I was given a seat on a UN flight that was heading out of the country (not restricted by the NATO no-fly zone). This was one of the moments that really opened my eyes to the power of the civilian defence sector, where money talks.

Alana gave birth to our daughter on the Friday. We took Mollie home, but we both knew that soon I'd have to go away again. I'd got six weeks 'gardening leave' from the date of my discharge from the military, and I still had a couple of weeks left of this. I was still being paid by the MOD, and in their eyes, I shouldn't be working; I got a call from one of the boys in the squadron to say that the OC was fuming that I was out in Libya.

To be honest, I think a bit of that was just jealousy. You don't end up in a sabre squadron unless you want to be on the ground in places that are bubbling with the possibility of adventure, and I think he was just a bit sore that I was there and he wasn't. I had to think about my family, though. Yes, I had six weeks' paid leave, but what happened at the end of that? You don't get paid up front for freelance security gigs. You invoice at the end of the job, and then you can expect to wait a month, and that's if there's no delays.

I wasn't about to risk my family's cashflow to spare the OC's feelings. There were only two people whose approval I needed, and there was no way I was about to turn down jobs.

'Got a call about a job in Guinea,' I told Alana on the Sunday.

She had our new baby in her arms. It was Alana's first child, and she was two days into learning about nappies, breastfeeding and sleep deprivation. 'Go,' she said calmly.

We needed money, it was my job, and so within seventy-two hours of my child being born I was sitting aboard a flight to West Africa.

I arrived in Guinea in the evening. I had another Brit with me, and we were met at the airport by Claude, a tall local who would be acting as our interpreter and de facto guide.

Our client was an Arab minister who was coming here to meet with Guinea's president and prime minister. As their private jet wouldn't be landing until the morning, I decided we'd use the time to recce the locations that we could be visiting, looking at everything from the fastest route to the nearest hospital to the normal pattern of life: if a packed street was empty the next night, that could be an indicator of trouble.

As it was, our presence the next day seemed almost silly. As the visitor was the guest of the president, the big man sent a huge convoy of trucks and police cars to escort him – and us – from the airport.

I don't know what it is about bodyguards in Africa, but they all seem to have a thing about wearing sunglasses indoors. They were big lads, and about fifteen of them stood in the circular lobby as we entered, their backs to the wall, facing in to the spiral staircase in the centre.

Working me and my guy out as the Brit security, one bloke put a hand on my chest to stop me at the bottom of the stairs; a lot of people in security carry ego, and here it seemed to be supercharged. They wanted to flex muscle and show who was boss. Fine. Kicking off would achieve nothing, as well as looking totally unprofessional, and so I smiled politely until one of the president's team came down to tell him rather sternly to back away. I don't speak French, but I didn't need to understand. Of course, if I let my own ego get the better of me, then that would be the moment to give him a scary look or a biting comment. Instead I put out my hand: it wouldn't be my ego coming in as QRF if any kind of threat emerged, it would be these people. Too often in security work – or life in general – people confuse being calm and reasonable with being weak. You don't need to beat your chest. When people see you acting calm and confident despite them pushing your buttons, that's when they recognise competence and leadership.

The minister's trip was short and he flew out the same night. Our flight wasn't until the next day and so I took the opportunity to conduct a post-op report. There'd been no 'action' in the Arnold Schwarzenegger sense of the word, but when you're on the ground in a new place it's important to pick up and collate as much information as you can. Who knows when I'd be coming here next, and even if I didn't, then it was knowledge that could be passed on to the next guys who did. I wanted clients to know that I was approaching the work they gave me with the same professionalism as I'd conducted my work in the squadron, and so I told our official point of contact that we'd be leaving the hotel to 'look around'.

They offered me a car with government plates, but I declined. I didn't want to attract any more attention than two white guys would already receive. Claude was with us too, but maybe his skin tone saved him from what happened next.

I was standing on the corner of a street with my team-mate, nonchalantly taking notes to include in the report. The next second we heard the roaring of engines and saw a bunch of trucks and jeeps flying down the road.

'They're in a hurry,' my mate said. 'Wonder where they're going?'

They were going to us.

Tyres screeched as the lead truck slewed to a halt and armed men in uniform began jumping off the back, shouting at us to put our hands in the air.

We'd been lifted.

I saw Claude running off down the street as we were put into the trucks. We were driven a very short distance into a camp, and as we weren't cuffed or blindfolded I could see everything and recognised that we were in a government facility. I breathed a lot easier then.

Soldiers kept barking questions into our faces as we were led into an office and parked in plastic chairs behind a desk. We tried our best GCSE French, but that amounted to 'bonjour' and not much else. They must have realised that no one can bluff being that shit, and they began to calm down. I imagine they were thinking who'd send a spy that can't speak French?

I had a gut feeling about why we'd been picked up. The drive to the camp had been incredibly short, and so I was assuming they thought we were casing their facility. In effect, our post-op report was doing exactly what it was supposed to do: identifying problem areas for future jobs.

Well, we'd certainly found one of those.

I wasn't scared, though. Not only had we come into the country at the invitation of the government but we had been trained in dealing with interrogators.

I pointed to the parachute wings on one soldier's shoulder. 'Paratrooper?' I asked him.

Just a few minutes later, using a mixture of broken English, French and gestures, the room full of parachutists had bonded over their common ground. I was almost disappointed when a representative of the president arrived: I was really enjoying the conversation!

She didn't hold back when she came to our 'rescue'. A big woman, she strode in and planted an open-handed slap across the commander's face that I'm pretty sure woke the baby back in Aberdeen. Then she launched into a verbal assault, the gist of which I was later told was: 'How dare you disrespect the president's guests like this?'

To be honest, I felt sorry for our new mates. In their position I would have done exactly the same, and I did my best to apologise and shake hands on our way out. A bruise on the cheek heals a lot faster than a bruise on the ego, and the last thing I wanted to leave behind was resentment.

We called the post-op a day at that point, and went back to the hotel. I wanted to get a workout in before we flew home, but I'd not long got started when Claude poked his head in through the door; he'd been the one to raise the alarm when we got lifted.

'There's someone from the president's office here,' he told me.

Shit. I was hoping there'd be no fallout from what happened.

This wasn't the kind of thing I wanted held against me as I looked for more freelance work.

I followed Claude down the stairs. My team-mate was talking to a man in a suit and smiling. I began to relax.

'I have brought gifts from the president,' the man said, gesturing at three wrapped items in front of him. 'Please, take one!'

I looked to my blokes. 'Leaders eat last' is the military mentality, and that ethos carried over into all things – the blokes go first. 'Go ahead, lads.' Claude and my team-mate went straight for a gift – they were suspiciously fast, and it wasn't until I unwrapped the remaining gift that I realised why.

It was a rugby-ball-sized wooden carving of a woman with huge drooping breasts. 'Erm . . . thanks,' I said to the president's man.

'It is a fertility statue!' he told me with excitement.

The airport security weren't so enthusiastic about it. They told me it could be used as a weapon, but with a lot of pleases and thank yous and name-dropping a president, I finally got it cleared through Charles de Gaulle Airport to join my connecting flight in Paris.

A couple of flights later, I pushed open the door of my home in Aberdeen. Alana was on the sofa, our baby asleep in a swaddle, and her eyes went straight to the big wooden lump in my hands.

'What the hell is that?' she asked me.

I held it up so she could see the drooping breasts. 'It's a fertility statue!'

Alana rolled tired eyes and pointed at the baby she'd been changing and nursing alone.

In hindsight, I'm lucky the president's gift didn't turn into a murder weapon.

10. BACK TO THE DESERT

During my first trip into Libya I'd been looking for a niche in the security market. There is no such thing as total independence in the industry – you'll always need the help or business of players from airlines to local fixers – but as far as possible I wanted to be my own boss. I knew from experience that the bigger the organisation, the more things got overlooked, and so with that in mind I began sticking my nose into things to find out what angle they were missing.

In the end I discovered that it wasn't that the companies had *missed* an angle but that they hadn't properly covered it. I'd found my niche, and it was in evacuation plans.

These were essential for any foreign organisation or business working in a country where disruption was possible, or likely. A place like Libya could go from peaceful to dangerous in a matter of hours, and it didn't have a hub like Heathrow where you could immediately book a flight and find a ride out of Dodge. Even if you did have a flight, how would you get from the hotel to an airfield? From an oil field to a port? From an office to a border crossing? Each stage of an extraction needed to be thought out and planned for. There had to be contingency plans for the contingency plans, and this is what business and organisations were paying the larger security companies to provide.

Except that they weren't. I looked into their plans and found that they were generic at best and lax at worst. No real depth of thought had gone into them; they looked like they'd been copied and pasted from contracts won in Iraq. Where was the local knowledge? Where were the safe houses? Where were the refuelling points? The alternative routes? The money for greasing palms and raising barriers? There was none of that.

Some people think that the Special Forces are all about taking out bad guys in an embassy siege, but we're a lot more than door-kickers. One of the reasons we are so successful when we operate in mountains, desert and jungle is our preparation work, and I saw my opportunity by applying this ethos to the areas that the big companies had just paid lip service to. After studying their lackadaisical plans, I knew all I needed to take out my competition was a few weapons.

Don't worry, I'm not referring to a Godfather-style hostile take-over; After talking it over with Alana, I decided to put all of my savings into buying fifteen AK-47s and fifteen pistols. Getting the weapons off the black market was easy, as Libya was awash with them, but with a civil war going on, finding the ammunition was a lot harder. Eventually, however, I had what I needed for the first step of my evacuation business model. After thoroughly oiling the weapons and packing them into damp- and sand-proof cases, I began burying them in strategic locations across the Libyan desert between Tunis and Egypt writing a report on each one so that they could be easily found – a practice known as caching. I now had the hardware in place should it ever be required.

Next up on my to-do list was to meet the local fixers who would supply vehicles, drivers, petrol and safe houses. Many security companies tried to make these connections, build relationships and secure contracts over the phone from a desk in London, but I met them all face to face on their own turf. I wasn't armed. I didn't have a team with me. I trusted my gut, and I trusted their honour. In neither case was I proved wrong, and they deeply respected the fact that I would come to their homes on faith of their word. Does that mean that I let my guard down? Of course not. I made a calculated risk/reward decision. I don't advise that just anyone go wandering around Libyan streets looking for business. These meetings came through people that I trusted – as much as you can trust anyone in this business – and without wanting to sound like a bighead, the truth is that I wasn't just anyone. I had had the best training that you could ask for. My senses were in tune. If I felt something was off, then I'd back out.

Ninety-nine times out of a hundred, though, the meetings were nothing but pleasant. It was a real honour to get to talk about more than just the job, to find out about the families, country and culture of the people that I'd be working with.

With is the important word here. I was paying them, but without the locals, there was no possibility of me getting anything done. They could do without me; I couldn't do without them.

Within a few weeks in Libya, I had my caches, contacts and plans in place. Now I just needed an opportunity to get them in front of the right people.

Some people in the private security industry choose to take a steady wage with a big company. You're placed on a rotation, given a salary and work the same job in the same place.

That didn't interest me. Not only did I want to build my own company but, subconsciously, I wanted variety in location and task. I needed to be active and challenged, and that's why I wanted to work freelance.

This is a lot easier to do when you've been a Tier-1 operator – the highest grade in the Special Forces world – because there are many one- or two-person gigs where people are looking to take on only those who were at the top of the military game. We had a hard-earned reputation, and like in any walk of life, that made us more desirable to hire.

This kind of work did require a certain switch in mindset, though. I've said before that we were more than door-kickers in the Special Forces, and that's true, but when it does come to direct action then there's no one better in the world. If you want a compound taking down and the bad guys to come out in body bags, then you call us.

Private security was different. If we got into a firefight, it meant that we had majorly cocked up. We were there to protect our clients and their interests, not to play at being James Bond. Discretion was certainly the better part of valour when it came to this business, at least for me and the people I worked with. You did hear of lads boasting with excitement when they got into a scrap. As a soldier, I totally understood that yearning for combat, but we were wearing plain clothes now, not camouflage. The army had paid us to do one job, and now we were being paid to do another.

That was one of the reasons I preferred not to have teams armed. If you put a firearm in the hands of an ex-squaddie, he defaults into the training that may have been drilled into him for decades. It's hard for him to switch out of that mentality and for muscle memory not to take over when he's holding that weapon. On the other hand, send him on a job unarmed and he has no choice but to start thinking about other ways of handling a situation. Default aggression goes out the window. If you're unarmed, you're hardly going to start gobbing off at a policeman armed with an AK, are you? It's just common sense.

Some of our jobs *did* require a bit of shooting, but not in the way that you'd expect. The hard-earned competencies of the SF trooper make him highly prized when it comes to training both military and civilian cadres around the world, and I took on a job like this in Kurdistan.

It came from one of the bigger umbrella companies. The Americans were pulling out of Kurdistan, a semi-autonomous region in northern Iraq. The people here consider themselves Kurds rather than Arabs, and they have their own language, culture and slant on religion. After Iraq fell to the coalition in 2003, Kurds were eager to break from the rule of Baghdad as much as possible. The West assumes that because the British had drawn some lines on a map that all the people of Iraq are countrymen, but the truth is that to the Kurds, the government in Baghdad was as alien and unwanted as one in Washington. They just wanted to get on with their own thing, after a long history of getting shafted – which is still continuing to this day. The US and the coalition had allowed the Kurds to build and maintain their own forces outside the Iraqi government's chain of command.

Up until 2012, the training of these forces had been conducted by US soldiers. The Kurds had played an important part during the surge in Iraq, and they would do so in the future in the fight against Islamic State. With the US pulling their men out, however, they needed some new instructors – and that's where we came in.

At first, we were simply there to train their presidential close protection team. Brits have a reputation as being the best in the world at this, and though the guys were already good, we were able to polish their drills and introduce them to our way of thinking: big blunt shows of force were not the only way to do things. Often, stealth and guile are the best weapons available for protecting your principal, and that's what we taught them.

The CP course went nice and smoothly. The guys were very keen to learn, and friendly. British Special Forces had built a fierce reputation in Iraq, and nothing gives your bonding a boost like a common, mortal enemy. At the end of the course, the Kurdish leadership approached us and asked if we'd be available to instruct them in the more direct-action aspects of SF work. As much as I wanted work, I wasn't looking to short-change anybody, and so I told them what we'd need in order to deliver an effective course, from large quantities of live ammunition to a sniper tower, a killing house and a drive-on range for vehicle drills.

I could see that the cost of it all surprised them. There was a lot of discussion, but eventually one of them asked, 'Can you come back here in two months?'

When I returned to Kurdistan, everything had been built as we'd asked – the Kurds weren't messing about.

Now that we had all the weaponry and facilities, the biggest issue we faced was the language barrier. Some of the lads could speak a bit of English, but it's one thing trying to understand a foreign language over a cup of tea and another when there's gunfire rattling around your head. We had an interpreter, but I began to notice that when I debriefed the guys on some poor drills – a polite way of saying that I gave them a bollocking – they'd still be sitting there grinning back at me.

'You didn't tell them what I said, did you?' I'd ask my terp.

'I did, Mr Dean.'

'Tell them again. Tell them exactly what I said.'

He spoke. They kept smiling. I shook my head.

The reason the interpreter wouldn't pass on my words exactly as I said them is that there is a strict hierarchy of family and tribe in Kurdistan (and a lot of the other countries that I worked in). The terp was the cousin of their OC, which allowed him to hold that position, but it would still be bad news for him if anybody took offence at his words – even though they were mine!

These rules of tribe and family complicated the course. One of the chefs in our dining facility had unbelievably good English – far better than our terp's – and I asked if he could be my mouth-piece. There was a lot of head shaking to that; he wasn't from the right tribe. Didn't have the right cousins.

It got even more problematic when we started putting the trainees through ranges and the killing house. Even though they had a chain of command modelled on our own in Western militaries, the power of rank carried less authority than the bond of family. Just like you and your sister might start arguing at Christmas dinner, two family members would start arguing back and forth with each other halfway through clearing the kill-house because they disagreed about which room to assault next. They might be a private and a sergeant, but it didn't matter. Before long it would be like any other dysfunctional family gathering.

Promotion was based on bloodline rather than ability, and this meant that even though individual guys were very competent, things would begin to slow and break down when they were put into a unit. It wasn't a problem that I'd ever really encountered in the UK military – a good reminder that even though you're doing something you've done a thousand times before, new challenges will always emerge, and that needs to be prepared for and dealt with.

We got a little bit of downtime while we were in Erbil, the capital of Iraqi Kurdistan. Not really knowing what to do with ourselves, the other Brits on my team and I got into the car and went for a drive around.

One of them was squinting into the distance when he said; 'Is that a *water park*?'

It was, an absolute monster of a place with pools and slides! Our decision was made: 'Let's go there!'

It was a strange experience being in a water park where all the women are covered up, and the kids and adults all stared at our white skin and tattoos like we'd dropped down from Mars. Or maybe they were just looking at us because we were running around excitedly like big kids: hands downs it was the best water park that I'd ever been to. Who'd expect that in Erbil, northern Iraq? It just goes to show that you never know what you'll find if you're willing to explore. Like a lot of people, I'm often guilty of assuming that life in countries like Iraq is all fighting and misery, but the truth is that most people just want to have a peaceful life and go down a bloody water slide now and then.

There was another moment in Iraqi Kurdistan when I had my preconceptions challenged. It was at the beginning of the

Above, left. Aged 6 in Bradford on my way to a birthday party.

Above, right. Boxing L/Cpl Wood at Middleweight in the Army Minor Unit Finals in Bicester (59 Commando Squadron v 518 Pioneer Squadron).

Below, left. Winter 1999 Op. Agricola (Kosovo) in an OP (Observation Post) gathering intelligence and imagery of the KLA training camp on the Kosovo/Serbian border.

Below, right. Diving task at Harstad harbour in Norway.

Cross training with the Norweigan Engineer Diving teams at a Fjord in Northern Norway.

Pistol shooting with the Sig. 226 while adopting various firing positions.

Standby Diver fully prepared to go on air.

Downtime in the accommodation block in Kosovo.

Jungle training in Ghana as part of the Brigade Recce Force: exercise Chamois.

On a helicopter ride back to base, following a live firing range package in Ghana.

Left. Kit preparation and being fitted with early generation NVGs (Night Vision Goggles) prior to deploying on an operation.

Below. After six months of arduous Special Forces selection. 'Badging' day – being presented with my SBS beret and belt from the Commanding Officer.

Talking in the Hawk aircraft for a low level CAS (Close Air Support) on the
Forward Air Controllers Course in North Yorkshire (August 2007).

Above, left. REORG conducting the ammunition and casualty statuses of the team before moving off.

Above. Humour was a massive part of military life by making light of dark situations.

Left. Rigged up onboard an AC-130 Hercules aircraft conducting HAHO jumps. This image was taken a few hours before my life-changing parachuting incident.

The Russian Mi8 modified as an air ambulance to transport casualties from the the front line in Tripoli to the Tunis border. My only mode of transport to get back into Tripoli.

Mentoring and advising a local security organisation in Somalia on sentry locations and arcs of fire.

Tripoli International Airport burning during the battle between militia and government forces during the Tripoli War (Summer 2014).

The aftermath.

course, during the opening address by the commanding officer. He had a map up on the PowerPoint screen showing the homeland of the Kurds. It stretched into what is now Turkey, Syria, Iran and Iraq. As the CO explained, that homeland had been chopped up and divided by a foreign power into these others countries, resulting in decades of persecution of the Kurds by their new rulers.

If you haven't guessed already, that foreign power was Great Britain.

To say I felt uncomfortable would be an understatement. There were a couple of hundred seasoned killers in that room, and a Brit with a skinhead sitting in front of them. The CO hadn't meant anything by it – he was just repeating the facts of history – but I did feel the sweat on my collar. This wasn't the first time I'd been to a war-torn country and heard that Britain had carved up territory that split tribes up, often resulting in them being ruled by an iron fist. In all of the countries that I worked in, I believed that what we were doing was important, but there was no denying that a lot of it was making up for past mistakes. I'm not a master of international strategic studies and I don't claim to be, but I've got two eyes and two ears, and what I saw during my time on the circuit was a lot of people with a dim view of British history. That being said, there was also an almost universal respect for our competence, particularly in military matters. People wanted to work with us, and I was never made to feel guilty – at least not deliberately – for things that had happened in the past. I wasn't taken at face value and was instead judged on my own merits, and I did the same: I wasn't about to condemn all Afghans, for instance, because some of them had been my enemy. I felt very privileged that in Afghanistan I had witnessed a part of the country that very few servicemen got to see. I saw families going about their daily business. Children going to school. People buying fruit. I saw vivid colours, and smiles, and a people who loved their families and simply wanted to be happy even though there was a war going on.

To be honest, I felt sorry for the soldiers who had spent their entire tours in patrol bases getting attacked and searching for IEDs. They never got the chance to really see the people they were fighting for, and I'm not surprised if some have a negative opinion of the place if all they experienced were threats and danger.

I knew that there would be a lot of benefits being in the Special Forces, but I didn't know that finding common connections of humanity would be one of them.

After the job in Kurdistan, I followed the usual routine of being home for about thirty-six hours before being sent on another job: this time to Mogadishu in Somalia.

A lot of the countries I was working in had oil and gas resources; Aberdeen is the oil and gas capital of Europe. I had enough mates working in the industry to have picked up a bit about how things worked, not to mention some of the lingo, and so it seemed like the perfect cover for me to use when I was entering these countries. It's much easier to pass through immigration when you show them a business card from your mate's oil and gas consulting firm than if you tell them you're there for security. When people hear the 's' word they assume that you're a mercenary coming in to start a civil war, and I didn't want to spend a day or two with a lamp shoved in my face.

The reason I was travelling to Mog was not to topple a

government but to recce the place for a security company start-up. In none of these countries can Western companies operate alone, and so there always needs to be links established with local security providers, and reports made on anything from the atmospherics to the availability of clean water and food.

The head of business development for the company had already come out on a recce himself, but the security provider who 'hosted' him hadn't shown him much beside the airport, which was where almost all foreign nationals and their security were based. He needed the recce doing properly, and so he asked me if I'd be willing to fly out alone: 'It's the only way you'll get to see anything.'

'No problem,' I said, and within a few hours I was starting on the chain of flights to get to Mogadishu.

Most white faces flying into the country are met inside the terminal by their security personnel, and so I got a lot of intent looks as I put my bag over my shoulder and walked past the last security guards and out into Somalia. It was only about a 400m walk to my hotel, but I got so many stares on that road that I felt like I was stepping out along a catwalk in Milan.

Even the manager of the hotel was flapping. He was worried that I'd get kidnapped either for ransom or a good old-fashioned beheading. Once we'd had a couple of drinks together, he gave me a rifle and a pistol for my own safety; you don't get that from your concierge in London!

I got a lot of the answers that I was looking for on my recce from the hotel manager and other guests, but I needed to see the ground, and so he arranged a car and driver for me. Nothing fancy – that's the easiest way to draw unwanted attention. We hit the streets, and though the city was run-down in parts it was not the total shithole *Black Hawk Down* had led me to expect. Like all cities it had its prime real estate and its less desirable parts. What I couldn't find, though, was the hospital.

That mystery was solved when I heard a huge explosion rip through the morning. I shouted for my driver, we ran to the car and I told him to follow the first ambulance that he saw.

We did, and when it came to a stop I saw a familiar scene: there was the twisted, charred ruin of a car in the centre of a ring of black dirt and debris. People milled about, watching as victims of the car bomb were helped into the ambulance.

'Follow him,' I said again to my driver as the ambulance pulled out, and sure enough we arrived at a hospital. It looked brand new to me, and when I started asking questions, I discovered that it had recently been built by the Turkish government. I asked if I could take a look around, explaining why, and they were happy to oblige: the facilities looked gleaming. Apparently, this was the largest hospital in Africa.

As we drove back to the hotel, I made a call to check in with the company. I did this on schedule every six hours to let them know I was alive and safe.

'I was just about to call you,' my mate said on the other end. 'Don't go out today, Stotty. There's been a vehicle-borne IED in the city.'

I couldn't help but smile. 'Funny you should mention that, mate. I've got some pictures to send you when I get back to the hotel.'

'How the hell did you get these?' he texted me later.

After an incident like that car bombing, there's always heightened tensions, and so I decided my next trip should stay clear of the city. Instead, I went to the airbase, where a number of US Special Operations Forces were training African Union troops for their fight against al-Shabaab. One SEAL Officer – a fellow frogman – offered to show me around. He took me to their field hospital.

'What do you think of that Turkish hospital?' I asked him.

He looked at me blankly. 'What Turkish hospital?'

I soon found out that, as in many of these countries that I visited, Westerners tended to stick to their compound in the 'secure' area. Personally, I always saw those sites as more of a target. Either way, you can't get the lie of the land unless you actually get out on the ground. Sounds bloody simple, but time and time again I'd see that get overlooked.

Like in Yemen, where I was privileged to be invited into the homes of the people that I worked with. I met the owners of the local security companies, and had dinner with them and their friends and family. They had a lot to ask me, and I had a lot to ask them. We all came away from the meetings with smiles on our faces and knowing more about the world; and the more I learnt, the more I realised that people everywhere want their families to be safe and prosperous, and that if you treat individuals with dignity and respect, then they will almost always return it.

Just before I left Somalia, my new friends took me to the south of the city. The area had once been a huge tourist destination for Italians, evident by the style of the architecture, and I could see why: golden beaches stretched into the distance. The water was clear blue and young lads dived down to catch the lobsters that we ate at a restaurant set back on the sand. It was a fantastic meal in beautiful surroundings, and with good company. Sitting there, I felt extremely lucky to experience it. Were there problems in Somalia? Absolutely, and big ones, but just like everything in life, you can't block out all of the positives just because there is some negative. The military is not all roses. Neither is cycling the length of America, or marriage, or friendships. Everything has its difficulties, but often that just makes the good bits better. The people I was sitting with at that beach could have hated me, the world and life. Instead, we got past the preconceptions and found great connections.

I was a happy man.

Gaddafi had been dead for a while now, but Libya didn't look as if it was about to calm down any time soon. The worst was yet to come, but even in the early days there was a need for lots of security operatives to protect the large numbers of diplomats, development agency staff and businesspeople. Understandably, the new-formed government there did not want all of these operators to be foreign nationals, and so I was hired by a company to train up a group of locals.

You wouldn't believe some of the people I had on that course. I'm not lying when I tell you that one was an astrophysicist and another was a university lecturer.

'What are you doing here?' I asked them when I found that out.

'There are no jobs for what we can do,' one of them told me in impeccable English – it was those language skills that had qualified them for the course.

They were bright lads. Far brighter than the security company, who only wanted to use them on an ad hoc basis and refused to pay them a retainer. As soon as I'd finished teaching them, they all left to open their own security companies. It just goes to show that no matter the circumstances, people with drive will find a way to get by, and even prosper. Those guys had been dealt a shit hand, but they didn't let it hold them back.

11. LET THE GAMES BEGIN

My next gig brought a big change of scenery. The Olympic Games were being held in London, and when you consider that the British government were putting troops on the streets for security, it's easy to imagine how big business was splashing the cash to ensure the best protection for their corporate tickets.

I landed a job with a huge sponsor of the Olympics, a major credit card issuer, and despite what I'd seen in Libya and elsewhere, I was still shocked to see just how deep those big business pockets were: they hadn't just taken rooms in a five-star hotel, they'd booked *the entire place*! The tickets they handed out to their corporate guests were the best going, and on top of that, they put on guest speakers at the hotel at a quarter of a million a pop. I won't name names, but let's just say that one of them had a thing for cigars in the office and the other was a Brit with a big grin whose hobby was starting wars.

I spent four weeks in that hotel, taking guests to the games and sitting beside them in the best seats. I'm a big fan of watching people pushing the limits of human capability, and so witnessing the Olympics was extremely humbling for me, and I was hugely grateful to be in that position. I almost had to pinch myself at times. I was getting paid more than I had in Libya *and* I was getting to watch Usain Bolt? It didn't seem real!

But it was, and that's when I had my suspicions confirmed

that more danger did not equal more reward in security. The industry is not risk/reward relative If anything, it was the lads taking on the lower-paid rotational work who were more at risk from shootings and IEDs. Bodyguarding for a VIP, you are usually at the centre of concentric rings of security. At the Olympics, you had people on £15 an hour searching bags, then cops and squaddies on £17–30K a year. And at the centre of all that manpower were people like me and their clients, and we were taking home more per day than the stewards would in a week. If there was a terrorist attack, chances are it would fall on the outer rings of security. If you're wondering why the guests would want to spend the kind of money they were on the likes of me, I'd say it's because they have very deep pockets, and even minimal risk is some risk. When you're sitting on top of billions, like our employer was, why not cover your bases with the highest-trained soldiers in the world? These people wore the best shoes, the best watches and drove the best cars. It follows that they'd want the best bodyguards too.

You'd probably never have known that that's what we were. You do sometimes see celebrities with bodyguards who stand out like a sore thumb, but discretion was the name of our game. We dressed like our clients. We appeared friendly and interested in the games – which we were! No mad-dog stares or shoving people out of the way. Even if there's no legitimate threat, shoving someone could start a fight out of nowhere – and you've just endangered your client for the sake of your ego. We wanted to blend in as much as possible, and it worked. At the end of the four weeks, as we were saying our goodbyes, one of my clients said: '*You* were our security? I thought you worked at the company!'

If you see me at the swimming pool, you'll see tattoos and a skinhead, and maybe you'll guess who I was and what I do. If you see me wearing nice shoes and a blazer, you'll just assume my hair fell out from worrying about the price of oil.

At the end of the Olympics I got a chance to go back to Aberdeen. Mollie was growing up fast, and even though I loved my time with her, I felt like my first obligation as a father and husband was to provide for my family.

'Where this time?' Alana asked me calmly as I put down the phone. I'd had an offer, and it was back to a country that was about to descend into chaos.

'Libya.'

12. FRACTURES FORMING

On 11 September 2012, the American Embassy in Benghazi was stormed by an Islamist militant group, resulting in the deaths of four Americans, including the US Ambassador. Even though it was well documented that Islamist terrorist organisations were operational in the country, this was an event that shocked the world. America is such a power that whenever it suffers a setback it's hard to get your head around it. A US diplomat had been murdered in the same streets where a year ago I had been chatting and drinking tea with the locals. At that time all I'd had to worry about was getting sunburnt, but now the situation was deteriorating rapidly.

I was in Benghazi when this went down. It sounds horrible to say this, but as a soldier and security operator, your 'right time, right place' often means that it's been the 'wrong time, wrong place' for someone else. I would never wish suffering on anyone so that I could profit, but the shit had hit the fan and because I had planned ahead, caching weapons and preparing escape routes and drivers, I was now in a position to act rather than simply standing back and watching events unfold.

An oil company were the first to call me. They had eight workers in Benghazi, and they wanted to get them out of there and to Tripoli asap.

You may be picturing the whole of the city in meltdown at

this point, but the truth is that the most of it was calm, with the incident contained in and around the US Embassy. That didn't mean that the chaos couldn't spread, though. Look at the Boston Tea Party. Look at the Arab Spring. Sometimes one incident is the spark that lights the bonfire. When these moments occur, it's almost like you can feel the city holding its breath, waiting to see what will happen next.

I didn't waste time waiting to find out the hard way, but there were no screeching tyres and slamming doors as the operation to get the Westerners home began. Fear is contagious. A leader – because that's what I was to my contractors and the people we were evacuating – should appear calm and unflappable.

'All right, guys?' I smiled at the Germans as we arrived to collect them from their offices. 'My name's Dean, and I'm here to take you home.'

That helped break the ice. These were civilians, not soldiers, and so they were naturally picturing the worst in their minds, probably expecting a mob to come for them. When they saw a smiling Englishman instead, unarmed except for his dazzling charm, it helped put them at ease. Imagine how they'd have been feeling if I'd raced over at a hundred miles an hour, and jumped out the car with an AK in my hand, screaming, 'We've got to get you out of here now! Go-go-go!' There'd have been a nasty smell in the cars, that's for sure.

I led our convoy out of the city. We had no trouble on the way. All of my drivers were local to Benghazi, and they advised me which neighbourhoods might be best avoided. I'd tried to pick up as much local gen as I could during my previous trips to Libya, but every little helped. Instead of taking the coastal road through the major cities, I took the less obvious route into the Sahara, using a safe house in an oasis town.

I'd stayed here with the owner when I'd been putting my evacuation plans together. He was happy to see me and made everyone welcome, further putting them at ease. I got as much information as I could from my sources, wanting to be sure that the attack was an isolated one and that anti-Western violence had not spread across the entire country.

Ironically, it was the safety of my local drivers that I was actually most worried about. Libya's system is tribal and militant, and after overthrowing the unifyingly hated figure of Gaddafi, these tribes were now beginning to look at each other a bit funny. There had been some sporadic violence between them, and my standard operating procedure was to keep them as far apart from each other as possible. It wasn't a risk I had to spell out to the Libyans.

'We are worried about driving into Tripoli,' one of them confided in me. He was the same man that I had had to teach how to turn on an electric light bulb – how much stuff at home do we take for granted?

'Don't worry, mate,' I assured him. 'Everything will be fine.'

He shook his head. 'They will know we are a different tribe. There will be trouble.'

'You'll be fine, mate.'

I don't know exactly how Libyans knew the difference between the tribes, but I expect it was the same way you can tell a Scouser from a Geordie. Regardless, despite what I had told my drivers, I was worried for their safety, and so I had another set of drivers inbound from Tripoli; we'd take the rest of the journey with them.

Happy that everything was in hand, I followed the army tradition of sleeping when and where I could and grabbed a couple of hours gonk on the floor. When I woke up, I had a hell of a surprise.

All of my drivers had shaved their thick beards.

The oldest of them smiled. 'Now maybe they will not recognise us, Mr Dean.'

Shit. I wish they'd still had those beards to hide their anger when the other drivers turned up. God knows what the two groups started saying to each other, but I don't think they were swapping weather reports from their sides of the country.

In the end, it came down to money. My original drivers were worried that they wouldn't get paid. When I told them that they'd be paid the same as if they'd done the entire Tripoli drive, plus a bonus, they were a lot happier; and we followed through on that promise. If you want to burn all of your bridges instantly, screw someone on their pay. Word gets around, and a lot of the time, your word is the only factor that will make people work with and support you rather than someone else.

With new drivers from the right tribes, the rest of the journey across the country was effortless. By the time we arrived in Tripoli I think that some of the Germans were even beginning to enjoy the road trip and seemed sad to see it end. I saw them to their destination, then went to work on my post-op report. I felt bad about the guys shaving their beards. They had grown them for religion, not because they're hipsters, and I thought about how I could deal with the situation differently next time. Knowledge of politics and demographics is of crucial importance when you plan, and I'd discovered a little more. When there are 140 tribes in a country, there's always something new to learn.

Not all companies operated this way. For many it was 'my way or the highway', and maybe that's why they ran into trouble, be it with their drivers not showing up or not getting warning of an IED. In the Special Forces you are taught that hearts and minds is the way to win. Giving back to the locals and getting them onside is the only way to complete the mission, and I found that no different when doing it as a civilian. Don't get me wrong, money talks too, but if you are disrespectful, then Arabs will feel no obligation to be respectful in return. They might take that money and you never hear from them again. On the other hand, if you act with humility, they will go above and beyond.

I watched the fallout of the attacks appear on the news at the bar in my hotel. I heard a lot of talk from other contractors about 'fucking ragheads' and 'dirty Muslims'.

I shook my head. If there's one certain route to disaster, it is in underestimating your enemy and alienating your allies.

After the attack on the US Embassy, I expected that I'd be in Libya for some time. Instead I was offered a job in Yemen, along similar lines to the ones I'd conducted in Kurdistan, training the security teams for government officials.

I spent six weeks in the capital city, Sanaa, which is 10,000 feet above sea level. The air was thin, which made physical activity harder going, but I enjoyed teaching the course on the basics of protection and battlefield medicine.

The main problem I came across in Yemen was that the locals all had an addiction to khat, which is a stimulant that the user gets from chewing the leaves of that plant. It seemed to be standard operating procedure that at 2 p.m. everyone would just stop and get off their box on the stuff. In fairness to my guys, they seemed to want to work rather than get munted, but their superiors and the movers and shakers were all jabbering and dribbling by 2.15. It was impossible in the afternoon to get anything done, and so I started running the course from 0500. Not everyone appreciated the early start, but it was the only way to fit in the course contents before khat o'clock. Any attempts to work after that were just met with a 'we'll do it tomorrow' and a wave of the hand. Considering it was supposed to be a stimulant, it seemed to turn them massively lazy.

I tried the leaf myself once, during our initial visit to plan the course. I was doing my thing of winning contracts by winning friendships and I didn't want to be rude, so when they insisted I try the leaf, I did. I can't say I saw what all the fuss was about. It just made me want to take a nap. Maybe you needed to have a gob full to really feel it, but I was quite happy to just stick to my brews and wets.

I didn't even get home to Aberdeen before the next job came through. I was waiting for my connection at Dubai when I got the call: 'Can you be in Libya tomorrow?'

I didn't ask what the gig was. 'I'm on my way home from Yemen, mate. No way I can get a visa in time.'

Libya wasn't one of those places where you could just turn up and pay ten bucks for a visa, and my own had run out during my time in Yemen.

'Don't worry about that,' the caller insisted. 'Just get to Manchester and we'll take care of it.'

I shrugged my shoulders and agreed, and then I called Alana to let her know that instead of being home for dinner that night I'd be flying into a country on the edge of civil war.

*

The company were as good as their word and by the time that I arrived in Manchester I had an e-ticket in my email inbox. They were sending me business class to Tripoli, which would be a nice chance for me to get some head-down before I arrived. I had no idea what job was waiting for me on the other side.

I got my first clue that this one was a bit different when I was met straight off my flight. This wasn't unusual in itself, as a fixer would usually be there to greet you and to help you through immigration. This time, however, he didn't just help me through the process: we skipped it entirely. I wasn't sure exactly how, but the logical answer was that someone who could skip me through a country's immigration process had to be working for the government.

I didn't find out any more in the car. I was driven to the Corinthia Hotel, and as we moved into the city I did my best to pick up on atmospherics from the passenger seat. The streets were still busy and people seemed to be getting on with their normal lives. Nothing that would hint at imminent violence.

I knew a bit about the Corinthia. A government pension scheme owned half of it, and this was where a lot of the new leadership of the country had based themselves after Gaddafi's fall. Now I was certain I was here at the behest of the country's top brass.

There was no need for me to check in, as my minder already had the keys to my room for me. I imagined that meant the room was bugged, but I'd be surprised if there wasn't a listening device in every room of the building. I'm sure my every word was heard by spooks from Libya, and all the way across to the CIA Headquarters in Langley, Virginia.

My minder gave me a bit of time to shower and change, and

then I was taken upstairs to one of the hotel's bigger suites. There were two men inside, and I knew instantly from the cut of their clothes and their confident demeanour that they were important men. One of them I recognised instantly.

'Good evening, Prime Minister.'

The prime minister of Libya gave me a firm handshake. He was a solid-looking man with a stern edge. The second man now introduced himself in excellent English as the health minister.

I hope I didn't raise an eyebrow at that. I had been in the business of fucking up people's health, and now I was in the business of maintaining it. I was used to meeting defence secretaries and generals, and if this guy started to talk about hospital waiting times, I'd have to politely tell them that they'd brought in the wrong guy. The only thing I knew about healthcare was what I'd learnt through my own experience in the MOD's medical system: don't lose people's bloody med-files!

As the health minister began to talk, however, I quickly realised two things: first that he was to be the interpreter between the prime minister and me, and second that I was definitely the man for their job.

'One of the militias has seized four oil terminals,' the PM told me through his mouthpiece. 'And I want them gone.'

It's not every day you get asked by a prime minister to make a problem in his country go away, especially a heavily armed problem. I asked a couple of questions to make sure I'd understood properly. There was no dressing up the answer. Armed militias had begun squabbling for power once Gaddafi had been killed. They weren't happy that the country's new leadership was largely made up of returning exiles, and when they got tired of talking, they turned to the weapons that had been supplied to them by the West for the purposes of overthrowing Gaddafi. Militias began grabbing whatever they could as bargaining chips, from airstrips to oil terminals. Libya's economy relied on the export of oil, and the militia had turned it off. Essentially, the country was being held to ransom.

I got as much information as I could out of the pair. Then, the PM asked me how I would deal with the situation. I gave my answer in broad strokes. Enough to give them an idea about how big an undertaking it would be.

'We'll have to hit all four terminals at once,' I explained. 'So that the others aren't alerted and have time to prepare.'

The prime minister just nodded, and so I went on. 'The good news is that we have the option of coming at them from the sea, air or land. They probably won't expect either of the first two.'

He nodded again.

'You could come at them from three directions,' I said, 'leaving one flank open where they could escape.' This was a favourite SF tactic. If you surround an enemy, he will have no choice but to fight on. If you leave him a way out, he'll quite often take it. Of course, you can set an ambush to take them out once they're running free of their defences, but that's not what I had in mind in this scenario. I thought the prime minister wanted the militia evicted rather than massacred.

I was wrong.

'No flank,' he told me through the health minister. 'No one gets out.'

*

I had a lot to think about. I went up to the restaurant on the hotel rooftop and got some scran. As the call to prayer echoed across the city, I wondered at the prime minister's words. Private security gigs were usually about protecting life, but there was no doubting that even simply advising on this job would tie me into *loss* of life.

I called the man who'd put me on the job. 'Who's authorised this, mate?'

He assured me that it was legit; after all, I was talking directly to the Libyan PM.

We discussed a few more things, including my rate of pay: over three times the standard that a Tier-1 guy could expect. For once, I was seeing that more risk *did* equal more reward. If I did have reservations, they disappeared when I thought about paying off a chunk of the mortgage.

The next day, the PM loaned his private jet to me and my team-mate so that we could fly over the terminals and get a look at them from above. We were too high to really see the kind of detail we needed for planning, but we enjoyed the ride and the food.

That night, we met again with the PM and health minister for what would be the first of many evening briefings.

'What do you need to make it happen?' I was asked, and I gave him the numbers that I'd decided upon with my partner: fifty Tier-1 operators, and seventy Tier-2.

The PM didn't even blink. 'Make it happen.'

That was easier said than done. Hiring like-minded, calm individuals who were the best at what they did meant paying big figures; we had that money in place, but it wasn't like I could just post on Facebook saying that there was a sneaky job going in Libya. A lot of these guys were like me, constantly out on other jobs, and so we had to put out feelers through trusted friends and contacts. We hired someone else that we trusted to handle all the paperwork. Everything from sifting CVs to overseeing non-disclosure agreements. My job at this time was more movie producer than door-kicker: I was calling in favours, sourcing kit, people and places – we needed somewhere to store equipment and house and train all the people we were going to have coming in. As far as paying for that went, I was essentially given a blank cheque book.

Our ops room began taking shape in a suite at the Corinthia. We'd been supplied with an entire floor, and knowing that the rooms would be bugged, we kept our more private chats for when we went into the pool or for a run. We weren't the only contractors in the hotel, and I knew a lot of faces in Libya at this point. As in any industry, people wanted to talk shop, and that began to be a problem.

'All right, mate' was how the conversation usually went. 'What are you up to on this trip, then?'

I'd feed them some line about looking over a company's evacuation plan.

'Really? Because I heard from so-and-so that you asked so-and-so and so-and-so if they could come out here for a gig, no fixed limit?'

Squaddies gossip like housewives, and they're just as bad when they get out of uniform. When word started to get out that our guys were being paid well just for being on standby in the UK, the calls didn't stop.

The blokes we could keep, for now, on standby in the UK,

but we needed to start bringing the kit into the country. During one of our evening pow-wows, I asked the PM if he had any ideas, and he offered us the use of Tripoli airbase.

The airbase outside Tripoli covers twenty square miles and was once the biggest US military base outside the States. When Gaddafi came into power, the base closed down, and since then large parts of it had been left to slowly decay. That can take some time in desert conditions, and as we drove around the endless tarmac we saw dozens of aeroplane frames that had been left for dead. Anything from Cold War-era fighters to the huge C-130 Hercules.

There were four of these big boys on the base, one of them with 'Sudan Air Force' written on its fuselage. We wondered if they might be of some use to us in planning and carrying out the prime minister's mission, but you didn't have to be much of a mechanic to see that they were unserviceable.

The trip to the airbase wasn't a waste, though. There was plenty of storage space available for our incoming kit and equipment and, as in any operation, we would need to rehearse our skills, drills and plan again and again and again before we could put it into action. The secluded parts of the airbase would be perfect for that, allowing our training to take place far from prying eyes.

The prime minister was happy about all of this when I told him. Then, through his mouthpiece the health minister, he informed me that he'd be going out of the country for three weeks; he had a conference to attend at the United Nations in New York.

I got the impression from his expression that there was more to it than that. The new Libyan government was in position because of the assistance of Western powers, and I wondered if this trip would also be one where he would meet with his new allies and ask for their permission to go ahead and wipe out the militias that were holding up Libya's crucial export of oil. Unlike most governments, the new leadership in Libya didn't have a standing army that they could call upon for security; they had to rely upon loyal militia groups instead. My guess is that the PM didn't want to use these guys to clear the 'bad guys' out of the oil terminals because it would probably lead to all of the infrastructure being damaged and massive oil spills: 'spray and pray' was the preferred marksmanship style in the area.

I gave the PM my assurance that we would continue the preparations while he was away, and that I'd continue to meet with the health minister and my heads of department every night to make sure that all was going to plan.

That lasted for about twenty-four hours.

The night after the prime minister left there was a new guy in the room, and he had that look that powerful people in the Middle East and North Africa often have: he was fat, with a moustache as thick as his shoulders.

I wasn't far into my daily sitrep (situation report) when this new addition turned to face the health minister and started tearing into him in Arabic. I didn't need to understand the words to know that he was, to put it mildly, not a very happy chap.

Eventually the man stopped his verbal assault and turned to face me. He didn't shout, but he was animated and angry. 'Who are you? Where are you with this plan?'

I told him that I was here because the prime minister had

invited me, and that I was putting the equipment, men and plan together at the request of the Libyan government.

The big man shook his head. 'I am the head of the Secret Intelligence Service, and nobody in the government knows anything about this.'

That wasn't something I wanted to hear. It just goes to show that you should never assume, even when that assumption is that a prime minister is speaking on behalf of his government.

'Do you want me to shut it down?' I asked him. I'd already made good money, and I didn't want to be in the middle of a lovers' tiff between the PM and his ministers.

Eventually, the big man shook his head. 'No. No. But can you slow it down?'

I tried not to smile at that. On my daily rate, this was about the best thing I could ever expect to hear.

'Look,' I said, 'I've got experienced guys here and people are going to start asking why. What if you provide us with men, and we'll run a training course for them?'

He liked that idea.

'How many guys do you have in mind?' I asked.

'Twelve hundred.'

I saw my mate's eyes go wide. That was the size of two infantry battalions.

'Why don't we try and concentrate on a smaller number?' I suggested, and after a lot of tea and talk, we'd whittled the number down, and I hope calmed the man's nerves too.

My own nerves weren't ringing alarm bells, but the meeting had unsettled me. Working for the British military, you don't question your orders from the government; you trust that they are just and legal. Having come from that environment, I saw the position of a prime minister in Libya as having the same sort of authentic authority, and it had been a rude awakening to realise that, actually, he could be playing his own game, with his own agenda.

The last thing I wanted was to be caught up in something that was backed by one part of the government and not the other. I realised that an operation like the one the PM was planning could instigate wider violence. If he came back from New York with the UN having sanctioned it, and got his own government onside, then I had no problem with doing what we had discussed – the country's economy was reliant on that oil export – but without those conditions being met, there was just no way I would go ahead.

If anything, it came as a bit of a relief when the PM didn't return from New York, even after several weeks. I met with the big man with 'tache again, and we decided to wind the operation down. The thrill-seeker in me was disappointed, but I had just about enough sense to know that it was all for the best. I'd made some good money for my family, done the same for other blokes, and no one had got hurt – that was win-win.

It took a couple of days to close it all down. There were flights to arrange, invoices, the return of equipment, and all that fun stuff. The night before we were due to fly back, I went up to the rooftop of the Corinthia Hotel to get some food at the Moroccan restaurant with my best mate and ops manager, TT.

We'd just started eating when we heard a distinctive drone in the distance. It was an unmistakable sound to anyone who had been in the military, and we looked at each other and raised an eyebrow: 'That's a C-130.'

There was no way any of the four Hercules we'd seen at the airbase were in flying condition, so we guessed that the sound must be coming from a charter flight bringing equipment into the country, or perhaps using it as a staging area before going on into central Africa.

We were wrong. It was a US military flight; that night Delta Force carried out a raid to pick up a high-value al-Qaeda target. According to the news, he had allegedly plotted the 1998 bombings in Kenya and Tanzania. They were in and out before the sun came up, but telling that to the officials at the airport was a hard sell; it turns out that a group of Westerners trying to leave the country after a raid looks a little suspicious. Though most Libyans are not fans of al-Qaeda, they're also not keen on people conducting operations on their turf.

Eventually, everyone was able to pass through and fly home, but the suspicion didn't stop there. Gossip spreads like a virus in the military and on the circuit, and I soon had friends and companies calling me to ask if we'd carried out the raid. By this point, everyone knew that I'd brought Tier-1 guys into the country, and they wanted to believe that it was for a Gucci raid for private gear on a HVT. The Americans eventually gave out a press release that they'd picked up an AQ bad guy that night, but it didn't do much to help me. Once someone has an idea in their head, it's hard for them to shake it, and I started to get a bad feeling that I was about to get tarnished with the unwanted title of 'mercenary'. What they weren't aware of was that the presence of our team, and the threat that we posed if sanctioned, was enough to bring the renegade faction at the oil terminals to the table with the government. By show of force, we had helped contribute to a bloodless solution for the country.

Unfortunately, that part of the story seemed to get lost, and things got worse when the prime minister finally returned from the US and was lifted from the Corinthia Hotel by one of the militias. Somehow, despite no longer being in the country, rumour control started to tie me and the others into that one too. We were guilty by association, it seemed, and I found that doors I had begun opening in the industry were now closed. I was still getting offered plenty of work, but the 'white collar' companies who want everything above board were cautious with me, even if all there was was a rumour.

Fair or not, I needed to find a way to clean up my image.

13. MY NEW NORMAL

With the label of 'mercenary' stuck to me, I knew it would be hard to win contracts for my own company, and so instead I took some work freelancing while I tried to think of a way to scrub the smell of the prime minister's job off me.

There was a high-profile court case about to take place in South Africa in the new year, and they needed somebody to head up the security for the defendant; basically, they were worried somebody would knock him off before he'd had his day in court. Believe it or not, both we and the defendant would be accommodated in a five-star hotel, and so even though it wasn't exactly where I wanted to be in terms of contract, I certainly couldn't complain. And even better, for the first time in years I was actually going to get Christmas and New Year with my family.

Alana and I had recently got married, and so it would be our first together as husband and wife. I'd hardly seen her or Mollie over the past twelve months, and I was looking forward to spending some time with them. Thanks to the South Africa job, I knew that I didn't need to worry about taking a phone call halfway through a meal and disappearing to the airport half an hour later.

Well, I was wrong on that one.

*

A few months earlier, my dad had been diagnosed with cancer. He'd been told he had about three months to live, and when I saw my sister's name on the phone's caller ID, my gut told me that the day had come.

'I think you should come down here,' she told me.

My face and my words were the same as any soldier's when he's confronted with something shit and just wants to push through it: 'Yeah. No drama.'

It was a couple of days before New Year when I took the flight from Aberdeen down south. I'd known that my dad was ill – terminally ill – but that hadn't pushed me to spending every minute with him. Our relationship just wasn't like that, and never had been. He'd been raised old school, and that's how he'd raised me. He didn't ever tell me that he loved me, but he didn't need to. I knew it. Why else would he have driven halfway up the country and back twice a weekend to see us when we were in Manchester? He didn't need to do that.

I was much the same way. My family all knew that no news was good news when it came to me. When I'd go on tour with the military, it would be one call on the way out and another six months later. That's how I was wired, and that's how my dad was wired.

I couldn't remember a time when my dad said he loved me, but I could remember as clear as day when he had told me that I wouldn't last two minutes in the army. I don't know if that was tactical genius on his part, because those words had helped push me on in everything I'd done since. If I had to guess, I'd say it was just a throwaway comment because he was angry at me chinning off my education, but the words have stuck with me to this day and taught me two valuable lessons: incredible amounts of drive can come from 'negative' energy, and words have huge power. Without doubt, that incident has led me to be extremely careful about what I say to my own kids, and how I say it.

I doubt my dad even remembered saying it. To be fair, once he saw I was serious about the army, I think he loved it. It was something we had in common. Soldiering had been his passion, and it was mine too. We'd talk once a week on the phone, and it was always about the military. We were both soldiers and proud of it.

When I walked into my dad's hospital room, two things hit me. The first was that he looked so different from the fit serviceman and football player that he would always be in my mind; it was almost as if he'd shrunk. His eyes looked red from exhaustion, and he was a little out of it from the drugs.

The second thing was that everyone else in the room looked just as knackered. My stepmum and sisters were hovering over him, tense and anxious as if they expected every breath to be his last. I could see their nerves were shredded.

'Bloody hell,' I said, going straight into squaddie mode. 'How long have you lot been like this?'

Days. I took one look at them, and knew that if they kept it up they'd be in worse state than my dad.

I went into the corridor and found a nurse. 'Excuse me. That's my dad in there. Can you tell me how long he's got, please?'

Bless her, she tried to give me all the hope and rainbows, but I just wanted the truth; 'It's fine, honestly,' I told her. 'I just need to know realistically so that I can plan ahead.'

Always planning.

She gave me a sad smile. 'A couple of days.'

I walked straight back into the room. 'I'm off to my mate's,' I told them, and they stopped hovering over my dad for a second to stare at me in shock.

'But you only just got here!'

'Yeah, and I'll be back in the morning. You lot can't keep this up for much longer, can you? We need to work a rota.'

It might sound cruel that I was putting a sentry duty on my dad's death bed, but what was the other option? Have everybody absolutely hanging out for days? I know what happens when people get tired. They become irritable. They argue. They can't make decisions. The only thing being eased by staying next to my dad's bed was people's consciences. It may seem heartless, but I knew the kindest thing to do was to give them space.

When I got back, I could tell that none of them had got any sleep. Their eyes looked like pissholes in the snow, and I insisted that they go home, eat and sleep. 'I'll watch Dad.'

The next eight hours was probably the longest continuous amount of time that we had ever spent together. We had a bit of a chat, but it was superficial; he was on painkillers, but that had never been our style anyway. He knew I loved him. I knew he loved me.

'Anything else I can do for you?' I asked him.

He told me he had a pain in his leg. I took a look and saw a problem with one of his pain-relief cannulas. It took a couple of seconds to fix it, and instantly he looked serene and nodded off to sleep.

When the girls returned that evening, he was still peaceful.

'I've never seen him look so calm,' my stepmum said.

'Well, that's 'cause he hasn't got three women fussing over him, isn't it?' I joked; every squaddie knows that dark humour is how you cope with death.

I stood up and gave my dad a pat on the shoulder.

'When will you be back?' one of my sisters asked me.

I shook my head. 'I won't. I'm going back to Aberdeen.'

They couldn't believe it.

'I've said my goodbyes,' I told them. 'And my family are up in Aberdeen. That's where I need to be.'

I knew it would be the last time that I saw him, and I was at peace with that. Back in Aberdeen that night, I got the news I'd been expecting.

'How's your dad doing?' Alana asked me the next day, at breakfast.

'He died last night,' I replied, and went back to eating my cereal. I was that blasé about the whole thing. I didn't realise it then, but death had been normalised for me. So too had my ways of coping with it: a complete numbing of my emotions. My father had passed away, and I'd given my wife that news in the same way I'd tell her that the kettle had just boiled.

Over the next week or so, I took control of the practical side of my dad's death. I helped arrange the funeral and made contact with the Royal Engineers Association so that they could be present. I wore my lovats, one of the ceremonial uniforms of the Royal Marines and the SBS. I wore my green beret, my medals, and my father's. It was the last time that I wore the uniform, and I suppose that was a fitting tribute in itself. My dad had been a huge part in me beginning my military journey, and now he was a part of its end.

'How are you feeling?' Alana asked me after the funeral.

'I need to leave the house at zero-six-hundred hours tomorrow to get to the airport,' I told her in reply.

In a moment when most people are racked by emotion, I was planning my travel for the job in South Africa. I was relentless, but in pursuit of what, and why?

14. WORLD CUP

For the 2012 Olympics, I'd landed a job that put me up in the best hotels and gave me the best tickets to the events, and so I could hardly believe my luck when the same company came calling for the football World Cup, in Brazil.

With such a big event coming up, I'd had my eye on it for an opportunity, but initially it seemed as though all the big companies were keen to use local security operations – there was already a bit of a stink in the country that the money generated from the event wasn't going to be fairly distributed, and the companies didn't want to exacerbate that.

Unfortunately, during the Confederations Cup, which had been held the previous year as a dress rehearsal, the local outfits proved themselves to be woefully underprepared and under-trained, and the big spenders now felt justified in bringing in outside assistance. Because of our success at the Olympics, they handed the gig straight off to us.

The World Cup would be played in several cities, and so we placed an operative in each one to be 'the man' for that location. That was a great job in itself, but I managed to go one better, travelling with the company's VIPs to all of the big events, from the opening ceremony to the final. There had been some concern that the protesting crowds could cause big trouble for the tournament, but Brazil is a nation of football fanatics and all the protests broke up in time for the locals to get to a television set and catch the games.

It was at the Brazil vs Cameroon game that I got a chance to catch up with a friend of mine. He was there representing the Football Association because his brother couldn't make it. Happy that my clients were secure with the other lads, I left my place and went to the presidential box to meet my mate from the army.

'All right, Stotty?' he said.

'How are you, mate?' I asked him.

We'd met back in 2007 at a Joint Terminal Attack Controller (JTAC) course held at RAF Leeming. There were eighteen students, and we'd been told to behave towards a certain individual as we would to anybody else in the forces; no special treatment.

It was on the second day that we hit it off, when we were being given our call signs. From the back of the room I'd made a joke at his expense, and there was a sharp inhalation of breath as everyone waited to see how he took it.

He laughed, and that was how I came to be paired up for the rest of the course with Prince Harry, who is one of the most decent blokes you could meet. He's a military man through and through, and I think part of the reason he loved the army so much was that he could just be himself. He was comfortable in this environment, and could handle his rank and job as well as any other soldier I'd met.

It was great to see him in Brazil. Not because he was a prince but because he was a comrade from my days in kit, just like any of the boys. One of the best things about the military and the circuit is that when you travel you quite often end up meeting a mate on the other side of the world. There's no better feeling than bumping into someone who's been beside you for the toughest moments of your life, and cracking a beer together in the sunshine. I've never been on a lads' holiday, nor have many of the soldiers I know. Who needs Ibiza when the taxpayer has sent you to work with the SEALS and a troop of you are let loose on San Diego's Pacific Beach?

Like the Olympics, the World Cup passed without incident for me, and that meant that we'd done our job well. I was extremely grateful for the work and the experience, and it would have been nice for my employment prospects if these kinds of thing went on all the time; but they didn't.

It was time to get back to the desert.

15. OPERATION BEAVER TAIL

As you might expect, the attack on the American Embassy in Benghazi sealed Libya's fate in a lot of ways. Many people in the West, both in diplomacy and in business, decided that the risk/reward ratio was just not worthwhile. There was a bit more to it than that in some quarters; some Westerners felt pissed off at the Libyans, quite frankly. There was an attitude of 'we helped them get free from under Gaddafi's tyranny and this is how they repay us?' While I do think it's true that intervention against the dictator stopped imminent ethnic cleansing, I feel that it's unfair to characterise and convict an entire nation based on the actions of a few hundred people. A lot of the Libyans I talked to in the wake of the embassy attack were appalled by what had happened. Appalled at the waste of life, and I think wise enough to know that there would be nothing good for their country in the aftermath.

Having been on the sharp end of diplomacy, I will be the first to admit that a country's involvement in a war zone is usually down to its own interests. That doesn't mean that it's not *also* in the interests of the countries in the war zone, but let's just be honest: no nation is going to spend billions of dollars, and potentially risk dozens or hundreds of lives, if there is nothing positive that's going to come back to it. That's the way the world works. In Syria, there was no oil, and therefore no intervention.

Embassies exist as much to promote trade and investment as anything else, and that, I think, is a good thing: if you do good business with your neighbours, then things are less likely to get messed up by arguing and fighting.

When the American Embassy was stormed, it showed that things in Libya had changed, but it wouldn't have been the end of Western involvement there if trade was on the table. That happened when the militias started fighting amongst themselves, closing off the oil that was the base of the country's economy and trapping Libya in bankruptcy. I was told by one group of diplomats that it would take *at least* fifteen years before Libya could now get back to the point of being a viable trading partner, and with embassies costing around $20 million a year to run, it just wasn't an investment that many were willing to pay. Pity, as Libya is the seventh largest oil-rich country in the world, and could be the Dubai of the Mediterranean if it had stability.

Diplomacy is a tricky thing, though. As in business, public relations are everything, and so a country can't just hold up its hands and say, 'There's no money to be made here – we're off.' What they need is an opportunity to pull the plug with a legitimate reason other than dollar signs. A moment that anyone could look at and say, 'Fair enough, mate. Didn't have any choice, did you?'

For the Canadians, that opportunity came in July 2014, during what was known locally at the time as the Tripoli War; this was the beginning of the civil war, which is still ongoing at the time of writing five years later. After months of posturing and chest-beating by rival militias, things came to a head when several of them began contesting ownership of Tripoli Airport.

This violence was significant for the Canadians not just because it was a clear demonstration of how far and how quickly the country was descending into potential civil war but because it gave that embassy a very real and immediate problem: the Canadians rotated in and out of the country through Tripoli Airport. This burnt down during the fighting, and it had been the lynchpin of their evacuation plan. With so much fighting going on in and around the area, flying out of there was totally out of the question, and so the Canadian government could say without hesitation that their position had become untenable; the order was given for the embassy to close down and come home.

That was where I came in. Unlike the bigger security companies, who relied on the airports, I had my own evacuation plans in place that could avoid the trouble spots thanks to the help of my network of local fixers. It was pretty well known by this point that I had weapons caches in the country, and after successfully evacuating personnel from oil and gas companies, I was beginning to shake off the 'mercenary' label that I'd picked up the year before. Westerners in Libya tended to congregate at the same hotels, and so I'd met a few of the Canadian staff, and they'd heard about me pretty often in the rumour mill. When I got their call, I was just finishing up at the World Cup. I'd been kept abreast throughout the Libyan escalation by my int. sources and fixers. As far as everyone knew, all the embassies had shut up shop and left. Only a handful were aware of the Canadians' situation, for obvious reasons, and I saw the chance to finally rid myself of the mercenary tag once and for all.

The Canadian Embassy was located in the Tripoli Towers, which was an interesting arrangement of blue and white buildings, with two of the high-rises connected by a decorative and religious-inspired arch. The decision had been made not only to pull out but with the acknowledgment that there would be no coming back for at least a decade, and so when I first visited, they were busy shredding all of their paperwork, and destroying anything else that could be deemed sensitive. Things were very orderly, though. It wasn't like one of those scenes where people are panicking and heaping papers into the fire. The Canadians were calmly and methodically breaking down their mission, and now I was told how they needed me to play my part in that.

Unlike many embassies, the Canadians' close protection officers are drawn from the ranks of serving military. In the Brit embassies, for example, the operators were all ex-forces, but they were now being paid and contracted by a security company hired by the government. With the Canadians, it was different, and using their own soldiers came with limitations. If they went out armed on the ground in Libya, then it was as if a military operation were being conducted, and you can imagine the headlines if something went wrong: 'Canadian Army fighting on the streets of Tripoli! Canadian soldiers killed! Citizens demand response!' The truth of the matter is that if a civvy operator like me is killed it doesn't usually make the papers. That civvy operator might have given twenty-two years' service to his country, but once he exchanges his uniform for a polo shirt and khaki pants then the newsworthiness of his death takes a nosedive. Diplomats are, by their very nature, concerned with *diplomacy*, and they knew that the headlines could be very different if the operation to close the embassy ran into trouble whilst being run as a military op or a civilian one. Perception is everything.

Of course, the reason that they'd come to me is that I'd built a reputation for getting things done quietly, and for taking on jobs when others won't.

Also, unlike their own military security, who only knew the ground within the city limits, I had an in-depth knowledge of all Libya by this point. It stands to reason that if you're evacuating dozens of people out of a country on the verge of civil war, then you'd like the guy leading the way to have done that route before, right? Time spent on recce is seldom wasted. Some of these people had been in Libya for a long time now, but what they knew of it was Westernised hotels and the same road they travelled every day. As you'd imagine, the unknown caused them concern; they were probably picturing the Libya outside their bubble as a Wild West.

To be honest, the diplomats were right to be cautious. When the militias began fighting, other people in the city started getting violent too. It always works like that in conflict. People start to act on impulse, particularly when there's no law enforcement or judicial system to stop them.

Early one morning, not long after dawn, I was driving with one of my fixers to visit a client. At the side of the road, we saw a carjacking take place; a blue car had pinned another in, and they forced the driver out at gunpoint before taking his car and driving off with it. The man ran after them until they fired warning shots; wisely, he decided to stop chasing them after that.

When I was part of Recce Troop, noting details in life had become second nature to me, and so the next morning I instantly recognised the same blue car, this time parked close to a quiet roundabout.

'Speed up,' I told my driver. 'Don't stop.'

He looked at me funny for a second, but then, sure enough, the blue car started to pull out so that it would block the entrance to the roundabout where, ordinarily, people would be slowing down.

'Foot down,' I said, firmly but calmly. 'Do not stop.'

I could sense his hands gripping the steering wheel, but he did exactly as I said, trusting my instinct. We shot through the gap, and I glimpsed an AK in an angry man's hands. I'd made the calculated risk that they were looking to make money, not to kill people for the sake of it, but that was exactly why I couldn't just stop and hand them the keys; if they were business savvy, they'd probably know how much the al-Qaeda operatives in the city would pay for a Westerner.

I looked over my shoulder and saw that they weren't about to give up easily. The blue car came racing after us, and like in an old gangster movie, I saw one of them leaning out of the window with a gun.

Believe it or not, I wasn't worried. I'd seen enough amateur marksmanship to know that in places like Libya they struggle to hit a target even if it's ten metres away and static. Moving target and moving platform? No point in even worrying. If I was unlucky enough to meet the Chuck Norris of Tripoli, then so be it.

'Just keep a steady speed,' I told my driver, not wanting him to red-line it. My gut told me that the carjackers had pursued us out of instinct and that once they realised it was a bad idea, they'd back off; the militias were everywhere, and approaching one of their armed checkpoints waving a gun out of the windows was really not a good idea. Sure enough, they seemed to come to that same conclusion and our short-lived car chase was at an end.

'All right?' I asked my driver.

He nodded. 'Yes, Mr Dean.'

'Cool.'

I didn't bring the incident up with Alana or the embassy staff. I didn't want to alarm either, of course, but I have to be honest; it just didn't strike me as being a big deal. There'd been some opportunists with a gun; we'd avoided them, and that was that. Move on. What's the mission today? What can I get my teeth into?

Paperwork was the answer to that question. You'd think evacuating an embassy would be all swinging in through windows and crawling through air-conditioning tunnels like John McClane, but the truth of the matter is that contracts needed drawing up, looking over by lawyers and eventually getting signed by yours truly. If I messed up and we all ended up as a political embarrassment, exploited on Al Jazeera, then everyone wanted to have a nice paper trail pointing at the guy to blame. I had no thoughts of failure, and so from my end I wanted to make sure I got paid. When I told them my fee for the job, the embassy staff thought I must have missed off a couple of zeros.

I shook my head. 'Seven grand,' I told them. Just enough to cover my expenses. They couldn't understand why, but my reason was simple: pull off a job like this and the business I'd get off the back of it would more than make up for the money. My goals in the security business were not purely financial. Of course I needed to support my family, but I also wanted to feel like I was making a difference in the world and having a positive impact on the places that I worked and the people that I worked with.

My plan to get the staff out was pretty simple. There's a single road along the coast that runs from Tripoli to Tunis, in Tunisia. For the most part it's desert and extremely safe. One of the biggest threats on it came as you approached the outskirts of the city, where a large militia had set up a camp and checkpoints. Days before our own operation, the British Embassy had evacuated along this route. It didn't look like they'd told the militia that they were coming or that they didn't plan on stopping at the checkpoints, and when the convoy of armoured Land Cruisers drove straight through, it initiated an exchange of gunfire between the security contractors and the militia. Luckily, no one was injured, but that didn't mean that there was no hurt pride. It also scared the hell out of the Canadian civilian staff, who must have been picturing how they'd have to run the gauntlet of a gun battle to make it out of the country.

I had a pretty simple solution for dealing with the militia's guns: talking. I went to visit their camp with one of my local fixers. Over a chat and some tea, I let them know that we'd be leaving town soon and that we'd have to take that road. I asked if it was all right with them if we passed through and promised to give them a heads-up on the day. Not only were they grateful for the notice but they offered to provide us with an armed escort, so that we wouldn't be stopped by any of their men at other positions or be at risk of threats like the carjackers I'd met the day before. People were on edge after the earlier incident, and people who are on edge pull triggers. We neutralised this with some pleasantries and handshakes. It really was as simple as just being human and seeing the problem from the militia's perspective. 'Put yourself in their commander's shoes,' I said to one of the Canadian soldiers. 'If that was your checkpoint, and you'd been ordered to stop and check all vehicles, then what would you have done when a convoy just tried to shove its way through without any warning?'

I saw it a lot in the security game, the hangover of imperial privilege. For a lot of operators, it had never sunk in that the militias were operating in their own country. We were the guests, not the overlords of the British Empire who could do whatever we pleased.

I knew that local understanding was the key to a smooth transition out of the country. At the time, the General National Congress was in power, and so I made sure that my fixer at the border was a well-connected member of the right tribe; pick someone from the government's opposition and at best we could have been held up for hours at that vulnerable point, just as a point of principle.

The Canadians had a fleet of vehicles that it would not be possible to leave behind, but it was also impossible for them to blend into the Libyan traffic. This in itself wasn't a problem, but in every embassy there is sensitive communications and security equipment, and this could not be left behind either.

'The problem with putting it in your embassy vehicles,' I explained to the diplomats, 'is that if we get stopped and searched, particularly at the border, then there's a very high chance that it will be impounded.'

That, of course, was the right of Libya and Tunisia. Unlike Western security services, the integrity of the people impounding the equipment could not be vouched for; it could quite easily 'go missing' and end up in the hands of people who were enemies of Canada.

'So what do you suggest?' they asked me.

I wish I'd taken a picture of their faces when I told them.

'Fish trucks.'

The fish trucks came and went from Tunis to Tripoli on a daily basis. The drivers knew the border guards and customs officials, and paid their daily bribes to go through without getting messed about. These men were close friends with my fixer and therefore the perfect choice to transport the sensitive equipment out of the country.

It took a lot of convincing but eventually the embassy staff were persuaded that undercover was best. The UK Special Forces reputation carries a lot of weight, and when I explained to them how I had conducted similar operations in the most dangerous places on Earth, they heard enough to be convinced; after all, the fact that I was still around to tell the story was good proof that the methods had worked for me in the past, and with much higher threat levels.

I don't think the military guys were too keen on the idea at first, and I don't blame them. Military blokes have big egos; we want to be in the lead, knocking the bad guys out of the way. They were probably looking at me and thinking I was some civvy dickhead who was going to lead them into a disaster, but I knew that the way to get them onside would be through establishing a sense of mutual respect and rapport. To that end, I held a detailed Orders Group for the extraction, just as I would have done if it was an SBS mission. When a set of orders is delivered well, it instils a sense of confidence not just in the plan but in the person delivering it. It shows that you have considered things from every angle, and then considered them again. There are contingencies, and then contingencies for contingencies. Everyone leaves that Orders Group with a full understanding of the mission and their part in it.

The final issue before departing was one that I didn't see coming. Like everything in government, there was stuff that couldn't just be left behind and needed signing for, as it belonged to the Crown. There was a large store of liquor in the embassy, and there was quite a flap about what to do with it, until a local German Embassy staff member volunteered to take charge of the alcohol. It was one of the most selfless acts of international cooperation that I've ever seen.

The vehicles were packed the day before the evacuation. I always give an early time of departure on my operations, because people are always late. By giving them a false time, I can get them going at the time I actually wanted. I knew that they'd be nervous, and nervous people are not the most efficient. It was my job to be the cool and collected presence that would stop butterflies in the stomach becoming demons in the head, and by putting out an air of calm I managed to leave with the twenty-two Canadians before first light.

As promised, the militia met us with a couple of heavily armed Land Cruisers, a show of force to anyone who might have considered messing with us. Thirty minutes behind our convoy came the fish trucks, totally inconspicuous.

Once we'd picked up the militia escort, my little car pulled out of the convoy and moved ahead. I wanted to be hitting every checkpoint ahead of the Canadians so that by the time they'd arrived they could be waved straight through. My fixers and I had been to all of these places in the days leading up to the evacuation, but there was always the chance of a last-minute balls-up, and getting out ahead of it could be the difference between a smooth evacuation and a shouting match between Libyans and Canadians that might escalate into an incident.

Thanks to our escort, we cleared the city smoothly, and then we dumped out on to the coast road that would lead us straight to Tunisia. For the Canadians, this was the first time most of them had been outside the Westerner-heavy parts of Tripoli. It was quite often like that for people in those kinds of job, and so, knowing that their blood pressure would be high from fear, I arranged for us to stop for lunch 100 kilometres outside the city. It may seem surprising that we didn't just go hell for leather for the border, but when people are stressed, tired and hungry they get distracted and make mistakes. I wanted to give off a sense of calm and tranquillity, and to make them all feel as comfortable in the desert as I did. Getting out of the cars may have been daunting for a few moments, but once they realised that the locals were not just pleasant but extremely hospitable, everybody's pulse rate began to drop, and they could take in the blue skies and palm trees and really enjoy the fact that they were in an interesting place at an interesting time. I didn't have any plans to run for the position of Libyan tourist minister, but I had come to really like the locals I was working with and I felt I owed it to them to give the departing Canadians a final impression that wasn't one of heavy machine guns mounted on pickup trucks.

Happy that the Canadians were comfortable and calm, I got back into my car to get a head start on them before the next rendezvous. I was confident that the biggest potential hiccups had been in and around the city (the next would be the border) – and so I couldn't understand why there was no sight of them in the rear-view mirror.

'Maybe they change a tyre, Mr Dean?' my fixer suggested, and I agreed with him. There was a lot of debris and potholes on these roads, and a puncture was one of the potential hazards I'd gone over in my Orders Group, but . . .

'How long does it take to change a tyre?' I wondered out loud, then made my mind up. 'Turn the car around, mate,' I said. 'Let's see what's going on.'

Thanks to the pancake flatness of the desert, we spotted the bulk of the convoy in the distance while we were still miles away; they didn't appear to be moving.

As we got closer, I saw why: one of the armoured trucks had hit a local car.

One of the Canadian NCOs was red-faced and arguing with a local man who had blood on his head. Neither understood the other's language, but I could grasp the Libyan's accusations: the Canadian wagon had hit him.

All of those vehicles were being driven by Libyan drivers I had worked with on several occasions. In all that time there had never been a single traffic accident. 'What's going on?' I asked the man who had hit the Libyan's car.

Except that he hadn't, as he explained. After lunch, the senior NCO in that vehicle had insisted that he drive the rest of the way. In the face of the Canadian's size and evident rank, my driver had conceded.

I was furious, but I made sure that I didn't show it. I'd been explicit in the Orders Group that only the Libyans – the trained drivers – would get behind the wheel. Unfortunately for us, driving an armoured car is different to driving a normal vehicle, as this senior NCO had just found out the hard way.

I turned to him. He looked tight and angry, but I expect that was a mask for his embarrassment. He probably knew that he'd messed up. My instinct was to say, 'Why didn't you do as you were told, you muppet?', but where would that have got us? Showing him up would only make him more angry, and lose me respect in the eyes of his comrades. What was done was done, and I expect the reason he had insisted on taking the wheel was because he felt like a spare part as a passenger. He wanted to feel like he was a more important cog, maybe. Perhaps he was scared, and keeping busy made him feel better. Either way, it had caused us a problem that needed fixing, and quickly.

The need for speed wasn't because I was worried about being on the side of the road; it was because our window was closing to make the border before noon. This was important because – in this part of the world – people are not especially enthusiastic in the mornings. Around noon the border crossings would begin to get busy, and I didn't want us to be a sitting target in the middle of that thick traffic. If I was a terrorist wanting to lift or attack Westerners, I'd be looking for choke points like that to do it in, so it was imperative that we got to the border quickly, before the midday rush.

My fixer had gone to work trying to calm the driver, who was irate. He kept pointing to the blood on his head and the damage to his car – which was superficial – and I knew what was going on in his head: accident + white foreigners = pay out.

No one was denying the Canadian driver had cocked up, but even if he hadn't, I would have paid the Libyan off anyway, just for a quick exit. My fixer and I took the man's details and promised he would be compensated. Using eye contact and nods, I got the Canadians back in the convoy and rolling away as we tried to de-escalate the situation.

I thought that the exchange of details and some money had done the job, but as we pulled away I saw his car following us, and sure enough he stuck to our tail. I could see him in the mirror and he didn't look angry, just determined; he could probably see a giant dollar sign rotating over the top of our car.

We reached the border crossing, and as I'd feared the traffic had begun to build. On the other side of the barriers we could see the Canadian Ambassador to Tunisia and a Tunisian police escort that would lead us through their country to the embassy, but we were forced to sit it out in the traffic and heat with the Libyan commuters – and, I expect, refugees getting out of the country in case the militia violence in Tripoli should spread.

I knew this choke point would be a vulnerable time for us, and I had instructed everyone to remain in the vehicles and to keep them literally touching bumper to bumper so that we would maintain convoy integrity. That part of the plan was all going smoothly, but now we had an extra vehicle in our midst.

After a lot of beeping, once we finally came to a halt in the traffic the aggrieved Libyan was out of his car and shouting for the police. This was not the kind of attention we wanted, and so I intercepted him with the fixer. The gist of the man's conversation was this: 'You lot are going to bugger off and not pay me.'

To be fair, I'd probably have been thinking the same thing if I was him, and it was hard to convince him otherwise. He was loud and animated, and I could see heads turning in our direction – not good.

I thought of a way to stop him swinging his arms around at least, and offered to take a look at the cut to his head. My fixer explained that I was a medic, and the man let me look at it; it was nothing serious, just a deep scratch, but I drew out cleaning and applying a plaster to it for so long that he probably felt like he was getting brain surgery. Maybe I have magic fingers, because it definitely did shut him up, and even though we still had onlookers, their eyes were just curious and not angry.

'Tell him again about the compensation,' I told my fixer. 'Make sure he's happy.'

I could see the blue lights of our escort just the other side of the barriers. I gave the man what money I had in my wallet. Seeing empty leather seemed to satisfy him. 'He'll get more,' I promised, and the Canadians told me later that they did follow through on that.

Right then, though, it was time to get passports stamped and cross the border. The Tunisian border guards had all been briefed, and there were no issues there. The Canadian trucks fell in with their escort and all of the embassy staff were blue-lighted to safety.

Not me. I found a nearby cafe and made myself comfortable waiting for a couple of fish wagons. It was a bit of a nerve-racking wait, knowing that they were both full of sensitive kit, and I knew that my success on the job would be determined by whether or not they came through. Get it done and I'd have established my reputation. Fail and I'd be pouring your coffee in Starbucks.

The time in the cafe gave me a moment to think about just what we were – hopefully – about to pull off. This was only the second time in history that Canada had abandoned an embassy, and they and their soldiers had effectively put their trust in a 'civilian'. As a military man, I could totally understand why the senior NCO had taken the wheel himself. He shouldn't have done it, but when you're trained to be the 'doer', it's hard to shake the habit. Often doing nothing is what requires the most discipline. The best course is not always the most obvious.

The fish trucks were a part of that thinking. They rolled up later that afternoon, all kit accounted for and zero issues in their journey. There were a lot of big smiles when I delivered them to the embassy. No doubt mine was the biggest. I'd ticked a few boxes in my life, and now I could say that I'd evacuated an embassy.

Not bad.

16. DEAD OR DIVORCED

During the time that I was working security it wasn't unusual for me to arrive home in the morning and be gone again the next day. A few times I even left again *the same day*. Because of this, my admin turnaround had to be squared away, and the first thing that I'd do after getting home and kissing Alana and Mollie would be to de-service and re-service my kit ready for the next job. In other words, get my laundry in the wash.

'There's blood on this shirt!' Alana said to me as she emptied my bag, seeing the effects of my first aid on the Libyan driver. There was a tone of worried questioning in her voice, but I didn't hear it.

'Oh, is there?' I replied, annoyed that the shirt might be ruined. 'Do you reckon it'll come out?'

That night, with Mollie asleep, Alana made me a steak dinner. It was a bit of a tradition whenever I got back, and as I poured her another glass of wine, she said, 'You seem more worried about whether the blood will come out of your shirt than how it got on there.'

I shrugged. That made sense to me. I was in one piece, so why worry? If the shirt was ruined, though, that was something I'd have to take care of.

Alana looked at me for a long time. I knew that she was

trying to figure something out, and I wasn't particularly comfortable with the scrutiny. 'What's wrong?'

'You know you just evacuated an embassy,' she said. 'On your own.'

I shook my head. 'I had help.'

Alana looked straight into me. 'You planned it. You led it. You evacuated an embassy, Dean, and you act like that's just normal.'

I didn't know what to say to that. I knew it wasn't something that happened every day but it *felt* normal. I was proud of a job well done, but: 'It was just a job. Got it done. No need to make a fuss over it.'

My wife put her hands on mine. 'You know that it's not normal to think like that? You should be blown away by what you did, and the ten seconds you talked about it to me it was like you were describing a chicken dinner.'

'It's not a big deal,' I repeated.

'*It is!*'

But it didn't feel like it to me, and Alana knew that.

'You're too used to this stuff. These are crazy events – huge – and you just shrug your shoulders and look for the next one.'

I didn't know how to answer immediately and so I took a gulp of my wine. I was feeling uncomfortable. 'Look, it's just my job,' I said in the end.

Alana nodded slowly. Her eyes were patient but worried. 'Aye, it's your job, Dean, and I'm worried that you're getting too used to it,' she sighed. 'You haven't even talked about your dad's death. You were straight off on a plane.'

'Well, what's the point? He's dead. I can't bring him back, so I've got to think about my living family. I've got to think about work.'

'But that's what I'm saying,' Alana pressed on. 'Your work isn't normal. It's dangerous, Dean, and you're so used to it that you don't even realise it. Going to these places isn't normal. Coming home with blood on your clothes isn't normal.'

I may have been detached from reality but I had no problem recognising the worry in my wife's every word. 'Look,' I tried, 'I know it's not a nine-to-five, but this stuff is what I'm good at. This is how I can provide for you guys.'

Alana shook her head. 'You can't provide for us if you're *dead*, Dean. Don't you know how much I worry about you when you're away?'

I didn't. It wasn't something I had considered. I had a family, and they needed providing for. I thought that meant earning as much money as I could, and I told her so.

'I don't give a shit about the money, Dean. I never see my husband. Mollie never sees her dad. And it's not like you're away at business conferences. Every time you go away *there's a chance you won't come back.*'

Alana's words stunned me. All my life I'd thought the man's job was to make what money he could and send it back home. I thought I'd been doing the best thing for my family. In my work, I prided myself on excellent communication at all levels, and here I was having failed to communicate with my wife about the most basic thing she wanted from me: not money but time.

'There's only two ways this ends if things don't change, Dean,' she told me with tears in her eyes. 'You'll be dead or you'll be divorced.'

The words were like a punch to my stomach. One of those fates scared me a lot more than the other. Being a soldier, I'd made my peace with death a long time ago . . .

But I didn't want to lose my wife and daughter.

'How can I fix things?' I asked her.

Alana's solution was simple.

'*Talk.*'

We talked until the morning. We'd emptied two bottles of port by the time we were done but the weight of the conversation meant that I never got drunk. I did not want to be dead and I certainly didn't want to be divorced, and so I listened to my wife as she told me about the stresses and the strains of being the one at home, how every phone call gave a shock of excitement, and fear. How a knock on the door could mean a postman, or a policeman, there to break the news that your husband had been pulled from a shot-up car.

She wanted to hear my side too. I was a lot more reluctant to give that than I was to listen.

'Why do you do it?' she kept asking me.

'To support our family,' I kept saying.

There was some truth to that – the work did pay well – but I was kidding myself that it was the only reason. I was an *addict*. I was addicted to war zones in the same way that some people get hooked on drugs or gambling. I needed it in my life, and it was only when it was missing that I felt uneasy. When I was out on the ground, I just felt *normal*. Being in high-pressure life-or-death situations had become so standard for me that I never felt uncomfortable when I was in them; it was when I was pulled out of that danger that I felt out of myself. Looking back on it now, I can understand that what I was suffering from when I was out of those intense situations were withdrawal symptoms. My body and mind were used to a certain amount of adrenaline and excitement. When I didn't get it, I was left feeling angry, grumpy and irritable.

But how do you explain that to your wife? Even one who loved me as much as Alana did. I knew what it would sound like: 'I get my thrills from war zones, not family.' That sounds bloody terrible. It's not that I wanted to choose one over the other. I thought that they could exist side by side, but I had been kidding myself: dead or divorced, that was the choice. If it could only be one life or the other, I knew which I'd choose.

'I want to be here for you and Mollie,' I told my wife. 'But I just . . .'

Alana put her hand on my leg and squeezed. 'What, Dean?' she asked me calmly.

I couldn't get the words out. It was hard even to formulate them in my own head. I was beginning to realise for the first time that I had never transitioned out of the military. The MOD weren't paying me any more, but in my mind I was still a Tier-1 operator, going out and executing missions. If anything, my tempo of operations had increased to way above what I'd be getting in a squadron; I'd spent fewer than four weeks of the last year at home! I was wearing collared shirts and trousers, but I was still a soldier where it counted.

'I can't get my head around this,' I told her honestly. 'Being a civilian.'

Where would I have been if I didn't have Alana? She was the one who'd squared away everything from council tax to the car's MOT. If I hadn't had her managing my life, I'd have probably been living full-time in a safe house in Libya, or been banged up in the UK for not paying my TV licence.

'Why are you smiling?' she asked me.

'I don't know how to do this stuff,' I admitted, and by that I meant *talking*, as much as anything. I was a squaddie, for God's sake. I was a man. When we lost a mate, we cracked a joke and had a drink. When we took lives, we shrugged it off and didn't even bother with the drink. I'd chosen a profession where good men die young, and the way that you deal with that is to laugh and never think about it too much. You know that there are risks – that's why there's such addictive excitement – but you push part of it down inside you, and the rest you try to control through your skills, drills and planning.

But there are some things that you can't control. I wanted to think that I was a superman who could balance family in one hand and war zones in another – I couldn't.

'I don't think I've ever accepted that I'm not Tier-1 any more,' I said honestly for the first time in my life. 'I was elite, and I can't let that go.'

'You don't need to be a soldier to be elite,' Alana told me, and I nodded but I wasn't really hearing her words. Instead, I was thinking about my accident. How that rigging had robbed me of my life in the Special Forces. Since that moment – since that year I had wasted away in hospital beds and on sofas – I had been trying to prove to myself that I was still the same guy who had jumped from that plane.

No . . . *better* than that guy.

'I know this can't go on.' I looked at her. 'But I don't know what else to do.'

My wife leant in and kissed me. She was my anchor, and without her my life would have drifted away and crashed on to the rocks. It could have been in some African town in 2030, but she was right. I'd have kept taking the jobs. Kept pushing my luck. Fortune favours the bold, but life punishes the greedy. As the old army saying goes, the enemy only has to get lucky once. Knowing that my family was the most important thing to me, I had to stop giving them that chance.

The security work had to stop.

Saying that and doing it were two different things. After a couple of days at home I had that familiar itch to be back some place where there was a cutting sense of danger in the air. For the first time since I'd been married to Alana, I told her this.

'You think I don't know?' She laughed. 'You're like a fidgety kid after you've been home a day. I'd get you a high chair to sit in at dinner if I could find one big enough.'

She was a star, and she was right. I just couldn't stop moving and thinking. I needed to be planning, and I needed to be executing that plan.

'We're still going to need money,' I told her. 'Until I get a new job.' Whatever that might be I had no idea. Absolutely none.

Alana wanted me home, but she was also a realist and she knew me well. If I took a few more jobs, it would not only bring in some more money but it would wean me off the gigs rather than going cold turkey.

When a job came in, I said yes without thinking, and with hindsight, I'm glad that it didn't come off.

Actually, that's not quite true. The task was the kind that I love, but for the sake of my family I'm glad that it didn't happen. I can't go into all of the detail, but it involved crossing into Libya under false pretences, and then a very close mentoring role with a militia that were fighting against a rival of the government. To put it bluntly, the militias were rubbish at urban combat, and we would be there to show them how it was done. As it transpired, there was a mix-up at either end about our cover story, and none of us was about to go into a job where we were already partly compromised. Instead, we pulled the plug, and I went home frustrated but in one piece.

The next gig to come up was a lot more palatable for Alana. A friend of mine had a workshop in Libya that fixed and maintained oil-drilling machinery. It was big business, but only when the oil industry in the country was up and running. Thanks to the war between the militias and the closing of the oil terminals, the country was bankrupt, and there was no need for drilling when there was no way to export it.

'I've got loads of kit there still,' my friend explained. 'I can't sell it because the economy has tanked, so I've kept it all in place with staff to watch it. I'm pretty sure they're stealing it, though. Would you mind going down there as operations manager? Two weeks a month.'

I was happy to oblige. More than happy, when he told me that I'd be on a steady salary.

'Getting you into the country's going to be a pain, though.'

All of the airports had shut down. Border crossings were tight, and driving across the country was not a clever idea: militias and criminals were active and trigger happy. Even if a bullet wasn't meant for you, it stings just the same.

In the end, I found my infil route via one of my trustworthy fixers. There was a Soviet-era helicopter that made daily flights in and out under the Red Crescent. The Mi-8 Hip is a flying washing machine, but it was better than swimming from Italy, and so I bribed my way on board.

When I first arrived at the site it was like a scene out of *The*

Scorpion King. Some of the staff greeted my unexpected arrival with over-the-top enthusiasm, while others literally snuck out the back door and disappeared. Most of them came back when they heard I wasn't just shooting people, but word quickly got around that their time of stealing was over.

Believe it or not, when you stop people thieving in certain countries they actually take it very personally, almost as though you're violating one of their job rights. For that reason I didn't stay at the site, but instead put my feet up at a safe house in Tripoli. Thanks to the fighting, there wasn't enough power to run all of the city at once, and so electricity was rationed to each neighbourhood for four hours a day. This meant I had to be on top of charging all my comms equipment, but also that air-conditioning was out of the question for twenty hours a day in the blistering heat of summer: not fun.

The site was a big one, and a couple of my weapons caches were buried there. Because of this, the employees knew me, and some were worried that I'd come to kill them for stealing; not a stretch of the imagination in that part of the world. I didn't keep to a schedule but dropped in and out to keep them on their toes. When I saw definite evidence that one of the staff had been taking equipment, I called him into his office, and told him, 'You're a *clifty*. You're fired.'

I didn't give him the Trump point, but the word 'clifty' did a lot worse. It's a local word that means thief, and the funny thing about the Middle East and North Africa is that, even though everyone knows that corruption is everywhere, no one likes to admit it. Everyone knew that this bloke was light-fingered, but by calling him out on it and sacking him, I had really escalated things.

All of the workers at the site were of the same tribe. Tribal loyalty is everything in Libya, which was partly why the country was so messy. Because of this, I knew exactly what to expect when word of the firing got around.

'Mr Dean,' their spokesperson said to me, 'unless you give him his job back, we must all resign.'

'No problem,' I smiled. 'I accept all of your resignations. If that's what you want, just put them on my desk by the end of the day.'

He left, none of them came back in with resignation letters and the *clifty* was forgotten.

After a couple of weeks at the site, I had things running as they should have been. 'I'll be back,' I promised, and the threat of me turning up at any time seemed to galvanise the workforce and things started working a lot more efficiently.

I hoped the same could be said about the flying washing machine that would take me out to Tunisia. As the fighting in Tripoli intensified, anyone with money was trying to exfil out of the country, and twice I got bumped off the flight for someone who evidently had deeper pockets, or better connections, than I did. When I did finally get a ride, the chopper was packed, and I made sure I was positioned by one of the small porthole windows. I doubt anyone else onboard had done the dunker drills – where a heli airframe is dumped into a dark swimming pool and you have to escape out of the hatches – and I wanted to be able to make as quick an exit as possible if we did set down in the sea. Sounds harsh, but there were dozens of people on board, and in a situation like that they would all be panicking and grabbing each other. There are times when you can save people and times where you can't, and that would have been one of the latter. If you're going to get on any mode of transport, make sure you know how to get off and get out.

Now, with Libya descending into chaos and Alana's words of 'dead or divorced' in my mind, I had to figure out how to take my own advice. I had to work out how I was going to get off the circuit and out of security.

I needed a job and Alana suggested that I come and work with her in the property development sector. It would be a chance for me to learn about something outside kicking in doors and sneaking people out of countries, and because I wanted what was best for my family, I gave it a go.

I think I was about an hour into it before I started to fantasise about launching myself out of the nearest window. Everything that I had done in my life I had done with the ethos of the unrelenting pursuit of excellence, and I tried to bring that attitude into the office, but something was missing.

That something was obvious to pinpoint, of course. Where was the *challenge*? What were the *stakes*? No one was going to die if I didn't get the photocopying done by five. Terrorists weren't going to kill architects if I was slow on reloading the stapler. Everyone I met was lovely enough, and I felt like a bit of a knob; I didn't want to give the impression that I thought what they were doing wasn't important or fulfilling. it just wasn't those things to *me*.

'How are you finding it?' Alana asked me at dinner.

'Good, yeah. Good.' I wanted to be a team player for my

family, no matter what. And I was an expert at suppressing how I felt, and compartmentalising. For my family, I could suck it up and be the best paper stacker in the country.

She laughed, seeing right through me. 'I saw your eyes glaze over about ten seconds into this morning's meeting.'

'I was just tired.'

'Liar.'

'Honest. I like the job.'

It was a lie, and we both knew it. Slowly, and without noticing, I began to slide into being grumpy and irritable. My replies were sharper than they should have been. Luckily for me, I'd married the right woman, and she didn't stand for that behaviour.

'What you need is some bloody exercise,' she told me, and she wasn't wrong; since leaving the squadron my fitness level had dropped; I'd gone from a finely tuned athlete to someone who'd struggle to pass a basic fitness test. There were times out on jobs that I'd crack phys – work out – with some of the other blokes, but when was the last time I'd pushed myself to the point of near-collapse? I couldn't remember. It had literally been years.

I've gone soft, I admitted to myself. Then I said to Alana those words that all partners love to hear: 'I think you're right.'

She gave me that look that says I know I am. 'Why don't you start cycling to the office?' she suggested. 'Ten miles each way.'

It was a great idea, and I was in Halfords that evening. I had never been much of a cyclist – well, that's an understatement. The first ten-mile ride to the office would be the longest of my life at that point – but running was out of the question after the devastation my leg had suffered in the parachuting accident. I reckoned I could handle a bike, though.

I must have looked like a right numpty the first time I took it out. I didn't know how the cleats fitted into the pedals, and the last time I'd ridden the gears were on a lever on top of the bars; now they were hidden inside the brake levers. I felt like an old man, but it's true what they say: you never forget how. I might have looked rusty but I stayed upright, and I made it to the office and back in one piece.

The effect that just this simple bit of physical activity had on me was staggering. Instantly I felt more alert, more happy and more driven. I had a goal, even if that was just to cycle to the office every day. Once I got the hang of the bike, I began timing myself, and every day I was trying to beat yesterday's time. It didn't matter that the competition was just against myself; the fact that I *was* competing, facing a daily challenge, had a mental as well as a physical effect on me. Forget the *bike*'s gears. I'd rediscovered my own!

'I feel so much better,' I told my wife. She'd seen it in me too, but . . .

'You're still not happy in the office, though, are you?'

I didn't want to break the spell, but that was the truth. I was beginning to live for my own personal race to and from the office. The time I spent there was eight hours of glazed eyes and watch-checking. As hard as I tried to find ways to compete with myself in the nine-to-five job, I just couldn't get it. While others were discussing the latest gossip and floor plans, I was staring out the window, thinking about contacts and evacuation plans.

As much as I liked the people in the office world, it wasn't *my* world.

Having someone in your corner makes all the difference in life. Who knows what would have happened if I'd been single, or with the wrong person. I was so fortunate in who I married. We were different in many ways, but Alana mirrored me in her drive, focus and need for challenge. (I suppose the latter is why she stuck with me, ha ha!) So she didn't ever take it as a personal slight when she saw that I was unfulfilled by my new office job in Aberdeen. Instead of getting offended, angry and trying to change me, she was the one that pointed me in the right direction and said: 'Go!'

'What's that?' I asked her. She had a book in her hands. A big one.

Alana threw it to me. 'Read it and pick something,' she said.

I looked down at what had landed in my lap; she *knew* me.

I smiled, opened the cover and began reading *Guinness World Records*.

17. A NEW CHALLENGE

Once I started reading the book of records I couldn't stop. I was like a starving man thrown a loaf of bread, and I was shoving it down me, instantly certain that in these pages I would find exactly what it was I needed to fulfil that desire for challenge that had burnt within me since I joined the army.

'We need to find you a challenge that doesn't involve burying guns in the desert and training people how to kill,' my wife agreed. 'What about this one?'

She pointed out another record that fitted my criteria, and I added it to my list. Running was out of the question, thanks to my wrecked knee, and so we were looking for anything where I could swim, dive or cycle. The fact that I'd never ridden more than twenty miles never entered my head. I knew that once I put my mind to something I wanted, it would get done. It was that simple.

I remember the moment we came across the Pan-American Highway record. Alana read it out: 'It's the longest road in the world, running twenty-two thousand kilometres from Argentina to Alaska. That's Land's End to John o'Groats fifteen times, or London to Sydney plus another four thousand miles! It crosses two continents, thirteen countries and two hemispheres, which means you have to pass through all four seasons to complete it.

'The record's a hundred and twenty-five days.'

'That's the one,' I said, confident that we'd found our challenge. And why not? It was only 21,968 kilometres longer than any ride I'd done before!

I grabbed Alana and kissed her. In my mind, I was already picturing myself crossing the finish line. The result was not in doubt; I'd beat the record – *smash it* – and that was that.

'Right.' I smiled at my wife. 'Let's get started.'

When I was a kid, if you wanted to break a world record, Cheryl Baker and Kriss Akabusi would turn up with a tape measure and a stopwatch and you'd be laughing, but in 2016 the application pack made *War and Peace* look like my supermarket shopping list. In effect it was a business plan, as I had to show how I would conduct the challenge in everything from the basics, like my route, to in-depth questions on sponsorship. It was a sales pitch and a plan rolled into one, and so I approached it as I would writing a set of orders; I'd put a lot of work into researching the challenge, and to be honest, it was kind of nice to get to show that work to someone. I wanted them to know that not only would I be attempting the record but I'd be smashing it, and the first item of evidence in getting them to believe that was the amount of research I'd done already, and of course the pedigree of accomplishments that I'd racked up in the past; tell someone that you've passed British Special Forces selection and at the very least they're going to hear you out.

I sent the completed application in on 16 April 2016, and at this point my sole focus in the preparation had been the planning. My physical state would be crucial to breaking the record, but it didn't matter how low my heart rate was if I got halfway through the ride and ran out of spare tyres. Before I worried about getting in the saddle, I needed to break down what was in front of me: where would I sleep? How would I stay hydrated? How would I deal with changes in climate? Do any stretches of the road cross cartel territory? The list was long.

Just one error could derail my chance, and I knew that *if* I didn't break this record, it would be down to a lack of planning and not my physical fitness. I could push myself over the line even if my lungs were dragging three miles behind me. I couldn't do that if my bike fell apart, though.

Before my first attempt at SF selection, I'd run up and down the hills a lot to practise, and that had led to me tearing my meniscus on the first week of Hills. The second time, I'd built up my training on the spin bike and got through selection without injury.

I knew that I had to take a similar approach to the Pan-American Highway challenge. If I flogged myself as though I was already on the record attempt, my body would probably be too beat-up when it came to the real thing. I needed to keep gas in the tank, but there was an important difference here compared to when I'd gone for selection; back then, I'd been an expert in yomping and map-reading. When it came to cycling, I was a total novice.

As much as I believe we have the capability within ourselves to achieve extraordinary things, I also recognise that we should think of ourselves as students, and be constantly looking to learn. If you want to break a world record, the place to begin is by studying someone who's already done it themselves.

To that end, one of the earliest 'phases' of my training meant finding whatever books I could about the Pan-Am Highway. *The Longest Road* had been written by a couple of Irish students who'd taken the trek on as a jolly, but their book still gave me great insight into what I could expect in terms of climate, terrain and people.

When I started my research, the record stood at 125 days, and I'd hardly got into my prep when someone else knocked it down to 117. His name was Carlos Santa Maria, and he was gracious enough to reply to my emails and answer my questions about my forthcoming attempt.

I love that, and I'm so grateful for his help. Just think about it: this man had busted himself physically and mentally to take a world record, and now here was some bloke in Aberdeen telling him that he wanted to knock him off the perch. Not only did he wish me luck, but he actively tried to help me to beat his own record! He could have held on to his secrets, and the things that he had learnt along the way, but instead he shared them with a total stranger. Moments like that make me happy and proud to be a human, and I hope I can live up to that standard of generosity when someone wants help in breaking one of *my* records.

Right from the word go, I knew that this record attempt would be about more than just giving Dean Stott something to do instead of being in the office. There needed to be a greater purpose. There needed to be a charity aspect to it.

Initially, the cause I chose to support was human trafficking. It's a problem that receives little exposure but it is a major scourge around the world; modern-day slavery ruins lives. Alana was a strong voice in campaigning to raise awareness of it, and with the route I'd be travelling it just made sense; a lot of human trafficking originates in South America and ends where you would never expect it: the United States and Canada.

With the cause in place, I now needed to set goals and financial targets. I'd become the SBS Association Ambassador for Scotland in 2015 and had been involved in charity events to raise money for the Squadron Association, and so I knew a bit about fundraising, but I was also fortunate to know an expert philanthropist: Prince Harry.

There aren't many people in the world who put in more time or have more knowledge of the way that charity works than the Royal Family. I'd picked Harry's brain about it during the charity events, but now I had my own record attempt and cause to raise money for, and so I texted him to let him know that any advice he could give me would be gratefully received.

He called me back that day. We had a lengthy discussion, and I told him that although the human trafficking cause was something that was dear to me and Alana, we weren't married to it; we just wanted to make the biggest impact that we could, however that was. Harry then told me that he was launching a new project with his brother, William, and Kate: Heads Together, a charity that would bring mental health providers together to ensure that people can feel comfortable with themselves, their friends and their families.

I took a moment to think it over. PTSD was becoming recognised as a real issue with soldiers. 'So it's a veteran charity?' I asked.

Harry explained that Heads Together was going to tackle all aspects of mental health, be that a soldier's PTSD or a new mum's postnatal depression. There are brilliant organisations helping in these fields, and they wanted to bring them together so that all their great ideas and useful experience could be passed around.

That made sense to me. No point in these charities having to learn the hard way if someone else has already found a solution.

Harry was passionate about it, and compared it to the way the army put standards in place across regiments, bringing people together into training centres so that there's the same quality across the board. 'What do you think?' he asked.

It all made sense to me. Just like I was going to the previous record holders to learn from the best, it made sense that an issue of critical importance like mental health should have some kind of structure where people could learn from others' experiences.

'I think it's a great idea,' I told him honestly, and he asked me how much I was looking to raise.

'One million pounds.' I didn't say it like Dr Evil, even if I did have the bald head.

Harry was fully supportive of my goal. When it came to a challenge, he knew that I was up for it. When it came to money, he knew as I did that there were some deep pockets on the charity scene. I'd seen some pretty big cheques changing hands at these events.

I hadn't picked the figure out of thin air. As soon as I decided that the Pan-Am was the record for me, I knew that the enormity of the challenge needed to be reflected in the sum raised. When you want to get people on board with an idea, you need to explain it to them in terms they can understand. Unless you're a cyclist, you can't fully grasp what that challenge of cycling 22,000 kilometres will mean, it just seems like a big number. On the other hand, almost everyone wants a million pounds, or can at least grasp how that figure fits in around their lives. Almost no one is going to hear that figure and think, 'Oh, a million? Yeah, no drama.' People will hear it and think: 'Bloody hell, you're raising a million? What the heck are you doing to justify that figure?' It's a big exclamation mark on the back of the record attempt. It's saying, 'This is not your ordinary charity target, and this is not your ordinary record attempt.'

'Will you help me promote the challenge?' I asked Harry, knowing that with his name and title involved I would be in a much better position to attract sponsors and donations.

He told me that he would, regardless of whether or not I chose to do it for Heads Together.

He was a good bloke for saying that – no pressure – but I was already seeing the great effect that his new endeavour could have, and my part in it. After all, wasn't the reason Alana had suggested this for my *own* mental health? Wasn't cycling to the office as much about sorting out my head as my heart and lungs? I was already realising that mental health issues could take many forms. You didn't have to be waking from a nightmare, screaming the place down. Maybe it was just that glazed look I had. The feeling that I was just slipping into a life of sleepwalking. This challenge had begun as a kick-start to my own mental wellbeing, and now I hoped that it could be the same for other people too.

When people think of prep work for a mammoth cycling event, they probably think of savage training sessions, drinking raw eggs and cold showers. *Rocky*-style training montages have their place, but so does sitting in front of the TV with a good box set. By watching *The Long Way Round*, I learnt a lot about how to formulate the strategy for sponsorship.

One expedition had first approached X Company about sponsoring them with bikes, but the manufacturer turned them down. Eventually another company gave them their rides, and in return their bikes placed in front of the eyes of millions of viewers. Great advertising for an insanely low cost: this was how I'd pitch to the sponsors that I wanted on board for my own adventure.

In 2016, the drive for mental health was gaining pace but it wasn't at the place that it is now, and so at first we thought the way to target sponsors would be by bigging up the cycling aspect of the challenge: provide me with spare tyres and it'll be written about in the cycling magazines and journals that will inevitably cover the breaking of one of cycling's biggest world records.

That all changed when Harry and I made a video promoting the challenge. The video looked slick and professional. His presence announced that not only was the attempt legitimate but *I* was legitimate. You can imagine that people were a little sceptical when a cycling novice announced that he was going to beat a cycling world record, but when Harry said, 'Yeah, he'll do this,' that made people sit up and pay attention. I didn't take that personally or as a knock to me. That's just how celebrity works. Who doesn't have a grill in the back of the kitchen cupboard because George Foreman said it was a good idea?

One area where I would definitely need sponsorship was for the support team that would accompany me; during my research I'd discovered that there was no distinction between breaking the record with or without a team, and so it seemed silly to not take one; as an amateur, I'd find it very useful to have experts on hand. I knew I could do the mental aspect and handle the pain alone, but choosing the right tyre for the road surface? That could totally stuff me if I made the wrong choice.

Before approaching anyone for this support, though, I wanted to have as much of the plan as possible in place. Yes, that plan would be adapted as experts contributed their ideas, but when I walked out of a meeting I wanted this thought to be stuck in their heads: 'He's professional. He's planned it. He'll smash it.'

When I began doing my research into the bikes themselves, I was blown away by how far the design and technology had come since I was a kid. I was pushing forty – and that wasn't a pleasant thought – but looking into the current cycling tech I felt as though I'd grown up riding windmills. Even when I was doing selection, the way that I'd gauge my fatigue level would be: 'On a scale of one to ten, how tired do I feel?' Now heart-rate monitors and power meters were the name of the game, particularly in cycling. The sport was a science, and I found myself learning about power outputs and zone training, two ways of optimising my cycling performance.

A little arrogance is a good thing in a soldier – you have to be able to back yourself – but get too cocky and you're just setting yourself up to fail. One huge combat indicator of too much ego is the inability to ask for or take advice from others, and I knew with this challenge that I'd fail before I started if I didn't check my ego at the door and look for some expert help.

The first company that I took on to help me had a pro cyclist on the books, and they offered online mentorship and guidance. That was fine by me, as I needed tips and tricks, not handholding. I should probably have seen a red flag when I sent them the charity promotional video and they offered me a whopping 0 per cent discount, but people have to make a living and so I let that go. At the time I didn't have any sponsors, and so the money was coming out of my own pocket, but that was fine by me: never ask anyone to do something you're not willing to do yourself.

I did my initial consultation via video – my coach was based in LA – and his eyebrows were raised so many times in that initial conversation that I thought they were in danger of flying off his head.

'The Pan-American Highway?' he asked me again. 'You know that's twenty-two thousand k?'

'I'm aware of that, yeah.'

'And you want to do it in . . .'

'A hundred and ten days.'

He didn't say it was impossible but the human face gives a lot away, and that bit of doubt threw some coals on to that fire that burns inside me. The fire where I torch statements like 'You can't' and 'You won't'.

Watch me.

'As of January, I'm training full-time for this,' I told him. 'So don't hold back on the schedule. I haven't got to balance this with a job.'

Alana and I had decided that if I was going to do this, it needed to be my sole focus. You don't take down Taliban compounds on the weekends between working in the office, and I was seeing taking down a record through the same sights.

My coach started sending me through my training plan. I took to the roads on my Halfords bike, but within a couple of days I was emailing him:

This stuff is too easy mate. Can't we crank it up?

He got back to me quickly, suggesting I try a century ride. The first time that you do 100 miles in one go is a big deal in the cycling community, kind of like earning a badge of honour, and he warned me that it might be too much, but at least it would give me an idea of how it felt to be in the saddle for a longer period.

I found an event that was running in Scotland, booked my spot and hired a more specialised bike. I was in the middle of the pack, which wasn't somewhere I was used to being, but ego aside I knew I was doing well for my first proper bike challenge. It was quite humbling to see old men zipping past me without any sign of strain on their face, and I realised very quickly that I still knew nothing about the finesse of cycling, like cadence – a fancy way of saying how many times I was turning the pedals. I was just pushing through like a young lad late on his paper round.

Talking with some of the other participants at the end of the six and a half hour ride, I told them what I had in mind.

'Are you bike-fit?' one of them asked, looking dubiously at my legs.

I shook my head. 'I've got twelve months to train.'

They laughed. 'No, buddy. Bike-fit means you get properly measured for your bike, so that your handles, pedals and seat are in the optimum place.'

'Oh.' I had a lot to learn.

My coach was sending me a programme of riding fifty miles a day, but it was getting stale and I found myself wanting to push on. 'Can't we push it?' I kept asking him, and eventually he conceded and I went up to a century ride a day. The only breaks I was taking were for occasional trips down to London, where I would brief a company's personnel on security before they travelled to a hotspot, but I was spending my time getting used to life in the saddle, and a good thing too. Harry had asked me if I'd include the Endeavour Fund as part of my training, and I'd agreed to lead a group of veterans on a cycle expedition from Lands End to John o'Groats. It was 874 miles, and six months away.

That night, I spoke to my coach. I told him about the mini-challenge to help the Endeavour Fund, and I heard him sigh. 'Look, Dean, you haven't done enough practice for that. If you don't get your miles in, you'll be doomed.'

Doomed?

DOOMED?

I didn't know exactly what to say to that. 'Yeah. All right. Speak soon,' is what I said in the end, and I hung up. For a long moment I just stood with the phone in my hand. *Doomed?*

Nah, mate, I thought. *I'm not having that on my time.* Either get on board or get out of my way. My coach's attitude had been negative and pessimistic from the start. I opened my emails; it was time to cut the anchor away.

> Thanks for your help, mate, but I think I'm going to try a new direction.

I went into my contacts and called one of the lads that had worked with me on the circuit.

'All right, buddy. What you doing tomorrow?'

'Nothing much, pal. Why?'

I couldn't help smiling. 'How do you fancy following me on the bike from Land's End to John o'Groats?'

Doomed, my arse.

The average cycle time from one tip of the UK mainland to the other is thirteen days. I decided that nine days would do it. I was three weeks into my training, and the decision may sound more reckless than relentless, but I knew my body and I knew my mind. I could have done those miles even before someone told me that I'd be doomed, but with that pessimism ringing in my ears, I knew that I could *walk* it if I had to.

I was self-aware enough to know that I was doing this absolutely just to prove to the coach that I *could* do it, but you know what? Negative energy does not always equal negative results. There was power in his pessimism, and I was going to use that as fuel. By the end of it I'd have a huge accomplishment in my pocket, and I'd be on the right track for the Pan-Am. If I tried to ignore his doubt, it would eat at me. Do you know how you get out of an ambush? You turn into it and fight through. That's exactly the same for mental ambushes as it is for ones involving AKs and RPGs.

I set off on the route a couple of days later. It was winter, and a bitterly cold storm had blown into the country. Not great cycling weather, to say the least – the long, narrow profile of your body makes you susceptible to gusts of wind – but to complete the Pan-Am I would have to bike through all four seasons as I went from one hemisphere to another. If I was to prevail, I had to get used to hostile weather, end of; for most of the Pan-Am I'd either be cooking or freezing, just as I had been on military deployments.

I came off my bike on the second day when I hit black ice. I can't say it was an enjoyable experience, but these things happen. There really was nothing else to do but get back in the saddle and ride the next thirty miles to a bike shop where I could get the buckled rear wheel repaired.

Those were a hard thirty miles, let me tell you. Point taken, though: you can't just pack a tyre repair kit or inner tubes like you did as a kid. On these challenges, you bring enough to build a spare bike!

With that lesson learnt, I pushed on through the cold. It was -8°C in Scotland, and if I wanted any motivation to cycle hard I got it through the need to keep pushing so that I wouldn't freeze to my bike! It's on days like that when you look back at the Arctic warfare training and feel glad that you jumped into a hole cut in the ice; there's a lot of comfort in knowing that things could always be worse, or colder, or hotter! The military had given me a great bar by which I could judge future experiences, and so I wasn't about to allow myself to be 'doomed' because of a bit of cold weather.

The ice had other ideas, though. I went down another two times, but you should feel more sorry for the bike than me. The poor thing had my weight come down on it twice, and the twisted frame looked like it had been hit by a truck. Lightly built cycles have the benefit of taking less effort to move through your own power output, but some compromise has to be made, and the light weight means the bikes can't stand up to much of a hit. There was no way I could just crack on like I'd done with the buckled rear wheel. The bike was now a K-kill, a total write-off, and so yet again I handed my credit card over to a cashier at Halfords and picked myself a brand-new bike off of the shelf.

My friend driving the support wagon – a camper van in which we carried the spares, heated our beans and got our heads down – asked me if we should maybe reconsider until after the storm.

I shook my head. 'I won't get to control the storms in America. I'll be cycling through Alaska, for God's sake. I've got to get used to cycling on ice.'

I didn't even know if such a thing was possible, but if people could skate on it, then I would figure out a way to bike on it, I told myself.

'Not sure the bike rental company will agree with you,' my friend said, looking at the mangled remain of the first bike.

I couldn't argue with him there. 'Yeah, fair one.'

I was pretty banged up from coming off the bike three times, and my left wrist was quite swollen, but I didn't think there was anything broken or worthy of being looked at by a doctor. I'd set myself nine days for the challenge, and bike shopping had set us back a bit, so there was no time for niceties like worrying about whether my wrist was smashed long-term; in the short term, it ached, but one benefit of cold weather is that it numbs the feeling in your extremities. There's always a silver lining somewhere!

My former coach's prophecy of doom was loud in my ears as I rode, but it wasn't like I was shouting 'I'll show you!' into the wind. I did want to prove a point, though. I wanted to prove that with the right mindset, no distractions and time to train, people could achieve things that would usually be thought impossible.

Think about it. I had the time to train. My family were behind me. Things were good at home. I had a mate willing to follow me and keep me company in the evenings. I had all of this great stuff behind me. When you think about it like that, is it really that much of a stretch to believe that I – or you – can accomplish what they say is not possible, so long as we have the time and our 'house' is in order?

After nine days of riding I reached the northernmost tip of the UK mainland, four days quicker than the average time for the run that most people take on in summer. I wasn't competing against them, though. I was competing against myself. I was about to take on the longest road in the world, and so to have this feat in my back pocket was an important milestone for me. I'd been riding for a couple of months, and I'd cracked a challenge that defies many people. That didn't make me any better or worse a person than them, but at the same time I took a moment to acknowledge the scale of what I'd just accomplished and, more importantly, how grateful I was to be able to do it. Not just thanks to my health – which could quite easily have gone to pot, or been much worse after my parachute accident – but down to people like Alana and my friend, who were supporting me in these endeavours. It made me feel extremely fortunate, which of course I was – and am.

Aside from teaching me that I needed bike spares from wheels to frames, the ride up the UK mainland drove home the point that there were technicalities of cycling that, as a novice, I was overlooking.

During that ride, my shins had become increasingly painful. Shin splints – or outer compartment syndrome, as it's known medically – are not unfamiliar to people in the army, particularly if you've been doing a lot of forced marches, where you have to open your stride more than you would at a patrol pace. I knew the symptoms – and I knew the pain – but I didn't know why I was getting it or how to alleviate it. I wanted a Yoda on my shoulder for my preparations for the Pan-Am. Someone who knew how to use the Force, or who could at least tell me how I could ride so that my shins didn't feel stretched out and aching. I needed someone who was as at home in the saddle as I was with a rifle in my hands. Someone who had spent decades fine-tuning and honing a craft that they lived and breathed. Above all, I needed someone who did not have terms like 'no way' or 'doomed' in their vocabulary.

It was Alana who found him.

'Look at this,' she said, pointing to the computer screen. I was standing at her shoulder, my usual position when anything IT-related needed doing; she was the brains in that department.

'A triathlon trainer?' I asked.

I looked over the company's website as she scrolled down the page. 'I don't know,' I said. 'They don't look like a very big company.'

I should have known better than to judge a book by its cover. I was dubious, but Alana was there to correct me. 'Dean, you don't even know how to properly dress yourself in this bike gear. It can't hurt to talk to them, can it?'

She was right. 'Fair one,' I conceded. 'Looks like they've got an open day soon. I'll go to that.'

The local man I went to see at Total Endurance was called Ken Bryson, a proven endurance athlete and coach. I didn't know much of that when I first met him, and neither did I know that his first impression of me was 'Who's this lump of a skinhead? He must be in the wrong place.'

The truth was I didn't think I was in the right place either. Ken runs a small operation, and I was under the misguided impression that I needed guidance from a company that had a host of professionals on the books. I clearly hadn't paid enough attention to *Karate Kid* or any other movie from the eighties: the underdog's sensei never comes in an obvious shape or size.

'How can I help you?' Ken asked me, after introducing himself.

'All right, mate. Yeah. So, I'm going to cycle the Pan-American Highway next year.'

He tried to hide his surprise, but I caught his head moving back an inch and a trace of shock on his face. Well, he hadn't heard it all yet . . .

'And I'm going to break the world record.'

Ken didn't know it, but he was on trial in that moment. Shock was something I could live with – and expected! – but if I saw doubt or dismissal in his body language or heard them in his words, I'd be out. Instead he said, 'That sounds awesome. How can I help?'

Boom. That was more like it. 'I haven't got much of an idea what I'm doing,' I admitted. 'I'll rag myself into the ground,' I said honestly, 'but I want to refine. I know the best out there are riding smart, as well as hard.'

I didn't tell him that I fully intended on being the best. At least, the best version of myself. I could tell that Ken just got that. Our interaction was only a minute old, but something about his manner told me that here was a guy who understood what the unrelenting pursuit of excellence was all about.

'Why don't you come in tomorrow?' he said to me.

'Sounds good. What do you charge?'

Once he found out that I'd publicly declared I was going to raise a million pounds, that figure was zero. 'Don't worry about it,' he'd keep saying whenever I brought it up.

Ken got to work with me straight away. At long last I was 'bike-fit', and I felt the benefits immediately: fewer aches and pains, a smoother ride, better times. I brought a lot of mental and physical strength and endurance to the table, and now Ken would help shape and fine-tune that.

Ken drew me up a training programme, and sent me off on to the roads. I was getting a lot of time in the saddle, but I had a problem.

'Ken,' I said to my new coach, 'I get that I need time in the saddle, but what's the objective of this? What's the goal?'

He looked at me a little funny, like maybe I had amnesia. 'For you to do the Pan-American Highway?'

'Nah mate,' I laughed. 'I mean each session. What's the goal of each session? I'm objective-oriented and driven, mate. I'm going a bit nuts in the saddle not knowing exactly what the purpose is.'

'Ah!' Ken got it then. 'So what if instead of saying a five-hour ride, I say a hundred miles? Or, your best mileage effort in a set time?'

I pumped my fist into my hand. 'Yes. Exactly that, mate. And don't hold back,' I smiled. 'I want a beasting.'

Ken obliged and came back to me with a training programme that had a clearly stated objective for each of my training periods. Sometimes I was covering a distance against the clock, or sometimes it was a set number of miles that I had to hit, but I had clear goals on a daily basis, and with my mindset I thrived under those conditions. The world record was the big challenge, but now I had a challenge every day. It brought out the best in me, and I felt energised and happy.

'This is brilliant,' I told Ken over the phone. 'I feel like I'm making great progress.'

Ken gave a happy laugh. 'I've never seen anything like it,' he said. 'I've been looking at your data on the app,' he went on, referring to Training Peaks, which recorded all my data, 'and whatever session I give you, you're completing it to the second, or the watt. Nothing either side. I can tell you're a military man.' He finished off with another laugh.

And I was. Precision had been – and still was – so important in my life. If you tell me you're going to clear the room on the right, but then you go left, what happens? If I tell you I'm beginning an assault at 0600 and you're not in position with the fire support group, what happens? If I say I'm going to cycle 100 miles to a rendezvous but instead I do 120, and we lose comms, then what happens?

The answer to all of those questions is: nothing good!

I couldn't get complacent. The unrelenting pursuit of excellence doesn't mean you just stick in a groove and stay there. You always need to be looking for ways to find that little bit more. That edge. When you're at the top of your game, a 0.5 per cent increase in your skill or output can mean the difference between victory and defeat. Once in my life those margins were the split between life and death. Now it was between successfully breaking a record and raising a million pounds for charity or going home with my tail between my legs, a failure.

'What do you think Dean will do if he fails?' someone asked my wife when the news about the challenge came out.

Alana's answer was not a joke. 'He won't fail.'

She knew that I'd ride myself into the grave before I failed, and so I guess the life and death stakes hadn't changed that much since I left the squadron and the circuit. That was just who I was, who I had to be. You can't deny your nature. You just have to harness it and put it towards a good purpose.

*

That good purpose was, of course, Heads Together, and just as I had to put time in the saddle to build my endurance, I also needed to build up the challenge's charity profile and search for sponsors.

One of the bike companies I approached had a brilliant reputation, and they had professional cyclists on their books. They thought the record attempt and the cause were both great, but unfortunately their UK arm didn't have the budget to take anyone else on to their strength. Because I'd be cycling across the American continents they asked me if they could pass on my pitch to their counterparts across the Atlantic, and of course I said yes; and so did the Americans! I could have my bikes, but there was one condition . . .

'We'll need a photo of Prince Harry on one of our bikes.'

I grimaced. Having the big man on board was opening a lot of doors, but back through those doors were coming a lot of requests for favours and backslaps. Those were things I was quite happy to do myself, but they were usually aimed towards the prince. Harry wasn't one to shy away from work or charity, but there are only so many hours in the day and taking a photo for a company's own PR campaign wasn't in the spirit of the challenge. We wanted sponsors on board who wanted to help for helping's sake, not because they saw a way of getting some cheap marketing on the side; giving us a donation was a lot cheaper than advertising spend. Of course I was quite happy to let them use me and the record attempt for as much publicity as they wanted, but . . .

'I'm afraid we can't do that,' I told them. 'Would you still be interested without the picture?'

No.

And so on to the next one. They weren't the first to lose interest as soon as they realised Harry wouldn't be their new PR mascot, and they wouldn't be the last. Fortunately, for every company that wanted a royal salesperson or bust, there were others who were keen to become involved because they loved the aim of the charity, the size of the challenge and the message we were promoting.

Just as Prince Harry's involvement was proving a double-edged sword, I was seeing a split in reaction in the cycling community when people found out about the record attempt, either because I'd approached them for sponsorship or information or when it came up in conversation. Once they'd heard the gist of 'I've been cycling three months and I'm going to raise a million pounds for charity by breaking the Pan-American Highway record' I'd get some variant on the following reactions:

'That's bloody amazing!'

'That's impossible!'

The sad thing is that most of the negativity came from people who were actively engaged with cycling and passionate about the sport. I wanted to be inspiring people, but quite often I sensed that I was just putting their backs up instead.

My local bike club was huge – hundreds of members – and I'd see them out on the roads decked out in the best gear you could buy. I'm not a paranoid bloke but I'd see them looking at my physique, and my bike, and they didn't seem happy with either.

'I don't get it,' I said to Ken. 'I'd have thought they'd have been happy to see someone getting into cycling and trying this.'

My coach gave me a half-smile. 'Yeah. People love seeing

someone come in and smash something in two minutes that they've tried for decades to get good at.'

He had a point. When I finally bought myself a proper bike I entered a race around Loch Ness. I was about four months into cycling then, and I came 120th out of 4500. My speed was improving but not, apparently, my standing with the local riders. Very few of them wanted to speak to me.

'It's like being back in high school, day one,' another rider said to me. She'd been riding only a few months herself, and also felt a little cast out. We'd got talking because we were both clearly loners. 'Everyone has their own little cliques. You can see them looking each other up and down, then talking about each other.'

Eventually, I think I was seen out on the roads and at races enough that I was approached by the local club. By this time I had all the gear, and was getting a small bit of the idea. 'Why don't you join the club?' I was asked.

'I'd love to but I can't,' I explained. 'You guys are riding evenings and weekends, and I've ring-fenced that time to spend with my family.' I was treating my training as a job; smashing it in the week, and then spending time with my family. That was part of the reason I didn't want to be part of any cycle club, and the other was that I would be completing the Pan-Am alone, and so I thought the majority of my preparation should be cycling alone: train how you intend to fight.

It still wasn't an easy decision to make, though. I didn't like the way cycling appeared to be a very cliquey sport, where you needed to have the right bike, gear and physique. Just riding to the office and back, I'd found tremendous benefits to my health – both mental and physical – and I wanted others to have access to the positive effects of the sport. Change is best effected from inside an organisation, and I thought that if I was inside a club, then perhaps I could help change the culture so that anyone would feel comfortable taking up the sport and joining a club, regardless of their age, size or anything else. In the end I decided that the best way I could change the culture was by breaking the world record; that would do the talking for me, and the best way to train for that record was to ride alone.

'Thanks anyway,' I told them.

I got a lot of dirty looks after that, and for every one I was thankful. More fuel for the fire, thank you very much. Turns out I didn't even need to be part of a club to get the motivational benefits!

Training with Ken was going great. After just a short time with him I was feeling as though we got each other's mindsets and were a great complement to one another; he had the expertise to put the training together, and I carried it out to the dot.

'I think we should get you measured up,' he told me.

'Bike-fit? I thought we'd already done that.'

Ken shook his head. 'We have. Now we need to measure your power output. I know a guy.'

That guy was Julian Widdowson, a sports scientist who works with international rugby players, and cyclists.

Julian was set up in Bath, and I went down to visit. Like Ken, he was offering his services pro bono because he believed in the cause. Top bloke!

Julian strapped me to a number of machines that measured this, that and the other. Do I know exactly what was measured and how? No idea! It was all a load of dark magic in my eyes, but I got the important points.

'Want to know something interesting?' the scientist asked me.

'Go on . . .'

'Your right leg's two kilos lighter than the left.'

I couldn't believe it. 'Two kilos?' My right leg was the one that I'd trashed in my parachuting accident, and I knew at the time I'd experienced muscle wastage, but it didn't look *that* different in the mirror. 'Are you sure?' I asked him.

He was.

'Bloody hell. I'm amazed I'm not cycling in circles.'

Julian passed all the data and recordings back to Ken.

'We think it'll balance itself out the more you ride,' my coach told me.

'I don't have to cycle with one leg then?'

Ken laughed. 'Actually, you do. All part of building up your cadence.'

A few months later I returned to Julian's lab. 'Your legs are now the same weight,' he told me. 'But the right hamstring has fourteen per cent less power.'

I pulled a face. 'I thought what didn't kill you made you stronger?'

'Not parachuting accidents, apparently,' he smiled. 'People usually have a dominant arm and leg though, so fourteen per cent is nothing to worry about. You could be the same if you were a snowboarder who preferred to lead with one leg over the other, or a right-handed tennis player, and so on.'

I didn't like leaving percentages on the table, but I took his point. Considering I could have lost the leg – or my life – a 14 per cent decrease in power output wasn't such a big deal.

*

As part of our fundraising campaign, we organised a dinner in Aberdeen. As guest speaker we had Fraser Brown, a current Scotland rugby international. The stocky hooker was a chatty bloke and we had hit it off the first time that we met. As you might expect, soldiers and rugby players find it easy to strike up conversation as we have a lot of common ground: we live for physical confrontation, painful challenge, teamwork and victory. What might surprise people, though, is how much we have in common once the boots are hung up for good.

'They told me my career was over,' Fraser shared with me. 'I badly injured my spine, and they said, that's it. You're done.'

The fact that he was the current international hooker told me how wrong that prediction was. 'What happened?' I asked. 'How did you get back on the field?'

'I just took it as a challenge,' he said. 'Oh, you don't think I can do it? Watch this!'

That sounded familiar. 'I know exactly what you mean, mate.' Then I told him about my parachute accident, and my record attempt.

'How did you feel after the injury?' Fraser asked me.

'Shit,' I said honestly. 'Really shit. I felt like I'd been robbed of my identity.'

Fraser nodded his head empathically. 'Mate, that's exactly how I felt. *Exactly*. I was, and I am, a rugby player. They were telling me to just accept it and move on, but that's like asking someone to forget his family or his country. It's a part of who you are.'

'A huge part,' I agreed.

'I know I'll have to stop playing eventually,' the rugby player said. 'But I knew I had more in me. I wasn't going to let it be an injury that stopped me.'

I knew exactly how he felt, but of course the Ministry of Defence had not asked for my opinion. 'They med-discharged me,' I told him, and I could hear the bitterness in my own voice. 'I didn't want to leave. I knew I could get myself back up to standard and do the job. I didn't want to leave the job, or my team. It was who I was, and what I wanted to do for as long as possible.'

I sat back against my chair as a realisation hit me. 'I hadn't really thought about it until now, but I think a part of me taking on a huge record attempt like this is a statement. Telling the desk jockeys who said I had to go, "Well, look at me now. You didn't think I could pass a personal fitness test. How's 22,000 kilometres?"'

Fraser smiled. 'They just don't get it,' he said.

'They don't. They really don't. That's why I'm so happy to be working with Heads Together,' I explained. 'Because everyone sees a soldier and they think PTS, but the reality is that it's the transition that messes you up as much as any blood and guts you've seen.'

'Losing your identity,' Fraser said.

'Exactly, mate. Exactly.'

It wouldn't be the first time I heard an athlete echo the same sentiments as a SF operator. When the team kit or the combats come off for the last time, each faces the same thing: their entire identity has been tied up in their profession. Yes, being a pro rugby player or a soldier pays the bills, but it's more than a wage slip. It's a calling. It's in your DNA. It's not as simple as just walking out of the camp gates or off the pitch and saying, 'OK, now I'm going to be a bank manager.' What we did is who we are, and talking to Fraser had helped reveal to myself that I was still carrying a lot of anger inside. Bitterness that I had been let go from my true calling, when I knew that I could still have done my job, and done it relentlessly.

Well, I'd have 22,000 kilometres to think about that, let it go or prove a point. Either way, I knew that my identity needed to change from who I was at one end of the highway to who I was at the other. I couldn't – and didn't want – to live a life with bitterness. I certainly didn't want to accept that my greatest days were behind me.

The day after I met Fraser, I pushed myself on the bike harder than ever. Like him, I would prove the doubters wrong, and I would do it for a reason that was better than resentment; I would do it to show others that they could do the same.

18. PROMO VIDEO

It was my friend Ian who came up with the idea for the video. We were discussing ways to raise funds and sponsors, and Ian had a lot of experience in marketing.

'You need a high-quality video,' he told me. 'A fully professional-looking summary of who you are and what you have planned. You can use it to spread the word online as well as showing it to potential sponsors.'

'I love that idea,' Alana said. 'It's your back story that makes this so interesting. Special Forces and no cycling background. That would make a great video.'

I found myself nodding in agreement. The Special Forces connection is a draw, there's no doubt about it, and without wanting to sound arrogant, I knew that I was unique in terms of the limited cycling experience. You don't get many people who try and cycle 22,000 kilometres within a year of getting on a bike for the first time. It just doesn't happen.

The SF reputation and my inexperience were my unique selling points. We had another on this campaign too, and that was the support of Prince Harry. After thrashing out some ideas with Ian and Alana about how the video would look and what it would cover, I sent the prince a text to ask if it would be possible for him to appear in it with me. Harry is about as A-list as it gets, and to have him endorse the video would make people all the more likely to watch it.

I wasn't surprised when he said yes. Harry was as enthusiastic about this challenge as I was. We both wanted to make a difference in the world. Nobody was forcing me on to the bike, and no one had forced the two princes and Kate to begin Heads Together. They had done so because they passionately believed in getting help to people early, before problems spiralled out of control, where they too often ended in tragedy. Heads Together was their mission to save lives, and the Pan-Am was my part in it.

I learnt more about the different layers surrounding the royals' work and their charity. When one of them gets or is presented with an idea for a charity – such as Heads Together – the Royal Foundation builds on the idea, gives it infrastructure and gets it in a position to launch. The now well-known Invictus Games was born out of the Royal Foundation, for instance. Once a charity reaches the level of success that Invictus has, then the Royal Foundation passes it on to new, capable management so that they can continue to develop other ideas.

The next crucial task was to find a team who could film the promo video. We had decided from the beginning that it needed to be slick and professional, and we began reaching out to production companies who would know how best to shoot and edit it. Alana and I had ideas for the look and the content, but you can't beat a subject expert for taking an idea to the next level. They'd know how to transition between the shots and build the story with our sound bites so that by the end of the film, hopefully people would be going straight to the 'donate now' button on their phones and computers.

It didn't take long before we found a great company to make the video, Artlab Films. Not only did we love the look of their demo reels, but they were extremely keen to help out a charitable cause. We insisted they take some money for equipment so that they weren't personally out of pocket, but they gave their time for free. Some people say that you get what you pay for, but I can tell you that that is not true. Artlab delivered us a top-quality video, and they did it pro bono because they were passionate about the campaign. I'm extremely grateful to them for that.

A couple of months after we first had the idea for the promo video, I went down to Kensington Palace to film the section with Prince Harry.

'Do I have to call you Dean?' he asked me on camera.

'Do I have to call you Harry, or just mate?' I replied, and we both laughed.

'Stotty,' Harry smiled back. 'Everyone's like, who's that?'

I put my game face on. 'Thank you very much anyway, for taking the time out.'

'I have no idea what you've got me into,' Harry said. 'So what are you actually doing?'

He knew exactly what I was doing, but he's a pro at media and he was setting me up to talk about the challenge. Harry led the conversation from there, insightfully picking up on what made this record attempt special. When Artlab got back into the studio, they would edit our conversation into an eight-minute video with cutaways to sequences showing my preparations, scenic shots of the terrain I'd be covering and photos of my time in uniform. We had a narrator to tie it all together, and the Artlab team did a great job of picking out my USPs.

'Dean needs all the help he can get,' the narrator says ominously as I pedal along a Scottish lane.

The video cuts back to Harry, who tries to hold back a smile as he asks me, 'How long have you been cycling for?'

'Erm . . .' is my only answer, before we both start laughing.

At the end of our 'interview', Harry turns to the crew and asks, 'Was that all right?'

We get the nod. Harry turns to face me with a smile. 'One take!' he says as he offers me a high-five. 'That never happens!'

That clip, and the initial conversation when we didn't know the cameras were rolling, almost didn't make it into the video. I think most people realise the prince is just another human being like me and you. Personally, I have the deepest respect for Harry but it has nothing to do with his title. It's because he's a good honest bloke who cares about others. He uses his position, and puts his time on the line to make a difference. He's even put his life on the line too. I think most people know that and respect him for it, which is why in the end we were able to include those clips. I think they helped a lot, for a few reasons. It gave the video something unique, because it wasn't just the 'media face' of the celebrity. In my opinion, it's hard not to watch that video and think: 'Prince Harry believes in this cause, and he believes in the person that's going to complete the mission to support it.'

19. WHO DARES WINS

I was in between visits to check on my client's company in Libya when I got an unexpected call.

'Dean Stott,' I answered, assuming I was about to be offered a security gig.

'Hi, Dean,' a man's voice replied. 'My name's Andrew Slater. I'm a television producer.'

I pulled a face at that. What did a television producer want with me? 'Going somewhere dangerous, Andrew?' I asked light-heartedly. It was the only reason I could think of that he'd be calling me; perhaps he was planning some filming in a hot spot, and wanted a team on hand to get them out of trouble if things went sideways. I had knowledge of journalists being kidnapped by the very kidnappers they'd gone to interview. Play stupid games, win stupid prizes.

'Nowhere dangerous,' the TV producer laughed. 'I'm putting together a reality show about the Special Forces. Your name keeps coming up, and you sound like the man I need to talk to.'

'TV's not really my thing, Andrew.'

'Fair enough,' he said. 'But will you hear me out in person? You're in Aberdeen, aren't you?'

I smiled to myself. He was keen, and if he was willing to

come to me, then I felt that I should at least hear his idea, out of manners, if nothing else.

'When did you have in mind?' I asked him.

A couple of days later I met Andrew in a coffee shop. He had a university look to him. Confident, but softly spoken. I could see that he was full of excitement about his project.

'We've got this idea that we love,' Andrew told me. 'We want Special Forces soldiers to take civilians through a selection process, doing the kind of things you do. It'll be a competition. Hardcore. Everyone loves the Special Forces, and this way we can bring in people from all walks of life, all ages, races and genders. The potential audience is huge.'

I sipped on my coffee while I thought over his idea. I didn't doubt anything he said, but . . .

'I've seen a show like that in the past. I don't mean to slag the blokes off that were on it, but I didn't –'

'– think they looked the part any more?' Andrew cut me off. 'I know what you're saying. No doubt they were bad-ass once, but when someone is overweight and grey, let's just be honest about it, they don't look the part any more, even if they used to. It's hard for people to buy in.

'That's why we want people like you,' the producer told me. 'Younger. Still in great shape, and still current on what's going on, and how things get done.'

I sat back in my chair as I thought about this. Andrew leant forwards in his. He was excited about the project, that was clear, and if someone is passionate about something, then that's a great first step. Personally, I had my reservations.

'I've heard about SF guys getting into the media and then becoming persona non grata at their old units,' I said to him. 'So, to be upfront with you, if it's a case of me continuing with my ties to the squadron or going on TV, I'm one hundred per cent going to choose the SF community.'

Andrew nodded in agreement. 'Of course,' he said. 'Totally understandable.'

'That side of it I'll have to look into,' I went on. 'And I can't make any commitments until then. That being said, here's a few ideas for you . . .'

I pitched Andrew a few suggestions for how he could set up the show to mimic SF selection closely, while taking into account that however much the civilian contestants might want to be on the show, they weren't soldiers or candidates for SF. They wouldn't have the ingrained years of training that a soldier has. I was certain there would be plenty who would have the grit and determination, but there is a reason soldiers have to serve a minimum of three years before attempting selection; they need to learn the basics of living in the field. Map and compass. Battle fitness. And more. All things needed to be considered in putting together the show's format, and its challenges. I told him about some of my experiences, and those of being an instructor at the Commando course.

'I love it,' Andrew told me. 'Dean, I've got to be honest with you, I think you're perfect for the job. You look the part, you talk the part and you have the experience. I'd like to offer you the part of chief instructor on the show.'

'I really appreciate that,' I said truthfully, 'but I can't commit until I get it cleared. In the meantime, I can start sourcing the other guys if you like?'

'Absolutely. Thank you.'

We said our goodbyes and I got thinking about who would be a good fit for an instructor on the show. Tier-1 guys are confident, but that doesn't mean that they'd do well on screen. Some hate the limelight. Some have a quiet confidence. Others let themselves go physically when they get out of the military, others mentally. I made my list, then added the guys into a Whatsapp group that I called 'Hollywood'. It was a tongue-in-cheek name. The show would pay about the same daily rate as a job on the circuit, and filming would last a couple of weeks. For that reason, I got a lot of people saying no straight off the bat; they were knee-deep in security work and didn't see any reason to upset the balance.

Many of the others asked, 'Has this been cleared by the MOD?'

I told them the truth. 'No. It's a work in progress.'

'Let me know if it does,' was usually the response. After hearing about former members of Hereford and Poole being excommunicated for talking to the media, lads were wary.

I had a few takers, though. They weren't on the circuit, and they were confident guys. They'd do a good job on TV, and now that I had enough guys to put together a team of instructors, I called Poole's security cell to let them know what was going on.

'We'll have to run this through MOD Disclosure,' they told me, meaning the department at the MOD who signed off on potentially sensitive material – including this book! 'Thanks for keeping us in the loop. I'd advise you don't move forward with anything until you hear back from them.'

That was my conclusion too. When you join UKSF, you sign

on the dotted line to say that you'll keep your mouth shut about certain things. It's not a blanket statement and exceptions can be made, so I held out some hope that we'd get the all clear. It wasn't that I had a particular yearning to be on TV, but Alana and I had had our big talk, and I didn't want to be divorced or dead. I needed a new job, and who knew what doors this could open? Until the MOD Disclosure got back to me, I'd keep an open mind.

A couple of weeks later, I received the letter.

It wasn't exactly a pleasant memo from the MOD. It cut straight to the point, telling me to step away from the project immediately. I read over the letter a couple of times to make sure I had everything straight, but it was literally in black and white: step away from the project or become persona non grata.

When it comes to decision making, I always listen to my gut instinct, and it was telling me loud and clear that I should comply with the MOD's wishes. I was the SBS Ambassador to Scotland and I enjoyed that role. I enjoyed the SBS Association charity events. I enjoyed being able to visit Poole, and Hereford. I had good mates still in both. Did I want to cut that away in a vain hope of becoming the next Jason Statham?

The answer was clear.

'I can't do the show, I'm afraid, mate,' I told Andrew.

'No worries,' he said. 'We thought this could be a problem.'

'Have you approached the MOD about the show?' I asked him. 'You're going to have the same problem with everyone unless the show gets cleared.'

Andrew thanked me for my advice, and then I messaged

'Hollywood' to let the guys know that the MOD had told me to drop it. A couple of days later I got a text from one of them: 'Do you mind if we still go ahead with it?'

He gave me a few names. They were lads that weren't working on the circuit.

'By all means,' I told him. 'But the MOD aren't on board. Good luck.'

The show went ahead, and as soon as it became public knowledge, there was a shitstorm at the MOD, and in Hereford and Poole. The production company and the guys had pushed on without the MOD signing off, and the SAS and SBS immediately declared them persona non grata; they were not allowed to attend any association events or to be on camp. To give you an idea of how seriously this was taken, I'd heard of a former general who was persona non grata being escorted off camp in Hereford from his own friend's wake.

I didn't want to see that happen to the guys, but it was their decision and not for me to question. Personally, I felt that the sense of community was important for my own happiness, and that wasn't worth giving up. I liked the lads. They are very close friends, and so I felt for one of them later that year when I saw him at a black-tie event held by the regiment. He'd come as the guest of someone still serving, but when the RSM saw him, he was asked to leave. He looked absolutely gutted, and who can blame him? It was in many ways like being cast out of a family.

So I was very hesitant a year later when Minnow Films approached me to ask if I would work on their TV show *Spies*, in the role of an advisor. Andrew's show was doing extremely well, but knowing that the guys had been made persona non grata was at the front of my mind.

'I'll consider it,' I told them, and I did that because I had already begun training for the Pan-American Highway. I'd cleared this record attempt through the MOD because I would be using the title of Special Forces soldier to help raise money for the cause. You may wonder what the MOD could possibly have against that, as I wouldn't be doing anything remotely military, but part of the reason the MOD are so stringent on disclosure is because once your name is out there in the public domain they can't protect your anonymity. If there's a terrorist with a grudge, then you've told them who you are. People think the MOD are trying to keep secrets, and in a sense they are, but those secrets help protect the lives of SF operators past and present and their families.

Now that the MOD had signed off on me 'coming out', and with Prince Harry publicly working alongside me in the campaign, the horse had bolted as far as keeping my identity hidden, and so I knew the MOD would have no drama with that. What they might object to was me giving away trade secrets that could compromise operations, and we went over in detail what I could say and show on the programme.

Honestly, it was nothing more than you could pick up from a John le Carré novel. The show's aspiring spies had to follow me as a target through the streets of Brixton. Being surveillance-trained, I then debriefed them on how they'd done. In my second appearance, I blindfolded the candidates and then put a gun in their hand loaded with live ammunition. I tried to pressure them into firing at a target. Of course, they'd been drilled to never fire at a target that couldn't be identified. It was a test to see if they would buckle under pressure, and they did well; they all kept their fingers away from the trigger. Off camera, I let them shoot watermelons. They were a good laugh, and for that reason I enjoyed the show. My appearances were brief, and I wasn't talking to camera, but it was my first exposure to the media.

When the show aired, I got a lot of messages from blokes that I'd serve with:

'What you doing?!'

'Are you mental?'

'You too??'

'Won't be seeing you at the boxing, then.'

I texted them all back with the same message: 'Watch this space!'

What none of the lads knew is that I'd been in constant comms with MOD Disclosure, and everything that I'd done had been signed off. Not only that but my appearance on *Spies* was designed to raise my public profile at a critical moment: we were going live with the Pan-Am challenge a couple of weeks later, releasing the video of me and Harry. To further build the hype, I was granted permission to do an interview with LAD-bible. Everything in it down to the photos was cleared by the MOD. It was all part of the plan to get the wallets open and money coming in to Heads Together. I was walking a fine line with the media and the SF community, but because it was for a good cause, it was tolerated by the MOD; I was going to smash a world record, living the Special Forces ethos: the unrelenting pursuit of excellence. They liked that, and instead of being ostracised I got a lot of support from the blokes all the way up to the head shed. I could have taken on the Pan-Am as Dean Stott of the Royal Engineers, but the truth of the matter was that if I wanted to raise a million pounds for charity then I needed to deploy every weapon in my arsenal. The SF title opened doors, ears and wallets, and so I used it. Because of my fear of being PNGed it was one of the hardest decisions in my life, but looking back, I wouldn't change it for the world. Some things are worth sacrificing for, and I was certain that the charity Heads Together was one of them.

20. CONTRACTIONS

In the summer of 2016, Alana gave birth to our second child, Tommy, and the way he came into the world couldn't have summed up my wife any better. I was on a Skype call, discussing promotion for the campaign, when she said matter-of-factly: 'Oh. My waters just broke.'

I started getting to my feet. 'Let's get you down to the hospital.'

My wife looked at me like I was crazy. 'Chill out, Dean, we've got ages yet. I'll come to your next meeting with you now. Stop looking at me like that. It's fine.'

She was that calm about it. Half the battle of being on military operations or breaking a world record is not being worried or distracted by what's going on at home. I knew that I had a rock-steady partner in Alana, but here was more proof. When I hit the Pan-American Highway, I wouldn't spend a second worrying about how Alana and the kids were doing without me. That wasn't because I didn't care but because I knew that my kids were in the best pair of hands in the world.

Once our meeting finished we made the drive to the hospital. We had the car packed ready to go – a maternity QRF – but there was no hurry. After going through this before with Mollie, Alana knew what to expect, and she had everything she'd need to see her through the short stay at the hospital. She wasn't the only one; I'd brought along *The Longest Road* so that I could get a bit of research done on the ward. I wanted to take advantage of the opportunity to learn, and when Alana's contractions began, I saw another chance appear.

'Fancy a game of Scrabble?' I asked her.

Alana gave me a funny look. Usually it was she who suggested the game, and with good reason: I'd never beaten her. Now, however, with her mind on delivering our baby, I reckoned I had a slim chance!

'Ya bugger,' she said to me, as she realised what I was up to; I'd see her next contraction coming and pass the iPad back to her at that moment so her two-minute time to find a word coincided with it. It made us both laugh, but if you think she gave up, then you don't know my wife. She's as competitive as I am and, contractions or not, I barely scraped the win.

''Ave it!' I punched the air, then screenshotted my victory. That might sound mental to some people, but Alana and I find fun in competition. We like to laugh at each other, and ourselves. We know that we're different to most couples, but that's why we work together well. We know each other's strengths, and weaknesses.

'I'll thrash you after this baby comes,' she promised, and she wasn't lying: that was the first and last time that I beat her at that game!

Alana safely delivered our second child, a little boy we called Tommy. I wanted to give him a gangster name like Ronnie or Reggie, but as he was born on the 100th anniversary of the Battle of the Somme, we named him after the British soldiers who had fought there. I was elated and relieved that both mother and baby were healthy. To be honest, relief was something I was feeling a lot of that summer. It came from knowing that I had found purpose through the Pan-Am challenge, which had recently been given the green-light by Guinness, but also because our house was in order. We had businesses that were all doing well, so there was no stress over money. As I said, knowing things are sorted at home is a huge factor in being able to operate at a high level, be that on the battlefield or on the longest road on Earth. Some people might have seen the birth of our second child as an obstacle to the record attempt, but not me and Alana. Our children fit in around our lives, not the other way around. That doesn't mean they get ignored, far from it; we ring-fenced time in the week to be together without the distractions of phones or TVs. I'm a firm believer that the moment you start killing your own dreams off because you have kids, you're in for trouble. For one thing, what do you think your kid would want? Would you want your parents to live with unfulfilled dreams? I know I wouldn't. Working on this Pan-Am challenge, I felt more motivated and energised than I had done in years, and that positive energy passed down to my children. How could it not? I was laughing, smiling and full of beans. Think back to what I'd been like not long before: sullen, miserable. Is that the person you want to be around your kids? Not me. A family is a united team, just like an SBS unit, and if one person is feeling low, it affects everyone else. On the other hand, one person's infectious enthusiasm can lift all the others, so that's why in our family we support and encourage each other in our goals, no matter how crazy they may seem to other people.

That being said, we don't try and preach or shove goals down our children's throats, either. Alana and I are big on charity, but we never beat the kids over the head with a moral stick and say, 'You must be this way too.'

I'm not sure if it's down to nature, nurture or a combination of the two, but that Christmas, at five years old, Mollie showed me that she was following in her mother's footsteps. Alana and I had contacted a national charity that helps families fleeing domestic violence. It's very hard for a lot of people to break out of situations like that, because quite often the violent partner is extremely controlling and so the abused partner will often have no money of their own and no independence. This makes it extremely difficult for them to leave: they have no idea how they will be able to feed and shelter themselves and their children. Eventually, they can get help from the government, but there is a period in between where they are extremely vulnerable. Unless they have family or friends to support them, they have to rely on charities.

A local one contacted us just before Christmas to let us know that a mother and her four children had fled their abusive father, and they were now at the local shelter. The mother had had no choice but to pack a bag for the five of them, and now they were starting from the beginning, with nothing. Needless to say, without a home and without money, the children would not be getting anything for Christmas. What they were going through would be traumatic at any time of the year, but during the festive period the difficulty had a spotlight shined on to it.

Alana took Mollie with her when she went down to the shelter to meet the family. She persuaded the young mother to let her take them shopping and picked up some gifts for the kids. It was nothing extravagant, but Alana wanted the woman to know that she was not alone in her fight. Mollie felt the same way, and told her mum that she wanted to give her own Christmas presents away to the children she'd just met. You can imagine how that filled us both with pride. We gave her a lot of chances to change her mind, guilt free, but Mollie was adamant and her presents went to her new friends.

I should probably take fundraising lessons from my daughter. In 2017, she raised £700 by having her hair cut off so that it could be used to make wigs for children with cancer. Honestly, I was shocked when she told me her idea. Kids can be merciless to those who look different – who am I kidding, adults can too. And here was Mollie volunteering to be the one that stood out, all so that other kids could get wigs and not feel different. Just like we had done with the Christmas gifts we gave her plenty of outs and chances to change her mind, but our girl was stubborn – the hair was going.

She did it at the Aberdeen Expo, while her dad was riding a stationary bike, trying to raise awareness for his record attempt. Mollie stole the show, of course, and then father and daughter both felt follicly challenged. She wore it a lot better than her dad, beautiful as always, and I was so proud of her that in that moment I felt like I could have cycled the Pan-Am on that spin bike – anything was possible!

I'd think about moments like that a lot when I was cycling the length of the Americas, but first I'd have to get there.

That seemed a lot more likely when I was contacted by a bike manufacturer named Orbea. They'd been sent the promotional video and they'd loved it, and unlike some other companies, they did not want Prince Harry or bust as their condition for partnership. What Orbea loved about the challenge was the huge £1million target, the story behind me and the fact that I was a novice. They wanted to bring more people into the sport that they loved, and they reckoned that the way to do that was to have an ambassador who was also a newcomer to cycling. Orbea were about to launch an all-road bike – which means the forks are spliced so you can fit in different kinds of tyres – and the timing of my challenge suited them perfectly for promoting it.

Within days of getting off the phone to them, I flew out to beautiful San Sebastian in northern Spain. There are beautiful beaches and cobbled streets there that any tourist would love, but I had packed my laptop rather than my bucket and spade, and I met with Orbea's marketing team to give them a presentation about myself and the challenge.

'You know, Dean,' one of the team spoke up, 'our factory here used to be used to make guns, for the war. When there was peace, they used the same machines that had made the gun barrels to make tubings for the frames. I think this is very similar to your own story.'

I thought about it for a second and smiled at the irony. I couldn't agree with him more. A machine made for war could be turned towards something peaceful. Just like a factory building weapons to kill, a man who had been trained for that end could put his skills to preserving life and bettering the world. I was proud of my service and felt like it had helped the greater good, but you couldn't escape the fact that being the best operators in the world means being the most lethal. Now here I was, trading my cammies for Lycra and high-value targets for high-figure charity donations.

I got an unexpected surprise in San Sebastian when I discovered that Orbea had a sister company, Orca. Orbea were a popular bike manufacturer in Europe, but Orca was the leading company *on the planet* when it came to bike clothing and fitting. Not only would I be getting my bikes, but I'd be getting everything I'd need to ride them too. I couldn't have been more grateful to them.

All along we had been certain that once we got one sponsor to jump in and get involved with the cause, then the momentum would build and we'd get a snowball effect. It was a big ask for somebody to put their time and money into a novice, but once other companies saw that Orbea had taken the leap, that gave me the proof of concept that we needed and offers for meetings began to flood in.

We were on our way.

21. JOGLE

In November of 2016, I had ridden from Land's End to John o'Groats to prove a point to myself and others. I needed to know that I could smash a big ride, because I had the equivalent of fifteen times that distance coming up with the Pan-Am. It hadn't been easy, and I'd taken a couple of hard tumbles on the way, but when I rode the length of the UK for a second time, in the summer of 2017, my time in the saddle was a lot more enjoyable.

I was doing it at the request of Prince Harry, who had asked me if I would be expedition leader for a group of veterans and celebrities as they cycled the route. A handful would do the whole trip, while others would drop in for a day or two as our group passed their hometowns.

The last time I had travelled the route, I had gone from south to north, and so this time I flipped it on its head. After months of training, I was now bike-fit and knew about cadence, and with a lot of miles under my belt I could enjoy this ride as a bit of fun with good company.

My fellow riders were ex-forces people who had suffered mental or physical injuries during their service. That was something I was familiar with, and I was honoured to be sharing the cycling experience with them. I'd been told that I couldn't tell people officially that cycling was a benefit to mental health because the clinical research wasn't there to prove it, but I knew how I'd felt before I got on a bike, and I knew how I'd felt after, so Dr Stotty had no problem with telling people that exercise and cycling was good for mental health.

The weather was beautiful as I set off with my new friends in Scotland. It couldn't have been more different to the raging cold and winds of Storm Angus that had smashed me off my bike back in November. The UK really has the most beautiful countryside, and to see it from top to bottom in the sunshine was an absolute gift. It also felt great to be in a position of leadership within a team, helping and encouraging my new team-mates to make the huge achievement of cycling 874 miles. Doing this route is a high point in many people's lives, and rightly so, but personally I needed to look at it like a training ride. I didn't think that way out of arrogance, but just because the harsh truth was that if I struggled doing 874 miles, then I could never cope with 13,870.

Thankfully, my training had paid off, and I found the ride well within my limits. I had sun on my skin and new friends at my shoulder. It was one of those moments in my life that made me realise just how fortunate I am to be able to meet such great people and enjoy such experiences.

After JOGLE, it was time to really step up the sponsorship push. Orbea and Orca had opened the door, and now I had an influx of messages from charities, companies and individuals who wanted to meet with me to talk about the challenge. Many of these meetings would take place in London, and that, I soon discovered, would throw up one of my biggest obstacles in training so far.

Ken and I had set 100 miles as my baseline for training each

day. I didn't want my London-based meetings to derail my mileage, and so I took my bike along with me. I soon found, however,
that the Big Smoke was not the countryside, and the stop-start
nature of cycling in heavy traffic was extremely frustrating. The
only way I could get my miles in was by finding a park and
doing dozens and dozens of laps. I got a little dizzy doing this,
but it was still a better deal than being inside on a spin bike.
To squeeze as much training in as possible, I also rode to my
meetings; I'd turn up at the front desk in my Lycra, including
at Kensington Palace. Oddly enough, I never got turned away
for breaking a dress code – they probably thought I was the
Deliveroo guy.

I was burning the candle at both ends during this period,
cycling first thing, cycling to and from long meetings in the
day, and sometimes driving to different towns in the evening to
prepare for the next day's meetings. In hindsight, this wasn't the
best idea, and I should have just structured some days to focus
on one thing or the other, instead of spreading myself thin.

One afternoon I got a call asking if I could take a meeting
with Mr David Bellamy, the then CEO of St James's Place (SJP),
a FTSE-100 wealth management company that donates millions
to charity every year. They were looking to get involved with
a project that benefitted mental health causes, and David had
become aware of me after one of their Scottish partners had
been to a talk that I'd given in Aberdeen.

I took the meeting, and heard how the company were used
to funding projects, such as building schools in the Gambia,
rather than backing challenges. I was a risk for them, and I'd
have to get cleared by the board to become the first individual
that they sponsored. Thankfully, the board loved the message of

our campaign, and a week later SJP were fully committed. They would put up the funding for all of our operations, including flights, hotels, media, events, any equipment outside Orbea and Orca's domain, vehicles, petrol, food, visas, etc. To raise money we were going to have to spend money, and SJP were going to enable us to do that. It was a huge moment for us, a real weight off the shoulders. SJP's purpose is to enable people to build better futures, and they were backing me to do just that. I was already fifty grand into my own pocket so far on the challenge, and this was the reassurance I needed that Alana and the kids wouldn't be eating cold beans while I was on the bike.

A few months later, I was speaking at SJP's annual company meeting, which is held at the O2 Arena in London. There were 6,000 people there, by far the biggest crowd I had ever spoken to, and it gave me a real buzz to be sharing the challenge ahead. Every time I told someone about what I had planned with my team, it just cemented my will to smash the record even more. Not break it. *Smash* it.

With SJP on board I didn't have to worry about balancing meetings and cycling in London's parks any more. We had our sponsors, and Alana took over the full-time running of the challenge while I concentrated on going to war with my body and mind, preparing for the greatest test of my life.

22. THE UNRELENTING PURSUIT OF EXCELLENCE

I was months into hitting 100 miles on the bike every day, and so it was time to visit Julian Widdowson and his sports science lab full of gadgets and gizmos again.

As I lay back on a table, Julian began pushing and pulling my legs in different directions, measuring their range of motion. 'You've got fourteen per cent less range in your right leg than your left,' he said. 'How much have you been stretching?'

Hmmm. Not much was the answer, and my expression told him so. Like a lot of active people, I was guilty of overlooking the after-care of my body once I'd put in what I saw as the graft. I found stretching to be mind-numbingly boring, but I'd need to adjust my attitude on that.

'With the distances you'll be covering, it's imperative that you stretch out your muscles and connective tissue,' Julian explained, meaning my tendons and ligaments. 'If you don't, the cumulative effect of the tightness will lead to injury.'

Julian then demonstrated a number of exercises I could do to stop that happening, including using a foam roller to hit the deep tissue.

Once he was satisfied that I had a grasp of each one, Julian stood back and asked me, 'So what's next?'

I stood up and put the foam roller under my arm. It looked like a giant blue Wotsit, but I knew that I would need all the edge I could get for the next part of my training.

'I'm going to Dubai,' I told him. 'Time to cycle across a desert.'

A year ago I had been a total novice to cycling. By November 2017 I had racked up miles, cycled from Lands End to John o'Groats and back and was feeling at home in the saddle. The thing was, however, that all of my training had taken place in the UK and the Pan-American Highway did not run through Aberdeen. Now that I was a confident rider, I needed to get out into the kinds of environments that I would be facing on my 22,000km challenge: huge mountains, sweltering jungle, frozen tundra, baking desert.

In fact, I had marked out the deserts of Chile as one of the most difficult stretches that I'd face. The Atacama Desert is one of the driest places on Earth, and its soil is very similar to that which is found on Mars. It even looks the part, and is often used for movies: you might recognise it from *2001: A Space Odyssey*. *Quantum of Solace* was also filmed there, and the spy in a suit was about to be replaced by a frogman in Lycra.

I'd spent a lot of the past eight years in such harsh, hot environments, and I'd never become a heat casualty, so I knew that my body wasn't about to just pack it in the second that I hit the oven. Some people's bodies just can't cope when they get into an extreme, be that one of altitude or temperature, but mine had always been solid for me, thankfully. I'd worked in soaring temperatures but I'd never cycled in them, and I didn't want to be going into the Atacama with no experience of that. Think of it like learning to drive. Do you want the first time you drive on ice to be in a storm or would you like some experience on a skid pan? In the Special Forces we trained for all environments, because that's how you ensure that you don't get caught out. Each environment has its own challenges, be they mental or equipment-related. Just knowing that you've done your homework and put in the reps is a huge psychological boost. 'What if?' can be a great thought to have when you're trying to think big, but those two little words can also derail you if they're in the back of your mind when you're attempting something new. What if this bad thing happens? What if that bad thing happens? If you've done the training in the same environment as you'll be 'fighting' in, those questions have already been put to bed and you can concentrate on the 'what ifs' that are positively impactful: like 'what if I smash the record by ten days?' Those are the kind of 'what ifs' you want.

Luckily for me, Dubai was fully embracing cycling, and they had thought typically big when it came to designing the facilities to support that sport. There was a fantastic 100km track of smooth tarmac that looped out into the desert. It even had cafes along the way.

Dubai is a high-tech place in a lot of ways, and for a surprisingly low price I was able to get a full-body ultrasound that showed up all the bangs and tears on my body. I was expecting my legs to be the problem areas, but the biggest tear was in my shoulder. It probably dated back to my time in the military, and we didn't feel it would affect me on the bike. We kept hold of copies of the test, as these would prove extremely useful if I had to get another during the Pan-Am ride; we'd have something to compare to.

On the challenge, my plan was to ride in stages of two to two and a half hours, resting no more than thirty minutes in between, and so that's how I rode around Dubai's track. At the rest stops I'd have my blood drawn: this was so that we could monitor my blood sugar levels at various points, and measure my recovery; Did I need shorter stages? Longer? How about my rest times? Did I need to eat more? Eat less? There were a lot of questions that we could get answered by looking at a blood test and putting those results alongside my own observations of how I felt. In the military, I had often just told the voice in my head to shut up as I pushed through. No doubt on the Pan-Am there would be pain barriers that needed smashing through strength of will, but that didn't mean that I couldn't be clever when it came to getting the most out of my performance. Grit and determination has its place, and so does careful preparation. With a synergy between the two, I knew that I could topple records.

Riding in the 40°C heat of Dubai was a challenge, but it was a welcome one. I love the scenery of Scotland, but the desert has its own beauty and there was something really cool about riding along a road where I could see the heat shimmer above the tarmac. It gave me a real kick of excitement. A buzz knowing that I really would be cycling through all kinds of different terrain. When you get into the day in, day out preparation for an event, you can lose sight of the actual enormity of what is ahead of you, and cycling in Dubai brought everything back into focus for me – I was going to cycle the length of the Americas and I was going to do it in record time!

After a few goes around on the desert track, I took on

Dubai's second purpose-built cycle route; a 21km climb into the mountains: yes, they have mountains in the desert, and they're blooming big! The air was just as hot, and I could feel my lungs getting toasty as I sucked in deep breaths on the steepest of the climbs. Again the scenery was just fantastic, and a lot of the time I found myself totally distracted from the aches in my muscles because of the stunning views around me.

There was hard riding in Dubai, but I had not struggled, and I felt confident now that I could smash the desert in Chile. Our trip to Dubai had been a total success, and I couldn't believe my luck when it got even better.

During our stay in Dubai, we got talking to members of its cycling community and told them what we were up to. You can imagine how surprised I was when somebody said: 'I know the guys who hold the record for the South American stretch of the Pan-American Highway. They're here, in Dubai. Would you like to meet them?'

I bit his hand off, and that's how I came to meet Axel and Andreas, a Frenchman and a Swede who had broken the record for the stretch between Cartagena and Ushuaia. I was very pleased to meet them, and even knowing that I was out to break records – theirs included – they did everything they could to help me.

'You're doing the right thing going south to north,' Axel assured me, having done things the opposite way. 'But you will hit some hard side winds to begin with.'

'But don't worry about that,' Andreas put in, 'because once you hit Peru you'll have a tailwind for two and a half thousand kilometres.'

I liked the sound of that, and that piece of information lodged in my brain; later, it would prove hugely valuable.

'Check out this app,' Axel said, showing me his phone. 'It's called Windy TV. It shows you all the weather fronts, wind speeds, etc. It updates really often and is way better than using news channel forecasts.'

'Thanks,' I said, downloading it immediately. 'So what are you guys doing in Dubai?'

It turned out they were there as guest speakers and to promote an ultra cycling event that they ran. Lucky for me!

'One more thing,' Andreas said before I left. 'You should just get in your mind now that at some point you *will* get food poisoning. There's just no way to avoid it.'

I'd thought as much, and I hated the idea of losing days because I was firing out of both ends.

They laughed. 'You don't need to miss days, man. It won't be fun, but you can still cycle. Just make sure you stay super hydrated.'

I thanked them both and left. I didn't realise it at the time, but that conversation would prove hugely useful for me once I was on the challenge. I was extremely grateful to them both, and couldn't believe my luck that we'd been in the same place at the same time. I would have liked to have stayed in Dubai with them for longer – maybe even got in a ride together – but I had a plane to catch.

I was off to Thailand.

My mate Mac manages CrossFit in Phuket and just like I'd visited Dubai to tick training in the desert off the checklist, it was now time to get into 100 per cent humidity and work up a sweat.

I'd be passing through jungle regions on my bike and I needed to be ready.

There was one slight problem, however, and that was Thailand's traffic. I'd never been to the country before, but just the short drive from the airport convinced me that this was not a place to go for a cycling jolly. Riding in London had presented its hazards but going out here just seemed like suicide, and I'd been through too much in my life to get taken out by a swerving tuk-tuk.

Instead I hit the bikes in the gym, but catching sight of the hardcore ninja classes that they had going on in the CrossFit section, I soon got pulled out of the saddle. To be an SF operator you need to be a team player and you need to be competitive, and seeing a group of people flipping tyres and thrashing ropes just got my juices going. I had to get amongst it, and once I was amongst it I didn't want anyone beating me. I'd done most of my cycling training alone, and for good reason – I wouldn't have a pacer when I was on the Pan-Am – but I missed being in a team, and one danger of always training alone is that sometimes the bar of competition against yourself can drop when it's the same thing day in, day out. I was all about living the unrelenting pursuit of excellence, and in that gym I saw a chance to supercharge that ethos. Besides the mental aspect, I'm a big believer in all-round fitness. Yes, I'd be cycling the Pan-Am, not smashing it with a sledgehammer, but hadn't I passed Hills Phase in selection when I'd trained on a bike? My coach wanted me lighter, but I was 90kg and still built like an operator.

I wanted that extra timber on my frame for a couple of reasons. I'd done periods of endurance in the military, on mountains and in the jungle, and I'd seen how weight falls off people.

The Pan-American was going to take me just shy of four months, and even if I lost only a little weight each day, that would add up to a heck of a lot over 110 days, which was my target. I wanted to go into it with a reserve. As Axel and Andreas had told me, I *would* get food poisoning, and nothing strips the weight off of you like a case of Montezuma's revenge.

I'd heard stories that the guys in the Tour de France use their elbows to turn off light switches. They do this to avoid picking up any germs, the reason being that they are incredibly light, and your immune system suffers greatly when your fat deposits are so low. The Tour riders were staying and eating in top hotels, but at times I would be sleeping in impoverished areas and eating whatever they had to offer. I needed my immune system to be the SBS of the germ-fighting world.

The ultrasound in Dubai had made me aware of the tear in my shoulder, but hitting the circuits in Thailand, I didn't feel it. I'm not sure if that's just because I'd had it a long time and got used to it, but whatever the reason, I was able to crack on and beast myself until I was reduced to a puddle of sweat.

I called home every night to speak to Alana and my children. I was away for a month for this training, but I felt very differently compared to when I had been on the CP circuit. For a start, I was here because I wanted to be, rather than feeling like I needed to do it to support my family. I could also leave and get a plane home at any time, and of course, there was the feeling that all of this was not just for my own mental well being but would help thousands of others thanks to the money raised for Heads Together. I missed my girls and my little boy, but I wanted my wife and children to be proud of me. In my eyes, that meant being a husband and a father who got off the sofa and pushed himself to his full potential, and I felt like I was a step closer to doing that thanks to the scorching heat of Dubai and the sweltering humidity of Thailand.

When I got back to the UK and hit the roads around Aberdeen, I immediately felt the positive effects of my month away. I was buzzing with energy; I was flying. I was close to where I wanted to be before taking on my challenge, but one thing was still missing from my preparation: climbing mountains.

The longest climb on road in the UK is 12km. The longest on the Tour de France is 21km. On my Pan-American ride, I could add both of those climbs together, then double them. I had a 67km beast to take on.

Someone had told me that the Pan-Am terrain was a lot like Europe, but on steroids. Everything was bigger, longer, taller and wider. In the Tour de France you get specialists – sprinters and climbers – but I needed to be an all-rounder. I'd always had thick legs – hill legs, I called them – and they'd seen me well through the military. The way I looked at hills was that every one of them was a mini-challenge, and around Scotland I'd seen people get off to push their bikes.

I knew that I couldn't do that. Even on the steepest climb, the physical and psychological momentum I'd lose by getting out of the saddle would be too much to bear when trying to cycle two continents. I needed to be the king of the mountains.

I needed altitude training.

I found it in an unlikely place: on my sofa.

I was watching a documentary with Alana about how Mo Farah had prepared for the 2016 Olympics. At night, to increase the amount of oxygen carrying red blood cells in his body, Mo slept in an oxygen tent.

'I need one of those,' I said to Alana, and immediately started looking into it, finding a supplier in London at a place called the Altitude Centre. I gave them a call and they told me to come in the next time I was in town.

With the amount of meetings I was taking for the challenge, that wasn't long. The centre was located near St Paul's, and I wasn't really sure what to expect when I got there, thinking that maybe it would look like some kind of James Bond villain's gym. Instead, it looked like many high-end gyms in London, with some serious athletes going to work. The manager explained to me that a lot of their members were high-flyers who – in their spare time – liked to smash mountain climbs like Kilimanjaro and Everest. I told them what my own plan entailed and asked how much it would cost to rent one of their oxygen tents.

'Nothing,' they said with a smile. 'You're doing it for a great cause. Just feel free to come here and train anytime that you like.'

As ever, it gave me a great spike of gratitude to know that people were rallying behind the challenge and Heads Together. I told them about the 67km climb I'd face on the Pan-Am. I would have to cycle from sea level to 4,000m in a day.

'Well, why don't you come in here and ride for ten hours?' they offered. 'We've got Wattbikes and a hypoxic machine. It's as close as you'll come to simulating that ride without leaving Europe.'

We shook hands on it and set a date. To keep me company and to promote the challenge, the centre let their members know so that they could join me on the day.

When the time came, I must have looked a right sight with

my Tesco bag full of bananas hanging from my handlebars. My goal was to complete ten hours cumulative on the bike, so apart from the odd call of nature I stayed pretty much in the saddle, pumping away to cover over '200 miles'. The lack of oxygen made a difference, but I had a mirror in front of me and a handsome lad staring back at me, telling me to push on!

As I pedalled away in the heart of London, I pictured myself on the other side of the world. I ran through the length of the Pan-Am in my mind, thinking of all the different kinds of terrain I'd been facing. At the end was Alaska, and even though I knew that would be a step up again, I was happy enough that winter in Aberdeen had given me some preparation for that. After all, I had cycled through Storm Angus, which had gusts of over 80mph.

When people find out that I was a Special Forces operator, a lot of them ask me how I cope with fear. They probably wouldn't believe that part of that answer was 'sitting on a Wattbike in London'.

A lot of fear stems from the unknown, and here I was proving to myself that I could do something and it wouldn't break me. I was taking the fear of the unknown away and replacing it with the confidence that comes from conquering. You cope with fear through training. Through acclimatisation. Thinking back to my dive days, the first step on all emergency protocols was 'do not panic'. Easy enough to say when you're reading it, but what about when you're living it? At first, when you go through your training, it's almost impossible not to panic; after all, you're a human being not a fish, and your brain knows that you can't breathe under water. But what about after you've done that emergency drill underwater five times? Ten? A hundred? You learn not to panic. You have proof of concept. You've been in that position before and you're still alive, so why panic? Why fear?

That's how I felt now that I had Dubai, Thailand and the Altitude Centre in my back pocket. I had taken the 'what ifs' that could mean failure and turned them into the 'what's possible' of a world record.

23. LAUNCH

The original launch date for my Pan-American Highway record attempt was 1 March 2018, but when St James's Place asked me to speak at their annual company meeting (ACM) at the O2 in London, I started to think that the date should be brought forward.

'I feel ready physically and mentally,' I told Alana. 'I'm good to go now. What's the point in going to London for the ACM, then back here a couple of weeks, then back to London for the media week?'

'It makes sense to do the media and ACM in the same week,' Alana agreed, and she looked at our calendar, to check for clashes.

She smiled as she spotted something. 'You know, if you did start straight after the ACM, then you'd be finishing during Mental Health Week.'

Boom! I loved it. 'That's perfect,' I said, feeling a tingle of excitement that the date had come even closer. 'Right, that seals it. Let's bring this forward.'

That would cause some admin, I knew, but Alana was an absolute machine when it came to organisation, and it wouldn't cause her any issues. Because training had been going so well, I had given my team a warning order that I may bring the date forwards, and so it wouldn't come totally out of the blue. For the challenge, I would be supported on the ground by a sports massage therapist, a bike mechanic, a medic, and a two-man camera crew who would be gathering footage to make a documentary about the event. It was a big team, but with the exception of the documentary crew everyone was doing it pro bono, and so it wasn't a huge strain on our sponsors. As well as Alana on the home front, we had an operations manager, who was helping organise such things as shipping. To cut down on airline fees, we were sending out a lot of our gear on a boat. From the UK to the southern tip of South America is a long ride, and so getting that container away was our immediate priority. I sent the operations manager a quick text to explain the new situation, and asked him to give me a call. A couple of hours later I was getting a bit impatient.

'He's gone dark on me,' I vented to Alana. 'I've tried him ten times now. What the hell's going on with him?'

After a couple of days of him ignoring his phone, I couldn't wait for him any longer.

'Can you do it?' I asked Alana, and true to form she was all over it like a rash.

'He's really pissed me off,' I told my wife.

'Don't let it get to you,' she said, trying to calm me.

I'm usually a very calm guy, but years of preparation were coming to a head here.

I am a man with high standards. I live by the ethos of the unrelenting pursuit of excellence, and so does my wife. That doesn't mean that I stand over my kids to watch how they cut up their lunch or thrash them over a climbing frame like they're on the Commando course, but when someone gives me their word, I take them at face value, and when they let me down, I get angry. I suppose that each person has their own definition of excellence, but I couldn't think of any acceptable definition of it which would include chinning off answering your phones.

Thankfully, I had Alana. In next to no time she had our kit in a shipping container and on its way to Chile. It was a weight off my chest and allowed me a few days to concentrate on what was really important.

I was going to be away from home for almost four months. That meant four months without seeing Mollie and Tommy, and so before I went to London I tried to spend as much time with them as possible. Instead of doing long bike rides in the UK countryside, I set up the Pain Cave – basically some gym equipment in my garage! The one bit of Gucci kit I had was a system that allowed me to put my bike in a static position connected to a computer, which could increase resistance to simulate hills, and so on. It was really helpful, and often torturous. Great place to catch up on *Peaky Blinders*, though!

Tommy was too young to have any idea what was going on, but Mollie could understand that her dad was going away, and she understood why and knew it was for a good reason. She was sad – we both were – but there was no anger.

In the six weeks leading up to my departure, I'd begun sleeping in one of the oxygen tents loaned to me by the Altitude Centre. They give you a programme to taper up on the simulated altitude so that you don't overdo it to begin with, but even so, it was quite hard to get to sleep at first, because it was warm and more difficult to breathe. Once I got used to it, however, the tent was brilliant, and I felt like it was a great weapon to have in my arsenal. The only issue I had was convincing Tommy that it wasn't a play tent!

The day to leave our home in Aberdeen came quickly. I can't say I was sorry to leave Scotland in January, but saying goodbye to your children is another matter. Unlike the war-zone days of the military and the CP circuit, I knew I would be coming back, but even so, it's never an easy thing to step away, knowing you'll be missing four months of your children's lives; Thank God for Facetime, is all I can say. I gave them both a big hug and a kiss, told them that I loved them and promised myself that the next time they saw their dad he would be a world record holder.

Alana flew with me to London for a week of media promotion prior to the launch, culminating in SJP's annual company meeting.

We kicked the week off with a launch party, which was our chance to say thank you to the dozens of people who had made my record attempt possible. They were sponsors, coaches, journalists and benefactors, and I wouldn't have been able to do what I was doing without them.

The launch was held at a beautiful penthouse above St Pancras Station, courtesy of Lord and Lady Fink. It wasn't the first charity event I had attended there, and it wouldn't be the last – the Finks are an altruistic couple, and I was very grateful that they opened up their property to us.

The launch was a funny evening for me. To everyone else, it was the beginning of the challenge, but to Alana and me it actually felt more like the close. All along we had been certain that if we could get me on a bike and on that highway then I could smash the record. What hadn't been so certain was getting sponsors and donations. Now that that had been taken care of, all that was left in front of me was cycling 22,000 kilometres, and

I could actually breathe a sigh of relief. I know that sounds a bit mental, but it had never been the physical challenge that intimidated me. If I'd lost sleep over anything, it was that £1million target for mental health charities.

St James's Place did a lot to put my mind at ease about that. After a few days of media activity – I appeared on Sky News and did an interview with *Hello!* magazine, to name just a couple – it was time for SJP's huge ACM at the O2 Arena.

I hadn't trained during the week in London, thinking that a few days rest was no bad thing, considering what I was about to undertake, and so I was relieved when, backstage at the event, I had no trouble slipping into my Lycra. That didn't mean I felt comfortable, though . . .

Pushing my bike, I walked out on to the stage in front of 6,000 people. Most of them weren't close enough to see the intimate outline of my skintight outfit, but the giant screen behind me took care of that. Waiting for me onstage was Claire Balding, the BBC sports presenter who covers Wimbledon, but the only balls on display here were . . . well, you get the picture.

As I took my seat beside her, and looked out over the crowd of faces, that little voice popped up inside my head and said, 'Well, Stotty, you've done some interesting things in your life, and this is definitely up there.'

Even on the doorstep of the challenge, I was still the stocky SBS operator in physique. My Lycra was blue, the colour of my main sponsor, and I looked a bit like the cartoon character The Tick.

Claire asked me a series of questions about the challenge, and after her enthusiastic interview the crowd gave me a standing ovation, which was something I'd never experienced before. I was used to a pat on the back, if that. 'You better not mess this up,' I said to myself.

As if reading my mind, Iain Rayner, the company's chief financial officer, shook my hand and told me, 'A former Formula One driver came to us and asked for three hundred grand to sponsor him for an event. We were already committed to other projects, and a good thing too. He crashed on the first corner.'

He said it with a laugh, and I knew he meant it as a joke, but I still had a vision of me flying over the handlebars and eating South American pavement on the first mile.

'I promise I'll wait until the second corner,' I said.

I went to the green room and changed out of my Lycra into a tux and black tie for the celebration dinner following the ACM. Altogether we raised £265,000, which SJP then matched: we were a half a million up and I hadn't even pushed off on the bike yet! I was delighted, but of course I felt every pound of that total sitting on my shoulders. The benefactors had done their part, and now I needed to do mine.

It sounds bad but I didn't want to hang around too long at the black-tie event. Usually I'd stay at those events until the death, but in the morning I would be flying out from Gatwick and I wouldn't be seeing my wife for months. There was no chance of us getting a private moment together at the event, and I just wanted to spend some time with Alana away from the hustle and bustle. To enjoy her company, and to carry a conversation away with me that wasn't about the challenge.

I'm not going to tell you what we spoke about – some things need to stay secret, even when you're writing a book – but I will tell you that I love my wife very much, and that I wouldn't have been in the position that I was in without her.

I didn't sleep well that night. I never do when I have an important event the next day. Too much going on in my mind, I suppose. Maybe there's adrenaline leaking into my system.

The ride to Gatwick was quite subdued. No one had slept like a baby, and we all realised the enormity of what lay ahead. I broke off from the team at the airport so that I could say goodbye to Alana alone. Neither of us are big on public displays, but she had tears in her eyes. For most people, that's probably the equivalent of her sobbing. Neither of us were wired that way, though. We cared for each other deeply, but we weren't inseparable, because Alana knew that for me to be true to myself I had to do things like cycle two continents. She let me be me, which just made me love her all the more.

'I'm going to miss you,' I told her. 'I'm going to smash this, I promise.'

'Don't forget to open your letters,' she reminded me. The night before, Alana had given me a stack of dated letters that I was to open in the mornings before setting off: they would prove to be an incredible motivation to me.

'You're already in the zone,' she smiled. 'I can see it in your eyes.'

She wasn't wrong. After kissing Mollie and Tommy goodbye at home, my operator's mindset had kicked in. Now that we were at the airport, it was running strong.

We hugged and kissed one final time, and then I walked towards security.

The journey had begun.

*

And it was a looooooong journey. In case you think the team and I were flying out business class, living a life of luxury as we headed to our destination, I'll stop you right there. We were scrunched up in economy because we wanted as much of the money we raised as possible to go to charity. One of the team had made the argument that we could justify me flying business class, so that I didn't tighten up, but I didn't see it that way; I'd travel the same way as my team.

Alana and I had been very firm on the point that we wanted to save as much money as possible on the trip, and so the flights she found for us were the cheapest, which, of course, meant that they were also the longest. It took us four or five flights to get to Punta Arenas in Chile, and I can't say that the journey was much fun, but we were on our way and that was all that mattered.

Stepping out of the airport, the first thing that hit me was that despite the sun there were very strong winds. And not the kind of gusts that you get in the UK but a constant, unending pushing and shoving from Mother Nature, like she was dead against the idea of you standing upright.

She also seemed dead against the delivery of our shipping container. We'd only been on the ground an hour when we got the news that the spare bike, spare parts, tents, medical supplies, winter clothing and other equipment may not reach us for two to four weeks. The winds were kicking up huge waves, and it just wasn't safe for ships to come into harbour. We had one bike with us, and some kit, but the majority had been put into the container so that we didn't have to pay airline baggage costs on so many flights.

'I'm going to go for a ride to clear my head and think,' I told the team, and I hit the road for the first time in the Americas.

The wind pushed at me hard whenever I was side on to it, but I hardly noticed it, thinking instead of the shipping container and what its delay meant. There was a lot of kit on board, but was it essential? Did we need it on Day 1? What was the alternative to pressing on; waiting weeks down here in limbo?

It didn't take me long to reach a decision: we had enough to crack on, and so we'd crack on. I'd begin on 1 February as planned, which at the very least would make it easier for me to count up how many days I'd been on the bike!

I was mentally primed, and I knew how important momentum was, not only in physical activity but in life. Being inactive and away from home would grate at the team before we'd even got started. The only choice was to go.

I had another restless sleep that night, but in the morning I was still certain I'd made the right decision, and so we drove from Punta Arenas to Ushuaia (not to be confused with the club in Ibiza). The drive took us across a desolate, windswept landscape. It was Dartmoor on steroids, and the wind never once let up.

Ushuaia is a resort town on the southern tip of Argentina, on the archipelago of islands known as Tierra del Fuego. In many respects it's the end of the world, but I loved it. Surrounded by mountains, it looked beautiful.

Thankfully, there were a lot of camping shops in the town and so we made up for some of the supplies that were stuck on the ship. Then we went to identify the police station that marked the start of the route in the eyes of Guinness World Records. There were five police stations in the town, which made identifying the right one a bit of a task, but in any case I intended on starting the route at the harbour, on the very first metre of tarmac of the Pan-American Highway. It was an uplifting sight, that point, and despite the strong winds I'd have to cycle into, I was excited for the morning.

That night we stayed in a rented home, where we charged all devices and made final checks on all the kit. We talked through our routines – all things we had already discussed, but after almost three days of travel, there was no reason not to freshen up on it.

You'd think after a couple of rubbish nights' sleep that I'd have been out like a lamp, but yet again I slept in twenty-minute snatches, and when my alarm did go off, and I went to brush my teeth, my eyes were tight and red.

'Just don't cream in on your first day,' I said to myself in the mirror, terrified of falling at the first hurdle. 'For God's sake, at least make it through your first day.'

I put my toothbrush down and took a long look at the man in the mirror in front of me. I'd come a long way in life, some of it on my own and a lot with the help of others. Now here I was, at the end of the world, with 22,000 kilometres of cycling ahead of me.

'In one hundred and ten days,' I said to my reflection, 'you'll break this record.'

And then I walked away to make it happen.

24. HIT THE ROAD

Shortly after dawn on 1 February 2018, I went with my team to the starting point of the Pan-American Highway. I had 22,000 kilometres ahead of me, and 110 days to do it. As we turned the last corner to reach the official beginning of my journey – the local police station – I couldn't believe my eyes: it looked like the entire town of Ushuaia had turned out to see me off! They had smiling faces, banners, and as soon as they saw me they started chanting my name!

'Stotty! Stotty! Stotty!'

Nah, only joking. There were no crowds. No big send-off. There was a sleepy dog and a friendly policeman, who graciously agreed to let me use his office stamp on my paperwork. The Guinness guidelines were as comprehensive a set of orders as I ever got in the military. It wasn't as though I had a referee riding piggyback on my bike, and so I was responsible for collating all the information that would back up my record attempt. There were witness books to sign, videos and photos to be taken at landmarks, waypoints to pass through and GPS data to record. If I messed up on any of the admin, it could mean the record being withheld from me, even if I smashed it, and so we'd planned ahead to get as much detail as possible, and one of the team had come up with the good idea of targeting official buildings and offices, as they were likely to have their own stamps, like the one the policeman was now inking before dabbing it down on to my virgin paperwork.

'*Gracias,*' I said, and I imagine the officer probably looked at me a bit funny then, because instead of heading north, I rode south, towards the harbour. I didn't want any mix-up with this paperwork, and so the 'start' would come at both places. The security guys at the harbour gate admired my Lycra and gave me my second stamp, and then I was away.

I'd barely got going when a bunch of feral dogs took a liking to me and decided to 'encourage' me out of town. I'd found out from reading other people's stories about the ride that the dogs could be a problem, but I didn't expect Muttley to try and make a meal out of me so soon into the ride.

I don't know if you'd call it luck or not, but the steep angle of the roads soon meant that the dogs had to drop back, as I found myself climbing into the mountains that rise like shark's teeth outside the town. I couldn't have asked for more amazing scenery as I started the climb. It was a total distraction, and any nerves that I might have been feeling went to the back of my mind as I was drawn into staring at the epic peaks.

I stopped for a short break after a couple of hours of riding, and breathed a sigh of relief that I'd got out of sight of Ushuaia. If I did spank in now, at least I'd got further than the Formula One driver.

This challenge was going to be a learning experience for everyone, and so we took the time to chat and make sure we were all happy with the plan. I knew myself, and knew that the biggest danger would come in pushing myself too much. I needed to know that my team would be OK with saying, 'Dean, you've already done X miles today, mate. Pace yourself. Let's call it a day.' We have to identify the traits of our personality so that we can tell our team-mates what we need from them. Some people need pushing, others need pulling back. Some people need someone in their ear, other people need peace. It's about figuring out how you work, and then communicating that, because the people around us aren't mind-readers.

After a short stop, I got back on to the bike and almost immediately the road began to change direction. The southern tip of Argentina is an archipelago, and the road out of Ushuaia begins almost due east. Now it was turning north, and as I followed it out of the mountains I hit the first hurdle of the challenge: the winds.

Now if you're a Brit like me, you probably think of a bad wind as that gust that knocks a plastic picnic chair over, but what I experienced on my bike that day – and for the next seven – was *wind.* There were no gusts, just a constant gale that almost threw me out of the saddle when it first hit me. I'd been expecting it, but that's like saying you expect to get punched when you box; it still hurts, doesn't it?

The wind was so strong that I had to lean into it at a near 45° angle. I'm not kidding, I really was almost cycling on my side. If there had been a break in the wind, I'd have come off my bike, but it was relentless. As far as the pursuit of excellence for wind goes, Argentina was top of the class.

At the end of that first day, I didn't have any trouble sleeping in the basic hotel. Part of me hoped that I'd wake up and find the place calm and tranquil, but one look at the trees told me that wasn't happening; the knotted wood is so blasted that the trees grow almost horizontally. It gave the place an alien feel, and two

HRH Prince Harry and me catching up at Kensington Palace prior to my departure for Argentina.

Alana, Mollie and Tommy (the Stott family) join me on the stage at the Wheels Down Ball fundraiser at the Hilton, Park Lane hosted by Martin Bayfield.

Left. Heat training in Dubai at the summit of Jebel Jais mountain after a 20km ascent.

Below. Elevated image of me cycling on the Chilean coastal road (Day 18).

Above. Cycling towards the Atacama Desert in Chile (Day 19).

Right. Tropic line of Capricorn, North of Antofagasta in Chile (Day 23).

Above, left. Time to reflect and focus on the objective during a lunch break in Peru.

Above, right. Drinking from a fresh coconut in Ecuador.

Below. One of the many mountains I had to ascend and descend in Colombia, close to the Ecuador border (Day 42).

Above. The view from the mountains of Ecuador at 4000m above sea level.

Right. A local policeman in Ecuador and one of hundreds of witnesses for the witness book.

Below. Local taxi style in Ecuador for descending the mountains.

Left. Coffee break in Santa Rosa de Cabal situated in the coffee growing region of Colombia, having recently passed through the city Pereira in the background (Day 44, and 4 days before breaking the South America world record).

Below, left. Finding the coolest place for a 10 min power nap in Costa Rica (Day 53).

Below, right. Guilt-free eating and replenishing some of the 7–9000 calories burnt each day.

Right. A black bear strolling in Canada and an arctic fox in Alaska.

Below. Finally reunited with Alana, Mollie and Tommy at the finishing point at Prudhoe Bay (Alaska), on the shores of the Arctic Ocean, (99 Days, 12 hours and 56 minutes).

Interviews in Prudhoe Bay while sat alongside both Guinness World Records.

Alana and I presenting a cheque for the first £500,000 raised to the CEOs of the Heads Together charity.

days into the challenge I started to think to myself, *If it's like this all the way, I'm buggered.*

The reason for that pessimism was my knee. On the morning of my second day, it felt like someone had lit a bonfire underneath my kneecap.

'This is supposed to be my *good* knee,' I said to my team. 'Let's check the bike-fit and my cleats. Make sure everything's measured and fitting properly.'

It all was, and I was losing time. I had no choice but to get back in the saddle and grizz it out. As I pushed on, the team would call a specialist in the UK, to see what they could find out.

I didn't enjoy the ride that day. The beautiful mountains were gone, replaced by featureless tundra, wind and pain. Not fun.

When I got off the bike at the end of the day, the team explained that the specialist had said the pain was caused by torsion in the knee; because I was having to lean so heavily into the wind, it was stressing the joint.

That gave me some hope. I knew this wind wouldn't last forever. A week, maybe. Just a week, and then it would be behind me.

We pushed on. The road was so featureless that on the third day, when I came to a roundabout, I had a near-panicked moment, thinking to myself, *What do I do?!* I'd got so used to just pedalling straight ahead, trying to ignore the pain in my knee, that I nearly went straight into the middle of it. At least a crash would have been a nice distraction from the constant white noise in my left ear; it felt like I was being interrogated at Guantanamo Bay!

Yeah, I wasn't a happy chap, but things can always get worse. I could have been one of the llamas or emus that I occasionally saw, trying to scratch out a life in that hostile climate. At times I saw where they had tried to jump a fence but ended up tangled and dead in the barbed wire, like a soldier in the trenches. It was sad to see, but gave me some perspective.

The southern end of Patagonia was sparsely populated, to say the least, and so we didn't come across any Welcome Break service stations as I pedalled up the Pan-Am. Instead, we ate out of our two vehicles, sheltering in the lee side from the wind.

'What's for lunch?' I'd ask, setting up the daily joke.

'Well, you've got a choice of cheese and ham or ham and cheese.'

'Hmm. Tough one.'

I had to eat a lot of those sandwiches. With spending so long in the saddle, and with the effort against the wind, I was trying to consume between 9,000 and 12,000 calories a day. Sounds fun, doesn't it, but it's hard to do when there's no pots of Ben and Jerry's to dig into.

One break in the monotony of the natural desolation of this part of the world was the border crossings. For some reason, the Pan-American Highway criss-crossed from Argentina into Chile three times, until I finally ended up on a long stretch in Chile, heading north towards the Andes. The mountains of Chile were like a beacon in my mind, because I knew they would mark the end of the barren lands, the winds and, hopefully, the pain in my knee.

Sure enough, after seven days of riding in conditions that tested my mental patience as much as my muscles, I began to see snow-capped mountains in the distance. As we got closer, I came across towns that had an almost Bavarian look to them, and if I'd dropped here out of the sky, I could easily have believed that I was pedalling into the Alps. The wind died down, the pain in my knee eased, and I felt the huge morale boost that you feel after going through something arduous and coming out of the other side. Yes, I had 100-plus days of cycling ahead of me, but I'd known coming into this challenge that those winds would present a tough obstacle, and now they were behind me. Stotty 1 – Winds 0 (I told you I'm competitive).

Now that there was some civilisation around, I began to see service stations. Not big ones like you get on the M6, but petrol stations with a cafe attached. I took my breaks in these, enjoying a hot drink and the looks of the locals. I'm sure they'd seen cyclists pass this way before – I'd passed a couple of road-trippers myself – but covered in the logos of my sponsors, I looked like the local meathead who'd been abducted and dropped into the Tour de France.

As far as the weather went, there was one day in that early stretch where it hammered down. The rain was absolutely icers, and unlike when I cycled in Scotland, I wasn't certain of a hot shower and a washing machine at the end of it. Most of the hotels we stayed at were up to the job, but on one occasion I was back to wet/dry routine, almost. Not pleasant, but one of those things you just have to crack on with.

Besides, it started to warm up about a week into the ride, and who doesn't like being outdoors in the sunshine? It was summer in the Southern Hemisphere, and soon the temperatures were in the high 20s and low 30s. During my breaks, I'd bask in the sun like a lizard, but I couldn't work on my tan; risking sunburn was not an option, and so I slathered myself in thick factor 50. It reminded me of the stuff you get issued in the army, and after applying a coat of that I looked so white people must have thought I'd been moonbathing.

We refined our drills as a team on a daily basis. We had two support vehicles, and we found that they were frustrating the traffic that wanted to get past. I didn't think this was very fair on the locals, and we couldn't exactly claim to be raising money for mental health when we were making the South Americans lose their minds, and so we came up with a pepper-potting system where one vehicle would drive ahead at normal speed, then find somewhere to park up. The support team leapfrogged in this way and we dramatically reduced the chances of a road-rage incident, which, joking aside, was something we needed to be aware of. In the territories that we were passing through, road rage was not going to be a red-faced banker in a Range Rover; it could mean a man with a machete, or a gun.

One day we received great news, and one of our vehicles left our little convoy and headed back down the Pan-American Highway to collect our long-awaited equipment from the port; our shipping container had finally been offloaded! To expedite things as much as possible, my mate Ivor flew in and took charge of the admin, and so by the time the vehicle arrived he was ready to load it up, and they quickly caught back up with me.

The timing couldn't have been better, because the next day, I decided to put my bike – and my body – to the test.

I was on the hard shoulder when it happened. That was where I chose to ride, anxious to be as clear as possible of any passing traffic. I was coming down a hill, and ahead of me I could see two lanes of traffic merging into one because of a closure.

Brilliant, I thought to myself. *I can go into that empty lane. The surface will be better than the hard shoulder.*

There was a sign at the end of the lane, supported on two poles, but it was nice and high in order for traffic to see it at a distance. I'd have to duck, but I figured that I could ride straight underneath it without needing to slow down from my 30mph. I was so intent on making sure that my head didn't touch that sign that I never saw the lower bar that ran between the poles.

SMASH! The bike whacked to a halt where it met the bar, sending me over the handlebars like I'd been shot out of a cannon. I had the Lycra for it, I suppose.

I hadn't seen the crash coming, and I think that kept my body loose as I crashed and scraped along the ground. My immediate thought was *Shit!* and my second was *Shit! I hope the bike's OK!*

The crew parked up and came running over to me. They were especially worried that I might have broken my collarbone in that kind of fall, but other than bumps and bruises I felt OK. There were three places on my body that really ached, and each was down to landing on the bits of equipment that I had strapped to my body: my GoPro, heart-rate monitor and tracking device.

'How's the bike?' I asked them, shaking myself off and walking over to look at it.

I put my hands to my head and swore. If that bike was a human, I'd have been ordering in a priority evacuation. It had a couple of punctures, but the worst thing was that the handlebars were totally trashed. I was so lucky that the shipping container had come in when it had, because now we had a replacement set; otherwise my challenge would have been ending because of a road sign.

I was a little scraped and sore after my tumble, but I still felt a lot better than I had done when the wind had battered me and my knee had been twisted with torsion. I told Alana as much on the phone that night.

'Sky News want to come and talk to you,' she told me from Aberdeen, to Atacama. 'They're doing a piece about Harry and Meg. They're covering the charity work that they do, and so they want to speak to you.'

'All right. No dramas.' I wasn't in the saddle all day, so I could certainly make time for an interview that might direct more eyes towards our cause. 'Where do you think's a good place to do it?' I asked my wife; the Atacama Desert may have made a great backdrop for Hollywood, but there was no airport in the middle of that Martian landscape.

Alana liaised with Sky News, and they settled on the coastal city of Antofagasta, the central hub for the huge copper-mining industry in the region. I was just over three weeks into the challenge when I sat down with them, and I felt confident about how things were going: I'd beaten what I expected to be the worst of the winds and was making good time. I was halfway up South America, and if anybody had been doubting me before, I felt like I was showing them that, novice or not, I was serious about smashing records.

'When will this come out?' I asked them when we were done, thinking that it would help raise more money for the challenge's charities.

'Oh, about a week before the royal wedding.'

I tried not to show my disappointment. I'd have almost finished the challenge by that point.

I'm sure Antofagasta has some lovely tourist spots, but like the other towns that I passed through, I didn't see them. My days were spent pedalling, eating and sleeping. Quite often I was passing great scenery or interesting sites, but they were lost to me as I put all of my concentration into turning the pedals and being wary of traffic. I didn't just have the challenge to worry about but my life, and on a lot of stretches I was so far from a hospital that I'd be brown bread if I got into a bad accident. I had to keep my legs pumping and my head on a swivel.

One nice break in the monotony came when I crossed the Tropic of Capricorn, the circle of latitude that contains the sub-solar point on the December solstice. Basically, that means it's the southernmost point where the sun can be directly overhead. I stopped to get a quick photo with the sign, and then I was back at it.

Riding through this stretch of Chile, I came across the giant mining trucks that were used in the copper industry. These things looked like they could eat a tank for breakfast, with wheels the height of a van. They must have been fifteen metres long and seven high, and they made me feel like I was stood next to a Tonka truck in *Honey, I Shrunk the Kids*. I found out later that these things were actually auto-piloted by computers. Incredible.

The ground around me on this stretch of the ride was baked red dirt, so dry that quite often the cracks ran like spiderwebs into the distance. It really did look like Mars, and I half expected Matt Damon to pop up and ask me for a seatie home to Earth. The hardest thing about cycling through this desert was obviously the heat; even though I'd trained for it in Dubai, it was still a hard slog. At least in Dubai there had been plenty of purpose-built shelters to get out of the rays for a moment. Here there was nothing. The vehicles were so full of kit that it wasn't much of a sanctuary in there, and we kept the air-conditioning low to avoid burning excessive fuel. Everyone was a sweat monster. Before the desert, we had stocked up on water and filled the petrol tanks, but we didn't want to be too liberal with either because we didn't know exactly when the next service station would be; they didn't signpost them in this part of the world, and so I'd lost the motivating countdown system that I'd had in Argentina.

As you might expect, after years in the military, your eyes get tuned to picking up certain things in the landscape, even when you're not looking for them, and mine picked out landing strips that had been set out in the dirt of the desert. I put two and two together, and reckoned that these must have been used to supply the observatories that were up in the desert mountains.

You could see why they'd chosen this place to make their exploration of space. At night, the sky was lit up like a Christmas tree. There was no light pollution, and the stars stood out brilliantly in unending billions. You could make out the thick cluster of galaxies. The constellations. It was really spectacular, but I was usually so worn out from riding that my stargazing was kept to a minimum. Once the sun went down, it was the inside of my eyelids that I saw the most of.

Four weeks since setting off from Ushuaia, and with the Atacama Desert now at my back, I arrived at the border with Peru. I was alone, which was how we planned it, because a man on a bike aroused a few questions, then got his stamp and was left to go on his way and clock up the miles. The vehicles, on the other hand, were stripped, and what the border guards seemed most interested in confiscating was food. I won't comment on why that might be, but let's just say they could have benefited from a bit of cycling themselves.

We hit a snag in Peru: we could only find one vehicle to hire that would be suitable for the journey to Colombia – the original vans we'd hired were from a company that operated in Argentina and Chile, but which could go no further. We were doing well for time, and so I decided that we would take a day at the border to sort the logistics. A lot of the items out of the shipping container were essential, but some of it we could do without, and so we stripped and repacked until we could get it all into one vehicle. We'd also need to lose two of the crew, but don't worry, we didn't just leave them in Chile! Ivor and one of the camera crew flew ahead to wait for us in Colombia, where we hoped to get back to two vehicles.

On my first day's riding I'd been chased out of Ushuaia by wild dogs, but thanks to the desert conditions I hadn't seen much of them since then. The canine community in Peru seemed to want to make up for that, and I spent most of my day either trying to outrun them or doing my own mad-dog impression, establishing myself as Dog Stott, the alpha male. I'd often see packs of the buggers running in ahead of me from the flanks to cut me off, and I'd have to do my old time/distance/ speed calculations to figure out how I was going to get past them.

A funny thing happened after a couple of days of this. Once I'd been chased by dogs enough, I realised that the times they started coming after me was when I was freewheeling, and the bike was clicking. If I was pedalling and the bike was quiet, they didn't seem bothered by me. From that point on, if I was in an area with dogs, I kept my pedals moving, and I didn't have any more trouble with them after that.

As it had done in Chile, the Pan-American Highway in Peru handrails the coast, following its twists and turns. When I saw the barrelling waves, I wanted to trade my bike for a board, and I promised myself I'd come back some time to surf.

After we crossed into Peru, the service stations seemed to dry up, and we found it hard to find shops where we could buy items like dried pasta that we could cook ourselves using bottled water, a preventative measure against food poisoning. We had no choice but to eat out, and being a seafood addict, I ignored the warning voice in my head and ordered seafood pasta. It was lovely, but not quite worth the horrendous spewing that I woke up with. I just wanted to curl up and watch a movie, but we'd already lost a day to sort the logistics and so there was no choice except to get back into the saddle; maybe cycling 130 miles in 30°C heat is good for a bad stomach?

The next morning I felt back to normal. That was a great psychological boost for me, but it was nothing compared to the one I got from now picking up the tailwind that Axel and Andreas had told me about. All of a sudden I felt turbocharged, and I was knocking off 150 miles a day. The higher the number, the more I wanted to keep going, and I needed my team to reel me back in. The local food also did its best to help, and gave me a second bout of food poisoning – from a pizza this time – but even with frequent stops at the side of the road, I was still flying. I was setting and breaking personal bests every day, and I was loving it.

*

A few days into Peru, one of the team told me that we were going to pass the Nazca Lines; in the area I would be cycling the next day, there were over 300 etchings in the desert sand. These things were giant, covering a thousand square kilometres, and dating back well over a thousand years. It sounded incredible and I wanted to see them, but . . .

But I wasn't here to be a tourist. I was here to smash records. I knew that, but I still felt a pang of jealousy as I saw all of the light aircraft up in the sky, giving the tourists the best view of the hundreds of figures. They're worth looking at, believe me, even if you can only do it through Google like I did!

The Nazca Lines were the first real tourist trap that I'd passed on the road. Obviously, the countries of Argentina, Chile and Peru have a lot of tourist attractions; they just aren't on the Pan-American Highway. That was probably a good thing for me anyway, because I'm only human and it would be hard to pass them by on a daily basis.

After the Lines, my next place of note was Lima. It's one of the largest cities in South America, with a whopping ten million people, and I was going to have to go straight through the middle of it on a bicycle: great plan, Stotty!

But the route was the route, and there could be no shortcuts (or safe cuts). To try and limit the danger, we pulled up short of the city the day before so that I could hit it at first light, when I hoped it would be quiet. I told the team to go ahead and wait for me on the other side, as them slowing traffic behind me would probably put me at risk as people violently overtook them.

Lima is not a cycling city, and I was the only one in the saddle as I started to push along the road, which was already busy, despite the early hour. Just like on operations, my head was on a swivel, but instead of looking for gunmen and IEDs I was looking for lunatics in the traffic – and there were plenty of them. Lima's bus drivers race each other to get ahead and pick up the next bunch of passengers, their conductor hanging out of the open door, waving cars back when the driver spots his next fares and pulls in. It was helter-skelter, and more than a few times I thought I was about to witness a pile-up. The support team had their own near misses too, but somehow we came through unscathed.

'Look at yourself in the mirror,' one of my team laughed at me as I arrived at the rendezvous on the northern side of the city. I did, and cracked a grin: the thick white sun cream I was wearing had turned a dark grey with pollution. In hindsight, not great for my lungs, but I'd got through one of the most dangerous spots for a cyclist on my challenge, and that was a reason to smile.

25. ONE FOR THE BOOKS

During the last two days of my cycle through Peru, I began to see a welcome change in the landscape. The arid desert was slowly replaced with vegetation, until I was surrounded by lush, vibrant greens.

The change was an expected one, as this kind of detail was written down in 'the Bible', a breakdown of the route into 500 stages of 50 kilometres each. It was packed full of information I had picked up during my research phase, anything from the expected weather to warnings about drug cartels. One of the things covered was the height climbed per day, and a member of the team – himself an avid cyclist – was very vocal about the doom that was awaiting me when I hit the huge mountains of Ecuador. It was something he brought up on a daily basis.

'Look,' I snapped at him one day, 'I don't want to hear any more about Ecuador until we're *in* Ecuador. There's nothing to be gained by flapping about it. I've got to go over those mountains and that's that, so let's just shut up about it.'

As we approached the northern tip of Peru, I could now see those mountains – the Andes – rising in the distance. They were the biggest mountains I'd ever seen, and I started to psyche myself up for pushing over them. There was no such thing as an easy stretch on this challenge, but I knew that this was going to be one of the hardest. When the ascent came, it was without warning: the road shot upwards, and from that point the mountain slog was on.

I climbed non-stop for the rest of the day. When we did eventually stop for the night, it was in a town that was blanketed within the clouds. It felt like some possessed ghost town, but after such a hard day in the saddle, I'd have been happy to sleep in the devil's own bed.

To be honest, after a month of getting toasted in the desert, it was a nice change to feel a bit of a damp chill in the mountains. Everyone expected me to be saddle sore after climbing so long in the dry heat – the Japanese flag was mentioned more than once – but my backside, legs and back all felt fine. What was falling apart on me were my lips, which had blistered in the hot air – I don't think even my own wife would have been up for kissing them. I thought that being in the mountains would bring them some relief, but I was wrong about that. As I went speeding down the hillsides, fat drops of rain slapped against my lips and stung like a bee. Desperate for some relief, I tried to curl my lips back so that the most blistered parts weren't as exposed. With my duck lips and a documentary team in tow, the locals must have thought that *The Only Way Is Essex* was passing through town.

Up and down. Down and up. Those mountains put the Brecon Beacons to shame. At points I'd drop out of them, even down to sea level, but I could see the next set of beasties waiting for me in the distance. Being from the UK, it was hard for me to get my head around the scale of it. I'd crack one set of mountains that felt like I'd just hit every peak in the Lakes, and then after a 50km ride through a seemingly unending banana plantation, I'd be up into the next thigh-burning climb that would last for hour after hour. At one point, above the cloud line, we came across a landscape of rolling hills *on top* of a mountain. This was after a 4,000m climb in one day, starting at sea level and in tropical heat, and ending up in a landscape that looked like Wales but at four times the height of Snowdon. In the morning there'd been iguanas basking on the roads, and by the evening I was seeing cows with bells around their necks. It added a *Twilight Zone* feel to the cycling, and maybe for good reason; I was at the closest point on Earth to the Moon. There are taller peaks in the world, but given its position near the Equator, Mount Chimborazo is the one that comes closest to our lunar neighbour.

The people of Ecuador had a distinctive look to them compared to the other peoples of South America that I had seen so far. Their skin seemed to be a lot darker, and almost thicker-looking. They wore brightly coloured ponchos and conically shaped hats that reminded me a bit of what you'd see a yodeller wearing up in the Austrian mountains. When you heard the cow bells jingling, it would be easy to squint and imagine yourself in Bavaria.

My team member had warned me about doom and gloom in the mountains, but I was enjoying them. Was it hard? Yes! But if it wasn't hard, how could I justify asking people to contribute money towards Heads Together? If I wasn't having to dig deep into my tank every day, then I'd feel like a fraud, and the idea of quitting never came into my mind. Honestly. How could it? Coming off selection the first time because of an injury, I had accepted it, because – as well as accidents happening – it was only myself that was affected. Not so on this challenge. There was a bigger picture here. There were people counting on me, and I wouldn't let them down.

The mountains liked to keep me on my toes. The scenery was beautiful, but those passes could be deadly. There was no time to switch off. The climbs into the ranges were so steep that my speed was slowed right down, almost to walking pace at times. For this reason, I took my helmet off on my first day riding into the peaks – the first time I'd done so on the challenge – but after a couple of hours I decided it needed to go back on.

The reason for this was the traffic. The road twisted like a serpent into the mountains, and you'd think that people would take their time driving along it and that they certainly wouldn't overtake on blind bends.

Ha! They took on that route like it was a Formula One track. I rode as close to the edge of the road as I could, and a good thing too – sometimes two cars or trucks would come around a corner, neck and neck.

Motorists weren't the only danger. Sometimes I'd come around a corner and there'd be a cow just chilling in the middle of a road. Other times I had to stop and wait for a family of feral pigs to cross. I was trying to make best speed, but I was constantly having to shadow my brakes for fear of unexpected obstacles. There were plenty of dangers, but I made it without coming out of the saddle. More to the point, my morale received a huge boost because not only had I bested the mountains but I had done so within schedule, and that put me in a great spot to keep pushing for the record through the next country: Colombia.

*

I arrived at the border with Colombia nice and early in the morning to avoid the build up of traffic that comes in the middle of the day. Despite the dawn start, however, there were still huge lines ahead, and I began to worry that my first day in Colombia was going to be a short one.

The reason it was so busy, it turned out, was that political violence and uncertainty in Venezuela had people seeking refuge in other countries, and many of them were using Colombia as their route out. Thankfully, using our best Spanglish, we managed to convey to an official that we were attempting a record, and they allowed me to go to the front of the line; the team would have to wait their turn.

I was about an hour into my ride in the new country, and coming down a hill, when I noticed that a car ahead was indicating and about to turn off the main road. I slowed accordingly, but what I hadn't taken into account was that the car following it – with no indication and with seemingly no awareness of me – was now about to turn too.

My brain did that split-second calculation of time/distance/speed and I knew a collision was inevitable, but I hit the brakes to try and slow my speed as much as possible. The car sideswiped me and I tried my best to jump away from the bike, landing on thick gravel that tore my Lycra and the flesh of my backside to shreds. Worse, because the stones were loose, I kept sliding down the hillside. By the time that I got to the bottom – no pun intended – it felt as though someone had poured hot water all down my back.

Anger is a great pain suppressor, and I quickly made my way back up the stones to the road. I was fuming, and the old couple in the car probably saw that and decided, 'Nah, not today, gringo.' They pulled back on to the road and away like they were in a *Fast & Furious* movie.

I'd always assumed that if I got into trouble in Colombia it would be because of drug cartels, not because of an elderly driver with bad eyesight. It just goes to show that it's not only the sensational dangers that can get you.

As I was checking my bike over, a couple from a nearby house came out to see me and offered me water to drink and to wash myself down. I was really grateful to them, and I began to calm down. I can't say that I was a very smiley Stotty after being smashed off my bike – especially after the driver didn't even stop to see if I needed help – but *c'est la vie*. I suppose I do make a fearsome sight when I'm in bright blue Lycra.

After thanking the couple for the water, I got back into the saddle and cracked on. Thankfully, neither I nor the bike was broken, but when the support team caught up with me, they couldn't help but notice my new fashion style of bloodstains and ripped fabric: 'We only left you for a couple of hours!'

Despite the rocky start, I soon got to like Colombia. After all, the way to a man's heart is through his stomach, and when we found a ranch-style BBQ, I ate to the point where it was painful to lie down. It was the best feed I'd had in over a week, since we'd found a Chinese restaurant in Ecuador. That place had been lovely too, and my order to the waiter had been a simple one to take down: 'Two of everything, please!'

For the first time on the ride, I was seeing signs of Westernisation creeping in; the road signs were getting bigger, as were the advertising billboards. The restaurants felt like they had the same vibe as you'd find in a Texas steakhouse.

A couple of days into the country, I saw in 'the Bible' a note I'd written, courtesy of the advice I'd gathered from Axel and Andreas. It was about a 2-mile-long tunnel that was closed to cyclists, but the pair had talked the guard into letting them through, in order to save them the 20-mile detour into the mountains. In Chile, I'd stopped at a similar tunnel and been denied, and that had cost me a long stretch in the peaks. I was really hoping that wouldn't happen today, because I was making such great time that it looked as though I had a great shot at breaking the record for the fastest cycle of South America! With that in mind, there was no chance I was going to lose the best part of a day to a detour, and so I borrowed a mantra from my mates in the SAS: 'Who dares wins.'

I saw the tunnel mouth in the distance, but instead of slowing down to talk to the guard, I picked up my pace. He saw me coming and came running out of his hut, waving his radio, but there was no way I was stopping. I zipped by him and into the tunnel mouth, shouting 'Hello!' in Spanish as I went by. The tunnel ran downhill, and I kept the pace going, doing my best to keep my breathing as limited as possible so that I didn't breathe in any more fumes than I had to.

I wasn't sure what would be waiting for me on the other side – the guard must have had his radio for a reason – but when I saw blue lights flashing, I started to think that maybe 20 miles in the hills would have been a better option than a night in a Colombian cell.

Better to ask forgiveness than permission, I thought to myself, and I decided that I'd use the same plan at the other end of the tunnel: hey, diddle, diddle, straight up the middle.

I came zipping out into the daylight, expecting to see a police car pulling out to intercept me, and I couldn't believe it when instead I saw that all the guards were watching me go, with smiles on their faces and cameras in their hands. Some even waved to me!

I was through, and the first record – *my* record – was on the horizon.

I had no idea how close we were to total failure.

26. CENTRAL AMERICA

During the last couple of days of my cycle through Ecuador, before I was knocked off my bike and got a very bruised backside, something was happening elsewhere that was more of a threat to our challenge than any lunatic behind the steering wheel.

Back when I had looked at how all the other record attempts had been cycled, the predominant successes had ridden the road from north to south, but this had still thrown up issues for them; for instance, the great tailwind that I got in Peru had been blowing in their faces, and they'd had to deal with the Andes and the Atacama Desert later in the ride, when they were already fatigued. Getting bike spares, and food poisoning also hampered them further south. For these reasons, I had decided to do the ride the other way around, knowing ahead of time that there would be one significant drawback: the issue of support vehicles.

As I mentioned earlier, it was not possible to bring the same set of vehicles all the way from the southern tip of Argentina to Alaska. In South America, we had to change wagons at almost every border. Then, once we had flown over the Darién Gap – a break in the Pan-American Highway caused by a large area of undeveloped swampland – we would pick up the road and our new support vehicles and take them all the way to the end of the road in Alaska.

In the military, we say that no plan survives contact with the enemy. In civilian life, it's fair to say that no plan survives contact with a country's bureaucracy.

Some time ago, my team, with the financial support of SJP, had purchased two vehicles in America that were to be shipped to Panama and used by us for the duration of the challenge, before we sold them to recoup what money we could at the far end. Unbeknown to me, when I was less than two weeks out from Cartagena and the end of my South American ride, Alana had been informed that the paperwork for the vehicles was incorrect, and that they hadn't even been loaded on to the boat from Fort Lauderdale to Central America.

'No problem,' Alana had said to them. 'What do you need?'

'Oh, it's not that simple,' she was told. 'The process takes four weeks.'

Four weeks – and I was going to be there in just over one.

I always say to people that with the time and the right team around them, anyone can break a world record, and Alana proved that. She knew that there was nothing I could do about it from my position in the saddle, and so she kept the problem from me, not wanting to burden me with any extra mental fatigue. Instead, she began phoning around my mates, trying to find a couple of lads who were clued-up enough to drive brand-new vehicles through potentially dangerous stretches of Central America. She had wanted SF operators, but in the end, the volunteers she got were just as up for the task: our personal assistant, Frances, and Matt, a member of SJP's marketing team.

Within a day, they and Alana were on a flight to Fort Lauderdale. It was Mother's Day, and she had to leave our children with her father, who stepped in to take care of them. Ivor, who was still with our kit in South America, would fly to meet them in Fort Lauderdale, and they planned to load the gear there, then drive the two vehicles 4,000 miles over eight days, getting to Panama just in time for me to hit the ground running and to keep up the pressure on the Pan-American record.

Alana and the crew arrived in the States, and straight away they got given a dose of hurry up and wait. The shipping company wouldn't load the vehicles to be shipped, but neither would they release them to Alana. In the end, Alana and the team staged a sit-down protest in their offices.

'They're our vehicles,' she told them, 'and if we don't get them today, I'm calling the police.'

Funnily enough, the company sorted the paperwork in no time, and the guys were on the road.

I'd been warned by previous riders that I could expect trouble and hold-ups at the borders, but other than hitting a little congestion, I'd had no dramas in South America whatsoever. Coming through Central America, Alana was finding out, was a different story.

Ivor had been a bootneck (a Royal Marine), but for the others, it was the first time they'd seen people casually strutting around with weapons at a border crossing. These men were often wearing civilian clothes, the only mark of their rank, the pistols on their hips. They were deliberately intimidating, seeing a nice chance to mess around the four gringos and pocket a little change. Alana had been through a close protection course, so she'd had some training in the basics of safety in such situations, but the dynamics of security are very different when you're in a foreign country, with a different language and the knowledge that things can go badly wrong there.

I was blissfully unaware of all this at the time. Alana had only told me that everything was going well and they planned to make it to Panama in eight days.

Cartagena was the city in my own sights. Guinness were flying in a representative who would check my data and – all being well – present me with the world record for the fastest cycle of South America.

Every day my team had been sending our data to Alana and Frances, who had been collating it all in a monthly dropbox for Guinness. Now that we were down to days not months, the evidence of my rides had to be sent in on a daily basis, and so as well as the driving, Alana and Frances had that on their hands. We considered switching it to my support team, but we had a system in place and with a record in our sights we didn't want to tamper with what had worked well so far and risk our accomplishment because of a trivial technicality, like a missed upload.

When I was a couple of days out from Cartagena, it began to dawn on me that I was about to break a world record. There was always the risk that something could go wrong, and no time for complacency, but realistically, I knew that I had enough time in the bag to deal with anything short of catastrophe.

The night before I would break the record, I called Alana.

'Will you be there in Cartagena?' I asked her; we'd hoped that she would arrive in Panama in time to make the short flight across so that she could see me break the world record.

'I'll be lucky to make Panama City by tomorrow afternoon,' she told me, and I could hear that she was upset.

'Don't worry about it,' I said. 'We'll still see each other tomorrow.' And when you boil it down, that's what's most important, isn't it?

I was up at 0300 the next morning. I'd told the crew to get a lie-in. 'You can overtake me, and set up the cameras to see me arrive and breaking the record.'

But I hadn't taken into account just how much traffic there would be, and even though they did overtake me, I overtook them again and arrived at the finish point of the South American phase as Billy No-Mates.

At least I had the officiator from Guinness to keep me company. After the pleasantries, I began showing her the data to prove that I'd done everything to deserve the world record. Through no fault of her own, she was no expert on cycling data, but explaining it got a lot easier when the crew arrived. She looked it all over, then gave me the nod, a thumbs-up and a handshake: I was an official world record holder, having smashed the standing record by ten days.

We smiled for the camera, and then went to an old naval fort around the corner to get a few more PR shots. I'd been so busy trying to avoid getting zonked in the traffic, and then explaining the data, that it was only now that what I'd accomplished began to sink in.

And of course, I'd only been able to do what I'd done because of the work of other people, and that made me a little sad that Alana hadn't been able to see me come in. On the other hand, that had never been the plan, and so I told myself not to get negative about something that had only become a possibility because of a shipping cock-up. I'd be seeing her later that day, and that was a big Brucie Bonus in itself.

I took a few minutes to myself and looked out over the waters beneath the fort. I'd ridden from the South Atlantic to the Caribbean, covering almost the entire Southern Hemisphere. I'd cycled through massive winds, scorching desert and mountains on top of mountains, and not only was I still standing but I felt amazing, physically and mentally on top of my game.

I breathed a sigh of relief, but soon told myself not to slack off. I had accomplished something, but not everything. My goal had always been the Pan-American record, and I should see this first record for what it was: a confidence boost in reaching the real prize. I was ten days ahead of the record pace, and I didn't intend to let that slip.

Within a couple of hours of becoming a world record holder, I made the short flight south-west to Panama City, where the Pan-American Highway restarts after the swampy break of the Darién Gap.

I checked into a hotel, took a well-overdue shower, and didn't have long to wait before my wife arrived with Frances, Ivor and Matt.

'What took you so long?' I said to Alana as I pulled her in for a hug and a kiss. Then, 'You stink,' I joked.

She wasn't laughing. Instead she looked shocked. 'What's up?' I asked her.

'You've lost so much weight!' she replied, looking me up and down.

I hadn't noticed it myself, but over the two months I'd been steadily losing bulk from my stocky frame. In all the years that she'd known me, Alana had never seen me looking like this. At least my blistered lips had got better!

The documentary crew had set up to capture the arrival of Team America, but after 4,000 miles in eight days, my wife wasn't in the mood for PR. 'I just want a shower.'

It was only after Alana and the others had a chance for a shower and a coffee that I began to get the full extent of what they'd gone through to arrive on time with the vehicles. Because they hadn't wanted me to panic, they'd kept quiet on how dodgy some parts were, but now they told all because it was important to use this information as a post-op report and draw some lessons from it; after all, I'd be passing through these same places within days.

'The Nicaragua and Costa Rica border was the worst,' Alana told me. 'We didn't think we were going to get through there, but then we found a customs guy who escorted us through when he got off duty.'

As is common in developing countries, there was the usual dance of backhanders and flattery. 'We gave out a lot of the challenge bracelets,' Alana smiled. 'You might spot the guys wearing them on the way back.' And I did. Whenever I saw the light blue rubber bracelets at a border crossing, I knew that those were my guys to talk to.

I was so proud of my wife. I really couldn't have done what I did without her, and she and the team showed that in dramatic fashion by bringing those vehicles across.

Does it feel great to break a world record? Absolutely. But doing it because your better half helped you, and was there to celebrate with you, is worth way more.

*

After spending thirty-six hours with Alana, I was keenly aware that I wouldn't see her again until the end of the challenge, which was months away; we were still short of halfway.

I needed to get back into the saddle and burn off my emotions, and so after a day sorting logistics, I was back on the highway and chasing *the* record.

Panama City was the first major population centre I'd cycled through which actually had any kind of traffic regulation; or should I say where people *followed* the regulations. I still had to be vigilant, but I wasn't riding with my heart in my mouth as I had been in some of the South American countries.

I timed my ride to hit Costa Rica in the evening, when I hoped that the border would have quietened down. After Alana and the team's experience on their drive from Fort Lauderdale, we knew what to expect, and I thought that it would be better to deal with any delays at the end of the day, once I had my miles under my belt, rather than getting frustrated in the morning with my ride ahead. If I started chasing time and miles, then I was setting myself up for an accident.

True to form, we were given the run-around at the border by people with pistols on their hips but no sign of any credentials. These places were a money-making machine for those manning the gates; in essence, they really did have you to ransom.

Our ace in the sleeve was a packet of paperwork that Alana and the crew had collected on their way in. We knew what was needed, and even when they told us it was wrong, we played the game. Lots of smiling. Lots of inflating their egos. And a little bit of 'here's a tip for not strip-searching me and stealing my bike'.

In South America I'd flown through the checkpoints on my

bike, but in Central America I wouldn't be given any special treatment.

Although it was a pain, we did get through, and I was looking forward to the ride through Costa Rica. We had a function on our website that allowed people to track my progress, and many people had contacted us, asking me to drop in on the way. I really appreciated the invitations, but it wasn't really possible, for the same reason I had to skip the tourist sites: I was on the bike to break a record.

Things worked out in Costa Rica, however, and we arranged a stage stop at a restaurant near to the ocean with an old friend of mine who now lived in the area. Believe it or not, we had gone through Engineer training together before going to the same regiment, and now here he was, a retired RSM living in Costa Rica! It was great to catch up, but I had to be disciplined and stick to our stage plan, and so the reunion only lasted an hour, with no beers, making it possibly the first dry reunion in the history of the British Army!

Costa Rica was beautiful, with thick, lush vegetation and palm trees all around. Of course, the price for that kind of scenery was sweltering heat, and I took to napping at the rest stops – actually just an excuse for me to lie on the cool tiles of a restaurant floor as we waited for our food. I looked like a tired dog, but the locals didn't seem to mind, and people just stepped over me.

A couple of days into the country, as I was coming down a hill, I saw a crowd of people on a bridge, looking over the edge. My first instinct was that someone must have jumped, but as I got closer I saw my crew, and they waved me down.

'Take a look!'

I did, and I saw crocodiles. Hundreds of them, basking beside a river in the hot sun. I made a mental note not to take a dip in any water courses, and then I was back on my way.

I had another impromptu meet with a Brit soon after the first. He was a Scotsman from Aberdeen, who had traded in my family's hometown for the sunshine of Costa Rica. He owned a juicery, and he was by the roadside with his daughter to meet us as we passed, with a freezer box full of fresh juices for me and the team: what a legend!

I don't know if many Costa Ricans speak Jockanese, but a lot can speak English. After my rendezvous on the route, and through conversation with locals when we stopped, it was becoming clear to me that we were drawing closer to the influence of the United States.

Honduras and Nicaragua were the next countries on the list, and they were much the same as Costa Rica: beautiful and boiling. In Honduras, the highway began to handrail the Caribbean Sea for a while, and as we waited for lunch to be served, I took a dip. The water was warm and it required all of my discipline to get back out. I didn't have much fear of food poisoning by now – I think my guts were hardened by this point – and so I tucked into a big pile of my favourite: seafood.

After all the previous stress, I was now really beginning to enjoy the ride. Not only did I have amazing scenery to occupy me, with new sights and smells around every corner – not all of them pleasant! – but I had become confident as a rider. I *knew* myself as a rider. There wasn't much I hadn't cycled over or through by this point, and I was ten days ahead of record pace.

Of course, something was bound to upset that.

*

We were in Guatemala, closing on the border of Belize. The documentary team and Ivor had gone ahead of me, and I was cycling alone as the night closed in. There were only seven miles to go to the nearest town, and I wanted to push on. Wherever I stopped would be where I had to start the next day, and that would involve the faff of driving back out here.

I passed a huge lake, with a whole host of restaurants along its bank. Those places were teeming with people and I could hear laughter, singing and music. Pickup trucks filled with smiling families were passing me, heading to the party. It looked like a hell of a good time, and I was jealous that I couldn't join them. I wondered if the team were thinking the same thing, because I saw them outside the van, waving me down.

'What is it?' I asked. They didn't look in the mood for a party. They looked nervous.

'You need to stop here,' one of them told me. 'We'll drive in.'

'It's only seven miles. I'm gonna crack on.'

They shook their head. 'No, Dean, listen. It's one of the most dangerous cities in the world.'

I pulled a face at that. Operating in some of the most dangerous countries in the world, often alone, I'd staked my life on being able to read the atmospherics of a place, and I'll tell you this: no matter what country you're in, people don't go out smiling to dinner with their kids if they think there's a chance they're going to get kidnapped, mugged or shot.

'Is this another armed bandit flap?' I asked. The day before, one of the documentary team had got it into his head that there were armed bandits around, and he'd posted about it. That had resulted in some concerned phone calls, but it had all been groundless. The result of an active imagination.

I called Ivor. He had gone ahead to check into the hotel in the 'danger town'.

'What's going on?' I asked him.

One of the documentary lads had found an article online saying that the place we were staying was one of the most dangerous places on the planet. I'd seen nothing about this during my planning of the challenge, and so I asked him to send me the link.

'Tell him this article's eight years old,' I laughed. 'And it's not even the same country! The towns just have the same name.'

Ivor did his best to calm the others, but I decided that in the morning I'd need to talk to them. Ivor was a bootneck, I was a frogman, but not everybody had our training and confidence. 'You're in good hands,' I assured them. 'But please, stay off the internet. That stuff's just click bait to scare you and make you read more.'

I was comfortable being uncomfortable, and sometimes I forgot that not everyone is wired that way. To reassure the team, I spent some time going over our standard operating procedures and emergency rendezvous plan. Sometimes all people need is the comfort of knowing that there's a plan if things go belly up.

And I needed my team to be OK with the idea of danger, because we were about to enter the battlefront of drug cartel violence: Mexico.

27. STARS AND STRIPES

For the first time in Central America, we had an easy time at a border: this one belonging to Guatemala and Mexico. Maybe the Mexican authorities were more concerned with their northern border, because by the spring of 2018 there was a lot of talk from President Trump about building a wall, and a migrant caravan was arriving at the border with California – a predecessor of the one that would make international news that autumn – but my route would take me further east, to Texas.

I wasn't too worried about cycling through Mexico. The cartel violence here was brutal, and there was always the chance of being in the wrong place at the wrong time, but one of the benefits of sticking to the Pan-American Highway meant that I wouldn't – or at least, shouldn't – follow the wrong path and end up in a slum where crime was possibly waiting around the corner.

As in the other countries that I had passed through, I found the locals friendly and smiling. It's so often the way. The headlines talk about beheadings in Mexico, but where are the stories about people making a positive impact in that country, even if that impact is just a smile and a wave as a stranger pedals by?

Despite the absence of threat, a couple of days into Mexico I did start to feel the strain of the challenge. It was my birthday, and I could feel my heart being pulled towards Aberdeen and my family. Because of the time difference, my calls to the children and Alana usually occurred in the morning or early afternoon. That day, my wife had told me that Mollie was upset; she felt awful that Daddy would be spending his birthday alone.

That gave the heartstrings a hard tug, and I felt like I was cycling through cement. Alana had let the team know that it was my birthday, and that night they arranged a cake at the restaurant: I scoffed the lot!

Despite the cake, there wasn't much of a party atmosphere that night. We'd smashed a world record but you'd never know it. Most of the time, the team were sullen, and I'd begun to dread getting off my bike. It had started slowly but the mood seemed here to stay.

It was time to address it.

It was time for tough decisions.

The problems within the team had begun as far back as Argentina. I wasn't really aware of them to start with, as they were mostly between members of the support crew on either side of the planet. Later, I began to notice the change in mood, and then people began to come to me as a middle man.

It a nutshell, the problem was this: my team had signed up to support the challenge pro bono, and that involved taking time away from their own businesses. They felt that consequently those companies should be receiving a larger amount of exposure on social media.

Alana was trying to explain to them that such promotion would breach charity law and to get the point across that they'd get that kind of exposure when the challenge was completed – known as the after glow – and there would be plenty of interviews to do, not to mention the documentary.

Alana did her best to keep all of this from me, knowing that it would affect my head on the road, but soon enough I was hearing bits and pieces from the team as they approached me with their grievances. Soon, I was hearing the whole thing: 'We want to change our terms and conditions or we're done.'

It all came to a head just inside Mexico. One of the team made dinner and practically threw the plate down in front of me.

'What's wrong?' I asked.

And then I got it, both barrels.

'We want our job titles to change from mechanic to operations manager and from soft-tissue therapist to performance manager.'

'But you're not the ops and performance managers. We've all got our roles, guys. That's what you signed up for.'

I tried to be as neutral as I could but these roles were very different from the jobs they were performing. Promoting an individual or company into a role that they were not qualified to perform would be false and potentially detrimental, and I was not willing to put my name and reputation in jeopardy like that. Just because you can pour a pint in a bar doesn't make you the bar manager.

They didn't argue about it then, but I could tell they weren't happy with my decision. I had a lot of time to think about it the next day, which turned out to be a slog. There was no way of avoiding the mountains I was passing through, but the mental bullshit seemed like something that could have been avoided. I'd expected that people would come on to the challenge to raise money for charity and that was it, but now I was seeing that people had their own agendas too, such as promoting their own businesses. Obviously, if breaking the world record would help their careers, I was all for that, but not at the risk of breaching charity law and putting the money raised for a good cause at risk.

My plan all the way through the challenge had been never to get off and push my bike up a hill, but that day was the closest I came to it. Other people's negativity was rubbing off on me. I was beginning to dread my rest stops, because I knew I'd be the middle man in another round of bitching.

Mark Beaumont, the world-record-breaking cyclist, had told me that he rotates his support team every four weeks. Now I could see why. I wasn't the only one who was tired. The team had worked hard, and they didn't feel as though they were getting the pay-off for that hard work. Something would have to change, and as I wasn't about to break charity rules to accommodate their business promotion, the other option available to me was rest.

We stopped in a town for a day, the idea being for everyone to get a little time to themselves and sort out any admin issues. The guys told me they were going to head out to the shops, and I asked them if they could pick me up a new set of cycling gloves. Instead, when they returned, they were holding paperwork in their hands: new terms and conditions, to go with the new job titles they had been pushing for. We had come to a 'take it or leave it' situation. They felt like they had all the leverage – they didn't think I could finish the challenge without them.

I saw it differently: if anything was going to stop me breaking the world record, it was being around negativity. 'I think it's time we got you guys some flights home.'

There was no animosity in what I was saying. I was extremely grateful for the contributions that they'd made, but the positive was being heavily outweighed by the negative at this point, and there was over a month to go. I couldn't afford to spend every day with my head feeling heavier than my legs.

Maybe what the guys didn't understand is that I'd had weeks in the saddle to think and rethink contingencies for this challenge, including what would happen if I had to go on alone. Because I was the person who'd done the planning, I was more familiar with the plan than anyone. I wasn't an expert at sports massage or bike mechanics, but soon we'd be in the USA and never too far from a sports therapist or a bike shop. Until then there was Youtube – and Ivor; like most bootnecks, he was more than happy to just crack on, and he could drive the RV loaded up with kit. The other truck would be left behind with the documentary crew, who would then catch up with us.

It wasn't easy letting the other team members go. We'd spent a lot of time together and there were tears, but the challenge had to come first. I had a mission and it *would* be completed. I was on that bike to raise a million for charity, and that trumped everything else: spending my birthday with my kids, promoting businesses. Everyone needed to make sacrifices for the thing to work.

The next morning, with only Ivor following me, I hit the road with a huge weight lifted from my shoulders. I felt invincible in the saddle that day. Now that the mental weight and negativity had been cut away, I was absolutely flying.

I'd been dreading my stops in the last couple of weeks, but now things were back to being fun. I'd have a good chat with

Ivor, talking over anything remarkable we'd seen in the last stretch, or doing what Commandos do best: spinning dits with a wet in hand.

Since that experience, I've heard of other people finding themselves in a similar position during charity projects. Going into future events, I'll make sure that everyone's motivations are clear from the beginning; if someone wants to promote their business, we'll try and find a way to make that work, but if we can't, then they just won't join the team. You could have ten people along to support you, but if the attitude even a couple of them brings is negative, you'd have been better off just cracking on alone. Like fear, negativity is contagious.

But so is positivity, and with Ivor I was soon laughing again. We had the same attitude of improvise, adapt and overcome. We were comfortable being uncomfortable.

That doesn't mean that Mexico was all roses from then on, however. One day, I saw a mass of flashing lights ahead, and at the side of the road was a body covered in a blanket. Next to it was a bike: a cyclist had been hit and killed.

That was a deadly reminder to me that I couldn't afford to let my guard down at all during the ride. I had to treat every day, every hour and every minute with respect.

A few days into Mexico we passed a bike shop, and as we were so far ahead of schedule I was happy to chill there for three hours while they fixed up our tubeless tyres and serviced the bike.

Having dealt with the second vehicle, the documentary guys caught up with us via plane. And as we drew up to the Texas border, I felt nothing but positivity.

*

The queues to enter the United States were huge, but that was fine by me. I saw the Stars and Stripes flying, and it signalled a huge milestone. It wasn't that I'd felt threatened in Central and South America, but I had been more alien than I would be in North America. Here I could speak the language, making the resolution of any issue easier. There were bike shops. There was easy access to doctors and sports therapists. I would be able to hold conversations that went beyond just the pleasantries, and those chats would help the challenge, driving up traffic on our donations site now that I could really explain to people what we were up to.

I'm a fan of the States, and the little things – like watching *Rocky* on TV before bed or eating a meal the size of a house – really helped pump me up mentally. This felt like the home straight for me. There was a whole continent still to go, but all the record-breaking riders I had talked to had told me that their issues had been in South and Central America, and I was through that, with fourteen days in the bag! The next morning, as I rode out into Texas and watched the endless freight trains pass across the plains, I was one happy man, with not a care in the world.

And then Alana called me.

28. THE INVITATION

I got instantly worried when I stopped for lunch and saw that I had four missed calls from Alana. Usually she would just leave me a message, asking me to call her back. I worried that something had gone wrong with the funding for the challenge, or worse still, that something was up with Mollie or Tommy.

I Facetimed her. 'What's wrong?' I asked.

'What do you wear to a royal wedding?' Alana said.

I had no idea what she was talking about. 'What do you mean?'

'What do you wear to a royal wedding?' she said again, then lifted up a card so that I could see it: Alana and I had been invited to Harry and Meghan's wedding.

'I didn't see that one coming,' I told her honestly. Harry was a mate, but a royal wedding isn't a few beers in the local. 'When is it?'

Alana smiled. She knew that I'd know the date I was due to finish in Alaska off by heart. 'Nineteenth of May,' she said, and I heard myself groan; that was four days earlier than I was expecting to break the world record. 'The last flight you can catch is on Day 102. You'd better put your foot down.'

'I suppose you'll be going one way or another,' I laughed.

'It's a royal wedding,' Alana grinned back.

Once we got off the phone, I thought about my new target.

I'd had things so comfortably in the bag, but at the flick of the switch I was now behind schedule! Of course, I didn't have to make that date, but like Alana said . . . it's a royal wedding. Harry had invited me, and I didn't want to let him down.

There was more to it than that too. I knew that if I could get it done in time and make the wedding, then it would be great PR for the campaign.

That knowledge sealed it for me, and I did the maths. I had budgeted thirty days for the United States and Canada; I now needed to take ten days off that.

Game on.

Of course, just because I had a plan, that didn't mean that Mother Nature didn't have one of her own. At the town of Lubbock, I hit 60mph winds, and we were forced to rest up for the day; a gust like that could take me off my bike and this wasn't the time to be risking broken bones, or worse . . . the sight of the dead cyclist in Mexico wasn't easily forgotten.

During my enforced rest day, I turned to Windy TV, the app that had been suggested to me by Axel and Andreas. It showed the weather in great detail, and I realised that I'd have to cover 360 miles in 36 hours in order to beat the next weather front, and its winds. Over the next few days, I would be using the app to play chess with Mother Nature.

I set off as soon as the winds had died down, and made good distance. There was still a steady wind, but even that dropped in the evening, and so I kept on going in the dark. There was barely any traffic to worry about at night, but neither was there anything to distract me. I couldn't see the scenery and so I listened to music. In the distance, I'd see the light pollution of the next city, and slowly but surely that blur would grow and grow on the horizon.

I must have been a strange sight on the roads, particularly at night, and more than once I was stopped by a cop or a highway patrolman. They were just a little confused about why I was out on my bike at 3 a.m., but once they discovered that the reason was a world record and not meth, they shook my hand and wished me luck.

I needed it. With wedding bells ringing in my ears, the target for crossing the US of A was only twelve days.

Back when I was in the Southern Hemisphere, I'd stuck to my 'bible' pretty religiously, hitting the designated number of miles every day, and staying in the towns that we'd recce'd via the internet and places we'd booked from the UK. The winds in America meant that I changed that approach, cycling as much as I could in between the breaks in the crosswinds, or further still if I could catch a tailwind. Also, since we'd picked up the RV, I had a bed on wheels to sleep in, which allowed us to save more money that could be put towards the good cause.

We made one exception to this no-hotel rule. Alana called me to let me know that I had to spend the night at the town of Raton Pass.

'Why's that?' I asked her.

'A church group has been following your progress, and they've paid for a hotel for you.'

There were a lot of people contributing money to the challenge – some in huge quantities – but to be able to see and pass through a town where people were supporting me meant a hell of a lot. It was a testament to the power of the internet and social media, but more powerful still, it was proof to me that people are people the world over, and no matter what fancy gadgets we have that allow us to track people crossing continents on bikes, the oldest and greatest parts of the human character – like charity and hospitality – are alive and well, despite what some doom-mongers would have you believe.

I arrived at the hotel after dark, too late to meet the kind people who had put me up, but the hotel's owners were real characters, an older couple covered in tattoos, looking like they'd stepped straight off the set of *Sons of Anarchy*. I would have loved to have met the church group members, but Windy TV told me that if I wanted to beat the heavy gusts that day, I needed to be out and on the road by sparrow's fart. Ivor would get the pleasure of meeting them, as I pushed on into Colorado.

The wind was no joke, and if I needed any reminder of that, then I saw it in the articulated wagons that had been flipped on to their sides by the high-speed crosswinds. I didn't think Guinness would accept my record attempt if I crossed America like Mary Poppins, but I knew that soon the highway would dogleg, and these crosswinds would become my tailwind. I caught it, and for the next few hundred miles I was like a Tomahawk missile blasting across the prairie.

The Colorado air was a pale blue that you could almost taste, it looked so good. Soon I began to see snow-capped peaks: the Rocky Mountains. Their range and size was daunting even from a distance, but it wasn't only nature that made things big out here; so did Uncle Sam. I passed the front gate of a military establishment – an air force base – and two hours later I was *still* cycling along the perimeter fence! It must have been some kind of training base, as I saw everything from gliders to fast jets, and the constant air show was a welcome distraction. I was – and always will be – a soldier at heart, and seeing those fast jets streaking through the air sent my pulse racing, reminding me of the time when I'd been on the radio to them, picking out targets and bringing in the bombs and gun runs. Dangerous work, because if you mess it up, you can put those explosives on your own blokes, but it was one of the most enjoyable things that the military had taught me to do. Cycling past that base, I realised that I did miss it, but the bike between my legs was a great reminder that I had a new purpose now, and that the military may be behind me, but all I had to do was look around me to see that I was living a new kind of adventure, and one that would benefit other people in ways that I wouldn't have experienced if I were still in uniform. After leaving the SBS and going through an identity crisis, I was now confident in my resurrected personality. In uniform or not, I was living the ethos of the unrelenting pursuit of excellence.

I'd been a little worried about Denver in the days before I hit the mile-high city. Lima had been my big worry in South America, and Denver was the population centre that I was concerned about in the North. I'd passed through several towns in the USA, but Denver is a beast, and in the back of my mind I was pretty sure that I wasn't even allowed to be cycling through it. I decided again to adopt the attitude that it's better to ask for forgiveness than permission.

Of course, hurting someone's feelings was not the big issue; safety was. The highway through Denver had six lanes of traffic, and I'd ride the hard shoulder. The problem would come at the regular intersections, where two lanes would merge in and out with the highway. To get to the next bit of hard shoulder I'd have to cross these two lanes of merging traffic, then cross the two lanes of exiting traffic so that I didn't leave the highway with them. I was a yo-yo bouncing back and forth between trucks, pickups and angry horn blasts.

I'd told Ivor to meet me at the north of the city, and so I was on my own. To put it into context, this idea was about as clever as someone cycling on the M25 around London, but I'd come to ride the length of the Pan-American Highway, and this was part of it.

Denver itself is a beautiful city, modern and sleek, and when I wasn't trying to avoid disappearing under a truck's wheels, I enjoyed my views of it, even stopping a few times to take selfies. The drivers passing by must have thought I was nuts. I wondered what they'd think if I told them I'd already cycled from the foot of Argentina, and wasn't stopping until I got to the tip of Alaska.

I pulled right on to the hard shoulder for another selfie, and moments later I noticed the flash of lights behind me; they were yellow lights and belonged to a recovery truck. The driver got out and came walking towards me.

'Hey, man,' he said, shaking his head, 'you gotta get off the road. You've been causing people to go all kinds of crazy.'

The recovery man was tuned into the station that other recovery drivers and the emergency services used to coordinate on traffic and accidents. Apparently, the 'psycho on a push bike' was getting a lot of attention.

'You'll have to come off at the next intersection.'

I did, and I can't say that I was sorry not to have to go through any more dance-of-death lane switches at every junction. I caught up with my team, which now included my mate Jonno. Like me, he was an ex-Engineer, but we hadn't met in the service. Our paths had first crossed on the DFID contract in Libya and we'd stayed in touch, and now he'd driven down from his new home in Vancouver to help me out until the end of the challenge. Unfortunately, no good deed goes unpunished, and on his first night with us, Jonno's pickup truck was broken into outside the hotel. It looked like a crime of opportunity, just a few tools taken, and the hotel staff told us with a shake of the head that there were a lot of junkies in the town.

Planning the challenge, I'd always figured that we'd end up being the victim of crime at some point, even if we were vigilant and prepared; when you're a group of white faces with strange accents, you stick out and draw the wrong kind of attention. However, aside from having to give a few bribes at the borders, we'd had no drama in countries like Mexico or Honduras. Our first break-in was in the United States. It just goes to show that crime can happen anywhere. You can't let your guard down.

After Denver I checked in with my new wife, Windy TV, and realised that if I could get to the city of Cheyenne by nine the next morning, then I would catch an epic tailwind. I pushed myself hard to make it, but it was worth every drop of sweat: the tailwind launched me into orbit and I covered 260 miles that day, and climbed 10,000 feet in 11 hours! That was huge for me, and it was the first time I'd really used Windy TV as a tool for finding winds to help me, not just to avoid the ones that would slow me down. It was a practice that I used as much as possible for the rest of the challenge.

After the scenery of Denver and the Rocky Mountains, the

state of Wyoming seemed endless and barren. Wyoming and Montana were my final two states to cross, and aside from day-dreaming that I was in an old cowboy film, there wasn't much that stood out about my ride through them. Like some of the stretches in Chile, it was a case of just zoning out, pedalling and hitting my miles.

An exception to this came in the town of Billings. A US military veteran and his family had heard about the challenge through a friend, and they'd been following me since. When they saw that I was coming through Billings, they extended an invitation for me and the team to come by for Sunday lunch. It was very kind of them, and it felt great to be sitting around the table with such kind and hospitable strangers. Meeting their children made me miss my own, but I hoped that when Tommy and Mollie were older they would understand why their dad had been gone for a few months and know that it was for a good reason.

I did a lot of cycling at night during this period – the winds dictated that – but I still tried to keep the balance between chewing up the miles and promoting the challenge, stopping at times to take calls from radio stations in the UK. This wasn't as easy as it sounds, as I'd have to make sure we'd be in a town that had phone reception at the scheduled time, and so we had to carefully plan my ride so that we'd hit a population centre in time to take a call but not so early that we'd have to hang around for a few hours.

I didn't talk about the royal wedding at all during these calls, and neither did anyone ask – why would they? They knew Harry was part of Heads Together, but no one expected me to beat the record in time to make it back for the cake and disco. Only Alana, Ivor and Jonno knew about the invitation, and we intended to keep it that way until I was on the flight back to the UK with a world record in my pocket. However, I did notice that my recent surge in miles was provoking comments on social media, along the lines of: 'He's rushing back for his mate's wedding.' I didn't reply to any of them, but they did give me a chuckle. After all, we'd stated publicly that we were looking at eighteen days to cover the United States – Alaska excluded – and I'd finished it in eleven and a half.

Things had started to get chilly during those last few days, even with the graft I was putting in on the bike. I had my thermals on underneath my Lycra, and thick ski gloves on my hands. When I arrived at the Canadian border, the immigration officer in short sleeves saw me and smiled: 'Hey, man. It's not cold.'

Maybe not for him, but when I hit 30mph and above on the bike, the cold air cut through me. I'd been lucky though – very lucky – and I'd hit a warm weather front. It was melting the snow ahead of me before we reached it; I could see the water running away in the deep drainage ditches at the side of the road. This thaw meant clear roads and good going, which made me feel a lot better about the stop we had planned at Calgary.

Since our sports therapist and mechanic had left in Mexico, we'd had to rely on finding local services to help tune up my muscles and the bike, but because I'd been playing my chess game with Mother Nature using Windy TV, we'd not been able to book ahead or find a place when we stopped. For that reason, I decided we'd take an admin day in Calgary, so that we could get the bike fully serviced and I could get the knots worked out of my muscles.

My first priority in Canada, however, was Tim Horton's, a chain of coffee and donut stores. I'd once been at Kandahar Airfield, which was run by the Canadian military, and they had a Tim Horton's there. It was soon an addiction of mine, and luckily we had a rule in our unit that if a guy messed up he had to go buy a tray of donuts for everyone else to enjoy. Some mornings, I'd come into work and there'd be stacks of the beautiful things just waiting for me to destroy. While the bike was being serviced, we also had a welcome visitor. My cycling coach in Aberdeen, Ken, had a close friend living in Calgary, and his wife brought us giant cookies, along with more Tim Horton's. As I stuffed another donut into my mouth, I hoped the mechanics were doing a great job on the bike's suspension, because I could afford no breaks or hold-ups.

It was time for home stretch.

29. GIVE IT EVERYTHING

Now that the winds had died down, I switched back to cycling during daylight hours, which I decided was a good idea so that I didn't bump into a bear in the middle of the night; I'm not joking! Cycling into the Grand Prairie of Alberta, I kept a can of bear mace on my hip.

I cycled towards the Yukon River, a beast of a river carrying glacial water towards the ocean. I saw signs for Dawson's Creek, which turned out to be a town at the beginning of the Alaska Highway, and not the set of the TV show. The Alaska Highway was the last stretch of road that made up the Pan-American, and it gave me a great boost to see it. The finish line was coming closer, and unless something catastrophic happened, I knew that I had enough days in hand to not only smash the world record but to make it back in time for the royal wedding too. Just 1400 kilometres to go.

'You won't see much civilisation for the rest of it,' a local in Dawson's Creek told me, smiling and friendly as Canadians so often are. 'You picked the best time, though. In a couple of weeks there'll be tourists all over here. Way safer for you right now.'

The safety issue he was referring to was on the roads. Tourists descended on this beautiful landscape with rented trucks and trailers, and unlike in the UK, they did not need to pass any extra test to tow them. That could mean trailers sliding out on to hard shoulders to smash someone like me. The other cyclists I had talked to in my research phase had told me about some hairy moments on the Alaska Highway, and so I was chuffed to see the roads mostly empty.

Maybe the fact that it was the home stretch made me feel this way, but the Grand Prairie was instantly my favourite stretch of the ride so far. As I cycled north, I began to see thick forests of pines and spruce, and in the mountains, range after range of white mountains. At first the warm front had been melting the snow, but as I climbed in altitude the ground was carpeted in white. I was coming up to the Arctic Circle, and in wild territory I saw road signs warning of bison, wolves and bears.

The roads were long, and often empty. On one of my first days on the prairie, I saw something in the middle of the road a long distance away. It stayed there as I got closer and closer. I guessed that it must be roadkill, but in the end it moved, and I saw that it was a wolf. I wasn't sure what to expect, and I doubt that she was, either. We watched each other respectfully as I rode by.

It was as if I was riding through a picture postcard. I saw moose. Herds of bison. Dozens of bald eagles. Deer. Wolves, and bears. All of the animals that I saw were huge, a far cry from the squirrels in Aldershot! If I stopped and really looked into the forest, it amazed me how much movement I saw going on: the place was *alive*.

The animals were used to traffic on the road, but they didn't know what to do when a cyclist came by. Usually they'd panic and scatter, but often that would mean that they'd end up running directly in front of me, rather than just moving off of the road. (I think they lie on the tarmac to absorb heat.) It was a bit like driving a Land Rover around the ranges in Sennybridge, except that these bison could smash me and my bike apart if they choose to charge at me, and so I had to hold back and keep a safe distance. In Dawson's Creek, I'd heard about a tourist who'd been killed by a charging bison, and there were other stories about people who had tried getting a selfie with a grizzly in the background, only for the bear to charge them. Bears are fast, and so I was always aware that at any time I may have to go into Tour de France sprint finish mode: no way was I going to come this far just to end up as something's dinner!

The road was beautiful, and when I discovered that it had been made by military engineers, I felt a sense of pride – and also, maybe, of destiny – that another army engineer was using it to bring home the record. Now that we were truly out in the sticks, there was never any phone service to be had, and the tracker system that people could use to follow me online was now useless. I had a military-grade tracker for emergencies, and so this was how Alana could keep tabs on me and find me if a grizzly took me off into the woods. Rather than relying on GPS, we picked up tourist maps on our way; these showed a fantastic amount of detail, from toilet facilities to camp sites. As we had done most nights in the USA, we were sleeping in the RV. It was back to basics, and I loved it.

Feeling that the record and the wedding were in the bag, we stopped at the town of Whitehorse so that I could get a sports massage. We'd only just pulled in when we saw the golden arches of McDonald's, and in we went. Was it perfect fuel for a cyclist breaking a world record? Probably not, but sometimes you just want a dirty scran.

I walked up to the counter. 'How can I help you?' the girl behind it asked, in a thick Scouse accent. I couldn't believe my ears.

'Are you from Liverpool?' I asked her.

'Yeah,' she replied with a smile, then pointed into the back. 'And they are too.'

'What are you doing out here?'

'One of us moved here, then we all came. It's beautiful.'

I'd missed the UK, and I'd never met a Scouser who couldn't take some banter. 'You mean you're all on the run from the law,' I smiled, turning to Ivor. 'Check my bike's still outside, will you, mate?'

The Brits all laughed, and we gave a bit more banter back and forth. Americans can take a joke, but aside from the Aussies, I don't think anyone has the same kind of humour as the Brits. We had a great little chat with the four of them, and then it was back on the bike (which hadn't been stolen).

I was in really high spirits after that chance encounter, but it didn't last long. We picked up some phone signal in Whitehorse, and I received a message from Andreas; as well as wishing me the best, he let me know that someone named Jonas Deichmann – holder of many distance cycling records – was aiming to become the first man to cycle the Pan-American in under 100 days.

Later that day, I had a sick feeling in my stomach, and it wasn't the fast food. Currently, I was set to come to the end of my ride on Day 102. I would be smashing the world record by 15 days, beating the target I'd set myself. I'd never come out with the intention of doing the Pan-Am in under 100 days, so why should it bother me if someone else did? Was it just my ego talking? Was it that I didn't want someone else to do it faster than I had done?

No, I decided in the end. It wasn't about Jonas but about me. I was working hard in the saddle every day, but was I pushing myself to the edge? Was I falling off the bike at the end of the day? I was so close to the end. So close to being able to do it under 100 days. That hadn't been the aim to begin with, but when I looked back in ten years' time, how would I feel if I knew that I could have gone for it, but didn't?

I knew myself well enough that the answer was clear: it would haunt me forever.

That evening, when I got off the bike, I instantly called the guys together. They looked at me expectantly.

'Change of plan.'

I told the guys about the situation and my thinking. I told them that it would mean long days and little sleep. They were all on board, fully behind me. We were all tired and bearded. Driving all day takes a huge toll, but there were no complaints. I worked out what our new schedule would have to be, and we now had our new target: 99 days.

The next day, looking over our tourist maps, I saw that we would be passing some natural hot springs. I made a remark about it, and I saw the guys' eyes light up, but they said nothing; they wanted to go there, but they didn't want to slow me down now that I had this new goal in mind.

We passed the springs later that day, but instead of pressing by as I'd planned, I made the last-minute decision to pull into the car park. My team joined me, and asked if there was a problem.

'Let's go for a swim,' I said, and their faces lit up. They had more than earned some downtime, and if it meant that I had to cycle harder for the rest of the ride, then so be it. You've got to take care of your troops if you want them to take care of you, and these guys had done an amazing job of keeping me in the saddle.

We spent a couple of hours relaxing in the steaming waters, and it was fantastic. I felt the tension run out of me, and it gave me a chance to talk things over with the team, who all agreed that going for 99 days was the right call. After the two-hour chill-out it was back on to the bike, and I felt alive, mentally and physically. The team all had huge smiles on their faces, and just like my days in the army, I realised that a small thing can mean a huge difference in morale, for good or bad. This was our pick-me-up for the final stretch, and when we stopped to camp that night, we were all still talking about the hot springs.

Now that we were in Alaska, the American military made its presence felt again. I cycled by another huge air force base close to a town named North Pole, which made me feel like I was hallucinating; the lampposts looked like huge sticks of candy, and the streets were called things like Rudolph Street or Mrs Claus Avenue. It was bizarre.

The perimeter of the base ran right up the roadside, and I could see the jets roaring away for take-off alongside me. It was like that scene out of *Top Gun* where Tom Cruise rides along punching the air, with the slight difference that instead of a motorbike and leather jacket in California, I had a bicycle and Lycra in Alaska. I gave it my best though, and tried to get some selfies, but because of the cold, my fingers were always a split-second slow in responding and I missed the jets as they thundered up into the air.

A big moment for me came when I saw the sign announcing that I was now entering the Arctic Circle. I just thought that was such a cool thing to see, and it made me think about all the famous adventurers who had cut their teeth and made themselves legends in the Arctic. Some of them, like Sir Ranulph Fiennes, were SAS men, and I felt a surge of pride knowing that I was living up to the Special Forces ethos. I hadn't come out here because I wanted applause but because I wanted to do something important and challenging. I wanted to show people what an SF operator is made of, even after he's injured and out of the service. There were tourists taking their photos with the sign, and when they asked me where I'd come from, their jaws hit the floor: 'You mean Argentina Argentina?'

'Yep.'

'Oh my god. Are you crazy?'

'Jury's still out on that one,' I admitted, then rode on into the snow.

I pushed further into the Arctic Circle, and the next small town that I came to was Fairbanks, the last settlement before Prudhoe Bay, my final destination. We found an all-you-can-eat Chinese buffet, and I really hope that I didn't put them out of business. My mouth was like a black hole, plate after plate of food disappearing into it with no end in sight.

Dalton Highway was where I'd be using that fuel, and I soon realised that I hadn't done the preparation on it that I should have. To be honest, I think that my attitude had been: 'It's the last stretch. It doesn't matter if it's a minefield, I'll deal with it.' There's some truth to that – I wasn't going to let anything stop me now – but with the added time pressure, the unknowns began to wear my patience. I was an angry man on that bit of the road.

For the first time on the challenge, we had to swap in the wide and thick gravel tyres to cope with the uneven surface. At any time the surface could go back to tarmac, and we'd swap the tyres again, but a few miles later it would be back to gravel, and another swap. The stop-start nature of it really grated away at my nerves, and my joints were getting sore from the bumps in the road. At one point I hit a forty-mile stretch of great surface, and I thought, *This is it! Smooth sailing!* but then it went right back to bumpy gravel, and I'd be surprised if Alana couldn't hear me cursing from Aberdeen.

It was around this time that I started seeing – and doing my best to avoid – the trucks that were made famous on shows like *Ice Truckers*. I'd see these guys in the distance, and get as far off the road as I could, because: They. Do. Not. Stop.

The Arctic country is all slippery, rolling hills, and once these guys build up momentum, they don't want to lose it, so no way are they touching their brakes. They come down the hills like a rocket so that they can get up the other side, and they do it in the centre of the road, their huge tyres throwing the gravel outwards like an exploding mortar round. It wasn't exactly a fun experience to have them go by, but I'll say this for the truckers: they'd smile and wave!

The temperature had dropped a degree or two a day as we went northwards, and now, with two days planned until the finish, it was at a rather nippy -18°C. I needed to do 150 miles one day and then 100 the next to become the first person to cycle the Pan-American Highway in under 100 days. As well as the usual fuel consumption, my body was having to generate so much heat to stay warm (even when cycling) that Ivor took his breakfasts to the next level: in the mornings I would put away eight sausages, eight rashers of bacon and four eggs. It was easy to want that much scran inside me, but because of the cold it wasn't so easy to make myself take on liquids, which were equally as important: you can still get dehydrated in the cold. When I'd been a military ski instructor in Norway we'd say to the troops, 'Start cold, get warm,' but that's a lot easier to say than to do. Leaving the warm inside of the RV to get on to the ice-cold frame of my bike wasn't something that I looked forward to, but I could comfort myself that the end was in sight, and my family would be there: Alana and the kids were on their way from Aberdeen to the finish line.

I needed happy thoughts like that in my mind as I struggled on the uneven surface. The days of smashing across the states with a tailwind at my back seemed like years ago; now I felt like I was pedalling through porridge. When I saw the support vehicle pulled over at the side of the road ahead, I wondered what the next issue would turn out to be. A flat tyre? Some kind of engine problem?

Turned out it was a lady in a hi-vis jacket holding a stop sign. I pulled to a stop – I wasn't going much faster than walking pace anyway – and noticed that the documentary team were filming.

'What's going on?' I asked them.

'The road's closed,' one of the lads explained. 'We can't get past.'

I looked at the woman's stop sign, then at the camera. I knew what was going on. Between me and the team we had a great level of banter, this was a wind-up. They knew that this would break me, and they were setting me up.

I wasn't going to fall for that one.

'All right. Nice try, lads.'

I went to ride on, but the woman wasn't in on the joke. 'Sir, the road's closed.'

I looked around at the team, and I realised from their faces that there was nothing funny going on here.

'What do you mean?' I asked her. 'For how long?'

'Until we finish working tonight, sir.'

I could feel myself getting angry. I tried my best not to show it. 'And what time's that?'

'Eight p.m.'

Eight hours away. I couldn't believe it, and it took every ounce of my self-discipline not to launch my bike into the dirt. I was so close, but the going was painfully slow. I didn't know if I could handle a four-hour delay, let alone eight!

I tried explaining my situation to her, and the lady said that she'd talk to her boss, but she made it sound as if the road was gone – wiped out – and wouldn't be passable until they got done working at eight.

I snapped. I walked away from everyone, heading into the RV. I was furious, but I told myself to be calm; there would be a way to fix things if I could get a grip of my emotions. Once I told myself that there was a way to still win, I calmed down quickly so that I could find it.

I got pen and paper, and starting working out my time/distance/speed calculations. I needed a new plan, and soon I had it.

I called the guys together. 'We're going to go straight for twenty-four hours,' I told them. 'Rest now, because after this, we're pushing on until the end. If we don't stop for more than short breaks, we can still make it in under 100 days.'

'All right,' the guys said; they wanted to hit the goal as much as I did.

I climbed up into my bed in the RV and tried to sleep, but it was impossible. It always is for me when I know I have something big coming up. It's one thing saying you have eight hours to rest, but another to be able to flick a switch and go dark on your thoughts and feelings when you know one of the biggest and hardest days of your life is about to begin.

The guys continued to try and persuade the work crew to let us through, but it was no use. Whatever they were doing was hidden from us behind a hill, and we assumed it must have been major damage. Like it or not, we were stuck there until eight. I passed those hours slowly, and with frustration.

When we were finally allowed to carry on, my blood was boiling: the offending stretch of track was about fifty metres long. I could have carried my bike across, and that short distance had cost me eight hours. That knowledge put me in a bad mood, and so did knowing that I had twenty-four hours left to cover 200 miles – and some of that was straight up into mountains. The cold was battering, and despite my desire to keep pushing on and not stop, I had to think of myself as an engine; I'd need regular stops to take on hot liquid and to warm up inside the RV.

One thing I had going for me was that, because we were almost on the top of the world, the night-time was bright, with red skies. It would have been beautiful to look at if I hadn't been doing my best to get the bike going at anything more than a slow running pace. At times I was doing little more than 6mph, and I felt like everything was against me. My mind was tired, my body was aching. The conditions were relentless, and if I wanted the record, then I would have to be that too.

I was already running on fumes and willpower when the Arctic winds picked up and started to shake me in the saddle. *It can't be far now,* I thought to myself as I came out of the mountains and was surrounded by a sea of flat, white land. The only signs of life I saw was the occasional truck, and they'd honk their horns as they passed. I hoped we were close to Prudhoe Bay; maybe they'd heard about the lunatic who was trying to reach them.

Jonno drove ahead to the finish line while the others stayed behind me in the other vehicle. He told Alana that he didn't think I was going to make it that night. She was waiting with the kids, and Jonno was spooked; he'd never seen me have to dig this deep. I was so tired I was hallucinating. The snow was horizontal and in my face, so I was riding with ski goggles, coming through the night looking like an escaped lunatic.

Alana and Frances drove from the hotel to the finishing point to see the conditions for themselves. When they got outside, the wind flattened them both. Neither thought I would make it to the collection of hotels and oil rigs that made up the town of Prudhoe Bay that night. There was a buffet there, and Ash loaded up on high-energy foods that he brought back to me to throw into my struggling body.

I scoffed it down, and for the first time I saw a flickering light in the distance: it was the flame of the oil rig, and I knew that if I could just cycle a couple more hours then I'd make it!

I threw myself into it for two hours, and . . .

The light seemed just as distant as ever.

One more coffee stop, I told myself. *It can't be that far if Ash drove it. Alana and the kids are there. You're not stopping. You're finishing this tonight.*

And seeing that I was serious, Ash drove back to the hotel, waking Alana and the others. 'I don't think he's stopping!'

Alana, my kids, Frances, and the official from Guinness piled into their van and drove out to the finishing point to wait for me. Visibility was shocking, and I came pushing through the snow in erratic bursts as the wind pummelled me.

Athletes talk a lot about visualisation, and how they had imagined their final moment of victory again and again and again. I'd done the same, but now that I drew close to the finish line, my moment was nothing like I had ever imagined it. This was no ride along the Champs-Élysées with me leaning back in the seat with my hands in the air. I clung on to my handlebars for dear life, hitting one patch of black ice after another. My face was covered in frozen snot, my muscles were shaking from fatigue and cold, and every blast of Arctic wind cut through me to the bone.

But I made it.

I skidded to the finish line and pulled my wife and kids into a hug. I was so exhausted that I can't remember what I said – and I was probably talking gibberish – but I'd missed them all so much and they got big kisses from their dad's cracked lips. Mollie was aware of what was going on, and full of beans, but Tommy was in a world of his own.

I thought I must be hallucinating again when I saw the lady from Guinness was braving the cold in tights and a skirt, but there wasn't an ounce of discomfort on her face as she presented me with my record. I was now the record holder for the fastest cycle of the Pan-American Highway, completing it in 99 days, which also made me the first person ever to do it in under 100.

I hugged my wife, but unlike Cartagena, this wasn't the place to stand around for a post-certificate photo shoot.

'Let's get to the hotel,' I told my family and my team, and we piled into the vehicles, leaving the frost-bitten finish line behind us.

30. WHEELS DOWN

I was so tired when I made it into Prudhoe Bay that it took me a while to realise that my father-in-law and our assistant, Frances, were among the people wishing me well in the hotel's dining area. I sat with my family and the team, slowly eating my way through the mountain of food in front of me, feeling . . . strange.

I was totally knackered, and so happy to see my family, of course, but my head felt like a washing machine filled with thoughts, all of them being tossed and jumbled around, making it hard for me to catch and hold on to any one of them. I know what had been in that mental laundry basket, though: two years of preparation for this challenge, 99 days on a bike, the expectation of others and my own fear of failure. It felt so weird to know that I wouldn't be back on the bike again tomorrow. Not good or bad, just weird. I'd got so used to reconditioning myself and my bike in the evenings that as I was eating this nagging voice in my head was saying: 'Get away and square your kit!' When you build a powerful routine, it will continue to speak to you even when the reason that you built it for is gone. That being the case, think what your life could be like if you brought a healthy routine into it, and had that strong voice in your ear!

That inner voice, drive and cultivated instinct had got me to where I was. It had made me relentless. The aim of the ride had been to break the existing record, but as I found new gears within myself, I set new targets to match them; I didn't allow myself to coast, even with the record in the bag. As a result, I was the first man to cycle the Pan-American Highway in under 100 days. My record may be broken in the future, but I'll always have been the first. It's a part of my legacy now.

I felt different to how I had on passing Special Forces selection. To be honest, when I'd been in the army, I think everyone had *expected* me to pass and get badged. That hadn't been the case with this challenge. For every one person that had believed in me, there have been many who said it couldn't be done by a novice, or by someone with my build, or by going south to north, etc, etc. The list of negativity goes on.

Had I cycled with a chip on my shoulder? Absolutely. That didn't mean that when I was riding I was angry and miserable, but there were times on a steep climb or a freezing day when I would look inside my motivational armoury, and I'd think to myself: *If you fail, think of all those smug faces telling you they knew that you would.* I don't recommend using fuel from dark places as your only motivation in life, but there are times when it can be useful to throw it on the fire and get yourself to that next level of achievement. This probably sounds crazy, but if everyone had been totally sure I would smash the record, it would have made things *harder* for me, because on the toughest days, I needed to get angry to keep going, and the doubters and naysayers kept my feet turning those pedals again and again.

As we ate, I noticed I was missing half of what people were saying to me. I was so used to being inside my own head most of the time, and just like a soldier who feels like his rifle is a part of his arm, I felt like I was missing a limb by not having the bike close at hand. Like a soldier's weapon, my bike had been my lifeline to the record. If anything had happened to it, I was done, and now I had a constant nag in my mind telling me it was missing.

'I said, you've lost so much weight,' Alana repeated, and she was right. When we weighed in, despite the fact that I'd eaten like a bear going into hibernation, I was 12kg lighter than when I'd started.

'Daddy, why do you keep looking at your watch?' Mollie asked, and I wondered if she was the only one to have noticed.

'Daddy's just used to checking it, sweetie,' I replied. That watch and my time/distance/speed calculations had been on my mind constantly, so much so now that it was a subconscious action to look at it. I'd experienced something similar when coming off training phases in places like the jungle, or off operational tours. Unused, the habit slowly fades away.

Sitting at that table, records secured, I had my first moment of worry that I would too.

We spent three days at Prudhoe Bay, de-servicing the kit, packing and doing general admin and attending to my sore body. I wanted as much time as I could with Alana and the kids, but a charity event doesn't end when you cross the finish line. There were a lot of photos to be taken for each one of my sponsors with their kit before it could be prepared for the trip back. Some things, like inner tubes, just weren't worth the cost of flying them back, and instead I swapped them with some cycling enthusiasts who lived at Prudhoe in return for cardboard boxes. It sounds silly, but when you're in a tiny place at the top of Alaska, finding boxes to pack a vehicle's worth of gear into is not easy!

There was a souvenir shop at Prudhoe, and when I went there to pick up the classic fridge magnet and a few other bits, I noticed that there were two bikes outside loaded with panniers; saddle bags – basically, like a cowboy would load on to his horse for a long journey. I got talking to the two Dutch owners of the bikes, and it turned out they did have a big ride in mind: they were heading to Ushuaia, where I had begun my challenge. It was a lifelong dream of theirs, and they'd given themselves two years to do the length of it. I gave them as much information as I could, and wished them a great trip. By now, I reckon that they're in South America, either coasting past beautiful beaches or riding awestruck through the massive mountains.

I flew out with my family and team on a small aircraft, and I think we probably took up 99 per cent of the hold's space with our bags and boxes. We flew into Anchorage, the capital of Alaska, and got to be tourists for a day. In the three-plus months that I'd spent in the Americas, that was the first time I'd been able to wander around with no schedule and relax. I got to be a curious visitor and a dad. It was great.

Those few days in Alaska acted as a bit of a decompression chamber for me, and so by the time that we flew to Heathrow I wasn't feeling quite so weird being without my bike or constantly checking my watch as if it was my heartbeat. I still felt a little strange, though; it was the end-of-tour feeling that I'd had in the military. Knowing that – even if I wrote a book about it – someone could never fully comprehend the experience unless they'd gone through it themselves. That can be great in one way – breaking a record isn't special if everyone's doing it – but on the other hand, it can lead to you feeling 'lonely'.

Knowing that it's such a unique experience, and one that can't be repeated, can leave you feeling quite empty.

Luckily for me, I had something to keep my mind off of it: the royal wedding. It was only when we checked into the hotel at Heathrow and I turned on the TV that I realised just how big an international celebration it was going to be, and the next day, when I went into London itself, I saw that the nation had gone down with wedding fever.

I had eleven interviews on that first day, all to promote Heads Together now that I'd been successful in my challenge, but inevitably they asked a lot of questions about Harry. I didn't mind that, as I wasn't there to promote myself. If it helped put money into the collection buckets, then I was happy.

The next day I went to Windsor Castle for another round of interviews. It was the day before the wedding, and the only time I had seen scenes like these was during the London Olympics. The streets were packed with smiling, happy people and there was a huge buzz of excitement in the air that didn't come across on TV, despite the fact that every station was mad for the wedding.

The media outlets were situated in marquees outside the castle, and I visited one after the other, giving my spiel about the Pan-Am, asking for donations and answering a lot of questions about Harry. I finished with Sky News, and the next stop on my media tour was with CNN, who were situated further away, down by the river.

To talk to the press, I'd had to pick up credentials that let me move around the 'backstage' area. To get to the river I had to walk down the main road, where they'd set up railings down the middle so that half the road was empty and accessible, while the other was packed with well-wishers who had come to catch a glimpse of the royals at the historic event. There were dozens of police, all calm but alert, and one of them caught my eye as I walked down the empty half of the road.

'Do you mind taking a seat for two minutes, sir?' he asked me politely, with a look towards the gates; something was going on up there, and I understood why they wouldn't want people milling around as it happened.

'No dramas, mate.' I took a seat on a bench and watched, the crowd stirring and beginning to cheer as they realised that something was going on. It was then that I began to notice SF operators and specialist firearms officers. I recognised some of them, and by the look on their faces, they knew me too. They had a 'WTF are you doing on that bench?' look, probably wondering if I was still serving in some capacity.

It was then that Prince Harry and Prince William came out and began to shake hands with the public who were cheering them. They began working their way along the railings, and it was William who spotted me. He nudged Harry, who looked in my direction, and then came bounding down the hill towards me, stroking his beard as he said, 'Oh, mate, you look skinny!'

We shook hands and he congratulated me on my records and the challenge. I wished him the best for the next day, and then he was back to the railings, to be instantly replaced by an army of Dictaphones and cameras shoved in my face.

'How do you know the prince?'

'What did he say to you?'

'He touched his beard. Is he shaving it for the wedding?'

I'd never experienced anything like it. Thank God I'd gone through interrogation training, or it could have turned into a shock-of-capture moment! As it was, I answered politely and tried to throw in as much PR about the challenge as I could.

The next day, suited and booted and with Alana looking fantastic at my side, we went to Windsor Castle for the royal wedding. My chance meeting with Harry the day before had not gone unnoticed, and on the BBC's commentary, Emily Nash of *Hello!* magazine said that as well as the known heroes, 'there are a lot of unsung heroes too, one of them being Dean Stott'.

We had to be in the chapel two hours before the ceremony began, and after spending months on a bike, my body was not enjoying the pews: my back was in clip, and I had to stand up and down, stretching as best as I could while we waited for the ceremony to begin.

I realised that I was in a special room, one of 600 guests, and it was surreal to recognise so many people around me without actually knowing any of them personally. Other than Alana, the one person I *did* know was the groom, and he looked very happy, which was obviously the most important thing to see, for me. The rest of it was a blur of cameras and handshakes and, 'look, it's so and so!' Alana and I had won Willy Wonka's Golden Ticket to be there, and it was a special day to share as a couple. Really, I couldn't have asked for a better way to mark my return to the UK, and back to my own wife. Everyone loves a good wedding, don't they? And that's what they got. The happiness was contagious. It was one of those days where every cell in your body is smiling.

I joined Lorraine Kelly, Emily Nash and a lady from the Kingdom Choir on TV. The idea had been that Lorraine and I would talk about the Pan-American, but the world had wedding fever, so that was the conversation. At any other time, I would have got a lot more press, and maybe more donations, but I didn't mind because it was having Harry on board that had really helped the challenge in the first place. Things had worked out well across the board, and I was confident we could still raise money even though I was now off the bike.

In one week I had become the first man to cycle the Pan-American Highway in under 100 days, then attended a royal wedding. It was a double high, and having been through similar exciting moments in my life, things like the Canadian Embassy evacuation, I knew I should now expect a double low.

Back in Aberdeen, I saw the same people in the same places. That's not knocking them, but it's something that is very jolting when you come home after a long time away, having experienced a lot. You expect that the world is put on pause while you're gone from it. You feel that everyone else has lived through this journey with you.

But they haven't. They've got their own journeys going on, and when you walk into the shop you're the same guy to them that walked in four months ago, except that now you're looking a lot skinnier.

I'd been told that, back in Scotland, I should taper off the amount of exercise I was doing, for two reasons: it would help fight off the inevitable attack of depression that would try and take hold now that I'd completed a two-year mission, continuing to give my body the feed of endorphins that it was used to. Also, it would allow my heart to return to normal; because the heart is a muscle, mine would have grown during the challenge, and if it atrophied too quickly that could cause issues with the valves and so on.

I picked a town that was about ten miles away and told myself that I'd cycle there for a brew. A nice gentle ride.

I'd hardly been in the saddle for five minutes before I was putting my foot down, trying to beat my personal best for that route. On the way back I was spotted by three cyclists, and they tried to race me. My relentless mentality was fully engaged, and I beat off the challenge, but back in the house I had to ask myself why I'd done that. The challenge was over.

I left the bike in the garage after that, because I needed a new objective. Beating my PBs was not a taper. I knew myself well enough to know that if I kept getting on the bike I'd keep pushing it. I needed something new to get my teeth into.

For the next six weeks, that would be the planning and execution of the Wheels Down Ball, a charity event that I would host in London to mark the end of my challenge and hopefully raise a lot more money for Heads Together.

I lived my life on the phone and on email, roping people into giving and participating in prizes, and selling tables at the event. It gave me something to occupy my mind, and I let myself forget about phys. During this time I went on what you could call a guilt-free diet. I'd lost 12kg, and I wanted it back. Alana had married an SF operator, not noodle-arms, and besides, I was constantly ravenous. I was told this was because my body was so used to consuming and expending calories at an incredibly high rate that it was pushing me to continue doing so in expectation of another physical onslaught.

Before the challenge, Kensington had said that Harry could attend Wheels Down, and I'd chosen the date for the event so that he could do that. I couldn't tell people he was coming to boost table sales, but I felt that having him in the room would lift the mood to another level. It would also just be nice to have dinner together, something that hadn't happened in years.

Unfortunately, Kensington informed me a few weeks before the event that something had come up and the prince wouldn't be able to stay for the whole evening. This was a bit of a blow, but I saw an opportunity.

'Can he still come for an hour or so?'

'Yes.'

Perfect. 'Would he be able to do a live Q&A with me in front of the guests?'

I was buzzing when they said that he could. We agreed that Martin Bayfield – former international rugby player, and a friend to both Harry and I – would ask the questions. The questions would mostly be directed to me, and Harry could jump in when he liked. I thought it would be a fantastic way to kick-start the ball.

At the beginning of the evening, Harry joined us in private at the Hilton, Park Lane, to meet my family and the challenge's sponsors. He leant in close to Tommy, a bit too close, and my little lad jabbed his hand out and caught the prince in the face. Harry laughed, jumped back and put up his fists. He's incredibly good like that at putting a room at ease, as people are always a little awed and starstruck when they meet him. From then on, the ice was broken and photos were taken, until . . .

Mollie tugged at Alana's dress. 'Mummy, I told everyone at school that I'd get a photo of just me and the prince.'

I couldn't let my little angel down, and so I went to ask permission from the comms team. They were good enough to give it, and so my daughter got her picture with the man the world was watching. Alana put it on her Instagram and it instantly went viral.

I led the way as we walked out to applause, and took our seats on a circular stage that would rotate as Martin interviewed us. This, and a number of screens around the room, aimed to give everyone in attendance a good view of the prince and his dashingly handsome friend, who was now looking more like his old self and less like a broom handle.

Martin asked the first question, but Harry being Harry, he was soon leading the conversation himself. Just like in the promo video that had kicked off the fundraising part of the challenge, what had been a 'scripted' session turned into a conversation between mates. It was a great start to the evening, and his presence did a lot to boost the auction prices later in the evening even after he'd left. It was great to see him, and I was very grateful for his contribution to the night and the campaign at large.

My good friend, Amanda, was at the event. Her company, Fireball Ltd, had helped to set up Wheels Down, this kind of ball being their regular gig.

'Dean,' she said, beginning an inside joke, 'what's the contingency if you don't do it?'

I laughed. She'd been asking me this for months before the challenge, and I'd never given her an answer. Now I could.

'There never was one,' I told her. 'If I knew that there was an out, I would have had the temptation to take it when things got really hard, so I didn't give myself one. My only option was to be successful.'

That had been the truth of it. I'd either smash the record or die trying.

At one point in the evening, when the auction was done, I nipped to the bathroom for a pee. When I came back, I thought for a second that I'd walked into the wrong room; the band had started playing and the place was a party. I even saw someone backflip on the stage! While the guests were sitting at their tables, I had no idea how much alcohol was going down hatches, but now that there was music, everyone was on their feet and dancing.

I don't know if it's the security instinct in me, or just because I was the host, but I didn't drink and I was the last one up. I couldn't switch off until everyone was in a taxi or a hotel room, and I had so much going through my head that I hardly slept; I was doing a lot of maths, thinking of what we'd raised, and I had that new question burning a hole in my skull . . .

What next?

The Wheels Down Ball and the Pan-American Highway Challenge were a success, and it was one of the proudest moments of my life when Alana and I got to hand over £500,000 to Heads Together. There was more money to come, but we didn't want the fund sitting in our charity's account when it could be helping people, and so we gave this first sum, and then followed it with many others as the money from the auction came in.

Eventually, it was time to draw the challenge to an official close, and I sent out this letter to everyone who had supported us in any way:

It is with mixed emotions that today we draw to a close the Pan-American Highway Challenge 2018.

As a husband and wife team we set off on this challenge with three goals:

- *Raise £1 million for mental health charities*
- *Break a world record*
- *Raise awareness of the issues surrounding mental health*

We close today with a final amount raised of £900K. While this is just under our target, it is a net amount with every single penny going to the mental health charities. This amount includes a pound-for-pound matched donation of £265K from the annual company dinner for St James's Place direct to the mental health charities.

We are extremely proud of what we've been able to achieve, especially given we have never undertaken anything like this before and were starting from the very beginning.

What we have achieved:

- *We have seen the opening of a new family school with the Anna Freud National Centre for children and families*
- *We have connected the charities to a number of new high-net-worth individuals and companies*
- *The Mix were able to answer over 2,000 calls from desperate young people, as well as provide over 300 counselling sessions, because of our donation*
- *Young Minds used the funds to their Parent Helpline and digital services providing much-needed support to parents in crisis*

- *Our donation supported the training of 8,000 allied mental health professionals with the Anna Freud National Centre for Children and Families*

- *Our support has enabled Help4Heroes to care for veterans with significant mental health and physical challenges resulting from their service*

- *The funds from PAH have provided further support to veterans and their families through the Walking with the Wounded programme*

- *The Royal British Legion have described their involvement with the PAH Campaign as 'the highlight of 2018'*

- *The funds received by the Royal British Legion have helped deliver high-quality care for veterans with dementia and supported younger veterans on their Battle Back programme*

- *We have seen the appointment of a new Suicide Prevention Minister*

- *A huge reform happened in children's mental health management*

- *A new 24-hour veterans helpline opened with Combat Stress*

- *Dean, new to cycling, brought home two Guinness World Records*

- *The first man in history to cycle the Pan-American Highway in under 100 days*

- *The fastest man to cycle the Pan-American Highway (99 days)*

- *The fastest man to cycle the length of South America (48 days)*

We have witnessed first-hand how the money has helped change the conversation and the impact it has had on so many lives. We knew it wouldn't be easy but had no idea of the hurdles and barriers we would face. As a family, we made huge sacrifices, suffered losses, dealt with illnesses, gained new family members and had amazing ups and downs along the way. This campaign took over our lives but we never wavered from our goals, even when things like having a baby got in our way! We faced many challenges and learnt a lot of important lessons.

Today, however, we have a new cause that is begging for our help and now is the time to move on and help them. We must say goodbye to the PAH, and put all the many lessons we have learnt along the way into practice for the next challenge.

We firmly believe our challenges along the way were all in preparation for what we have coming up, and this next challenge requires strength, resilience, thick skin and a strong heart. Every single moment will be worth it in order to save even one person.

Finally, and most importantly, we want to say a huge heartfelt thank you for your help and support. You have supported us from the off – a true friend – and we really would like to say a huge thank you for everything.

This would not have been possible without our sponsors, donors and supporters. We have witnessed such an incredible amount of support from so many companies and individuals and each and every one of you contributed to the success of this challenge. From the guy who donated a pound a day, every day, without fail, throughout the challenge right through to our incredible main sponsor, St James's Place, from the bottom of our hearts . . .

THANK YOU.

Dean and Alana Stott

And with that letter, Alana and I finished the greatest adventure of my life.

EPILOGUE

In the crowded market, surrounded by locals, I reached for the weapon beneath my seat. I could feel H tense up in the passenger seat; as soon as I pulled out the sub machine gun and initiated the compromised drill, we would be in a fight for our lives.

My hand wrapped around the pistol grip, my eyes on the car's mirror. Behind me, I saw our second vehicle inching into the bustling space, where the locals continued to point at me, some tapping the glass of my window. They'd seen through my disguise. The enemy would be on their way. I had only seconds to act. Now or never.

Three . . .

Two . . .

'STOP-STOP-STOP!' The words came loud and urgent in my ear. 'Stop-stop-stop!'

I paused, caught between fight or flight; why was someone telling me to stand down on my drill? I didn't have time for delays. The locals were still walking by, looking straight at me and tapping the glass.

And then I heard it.

'Your clothing is caught in the door!' my mate in the rear vehicle told me. 'They're pointing it out!'

I felt relief wash over me. Relief, and embarrassment – I'd almost started an incident because I'd assumed the people around me were hostile. I'd looked at friendly faces, and seen enemies. I'd assumed hostility, not hospitality. I'd judged by race and religion, not acts and deeds.

I promised myself that I would never make that mistake again, and I hope that in telling this story I have managed to convey that no matter where I have been in the world, and no matter what the circumstances, I have always found *good people*. There is no end to my appetite for meeting people around the world. In the wake of my challenge, I returned to Moss Side to talk to school children, and their infectious enthusiasm could easily have belonged to the children of my friends and fixers in Libya. It's one of the reasons that I can't give up on challenge and travel; there are so many places to conquer, and so many people that I want to do it with.

And none more so, of course, than my wife, Alana.

'What are you going to do next?' she asked me, knowing that I was no closer to being able to accept a nine-to-five life than I ever was.

I'd given a lot of thought to that since I'd crossed the finish line. I'd dipped my toe into cycling, but it was time to take it back out. Whatever I did next, I wanted to be the underdog again. I wanted to be the novice, not only to raise the stakes and make the challenge all the harder, but because I want to encourage people to try something difficult, even if they have no experience in that field. I'd looked at mountain climbing, but I soon realised that there were a lot of people tackling the summits, and I wanted something unique.

'I'm going to do something on water,' I told Alana, my mind made up, and after some more searching, I knew exactly what. 'I'm going to solo kayak the length of the Nile.'

My wife didn't even blink. 'Has anyone ever done it before?'

I shook my head. 'No. No one wants to touch it.'

Which made it perfect for me.

That's my next challenge. What about yours? You don't need to cycle 22,000 kilometres to push yourself. You can find ways of doing it every day. What's your baseline? If you're not doing any exercise, start by doing ten minutes of walking a day. If you're running 10ks, do a marathon. If you're lifting weights, give CrossFit a try. You don't have to stick to these things forever, just like I'm not sticking with cycling, but try something that takes you out of your comfort zone; if you do, you'll be amazed how it carries over into all aspects of your life.

Whatever you do, whatever you choose, just make sure that you do it to the best of your abilities. You have it all within your control. It always has been. The only limitations are the ones that you set yourself. Starting today, break your own records.

Thank you, and I look forward to you joining me in the unrelenting pursuit of excellence.

Dean Stott

Acknowledgements

There simply is not enough space to thank all of those who I have met both in the military and civilian sector, all of whom have left a mark and played a part in carving my path.

I would like to thank my literary agents, Neil Blair and Rory Scarfe, who identified the uniqueness of mine amongst other competing projects. I'm grateful to the contribution of Gez Jones, everyone at Headline publishing, SF Disclosure and the lawyers in making this possible.

Thanks also to the Royal Foundation and the Heads Together charities, who believed in me and the PAH18 project. A special thanks to Nicky Turley, our fundraising manager, whose knowledge was priceless in guiding us through the politics of charity; on the way we found a lifelong friend. Thank you to Jo Peebles (née Livingston) and Freuds for their PR advice and expertise.

Many thanks to Amanda Heathcote and Fireball for their professionalism and delivery of the Wheels Down Ball.

Thanks to the several sponsors who gave material support: Total Endurance, True Start Coffee, Orbea, myvitamins, Schwalbe, NXG, the Visa Team, KitBrix, SBomb, Dozzers Smokehouse and Grill, Aberdeen Sports Therapy, the Altitude Centre, Julian Widdowson, RPX and MilDef.

A huge thanks to the financial sponsors St James's Place Charitable Foundation for their support on this challenge.

Thank you to David Bellamy, Andrew Croft, Steve McKnight and Iain Rayner for believing in this project and the impact it could have in changing the stigma surrounding mental health and help those in most need.

I must thank Ken Bryson from Total Endurance for his positivity and for teaching an old dog new tricks.

And Ivor Morgan and Jonno Adams for their selfless assistance on the ground ensuring I was fed, had a bed and the morale was high.

Huge thanks to the Duke and Duchess of Cambridge and Duke of Sussex for their vision in changing the way mental health is accepted and ending the stigma.

I am so grateful to the Duke of Sussex for his personal support of the PAH18 project, from the initial idea through to the Wheels Down Ball.

Finally, I must mention Alana Stott, Frances Race, Ivor Morgan and Matt Cordas for grabbing the bull by its horns and taking risks to ensure we had the vehicles in Panama and kept the challenge alive.

INDEX